ALL NEW 100 MATHS LESSONS

Licence

D1101768

YEAR 3

Ann Montague-Smith

Ann Morgan

00 785050 09

Contents

Acknowledgements

Extracts from the National Numeracy Strategy *Framework for Teaching Mathematics* © Crown copyright. Reproduced under the terms of HMSO Guidance Note 8.

Designed using Adobe Inc. InDesign™ v2.0.1

British Library Cataloguing-in-Publication Data
A catalogue record for this book is available from the British Library.
ISBN 0-439-98469-6   **ISBN 978-0439-98469-0**

Published by
Scholastic Ltd
Villiers House
Clarendon Avenue
Leamington Spa
Warks. CV32 5PR

© Scholastic Ltd, 2005
Text © Ann Montague-Smith
and Ann Morgan, 2005

Printed by Bell & Bain
3456789   5678901234

Series Consultant
Ann Montague-Smith

Authors
Ann Montague-Smith,
Ann Morgan

Editor
Nancy Candlin

Assistant Editors
Aileen Lalor and
Charlotte Ronalds

Series Designer
Joy Monkhouse

Designers
Catherine Mason, Micky
Pledge and Helen Taylor

Illustrations
Garry Davies and
Mark Ruffle
(Beehive Illustration)

CD development
CD developed in association
with Footmark Media Ltd

Visit our website at
www.scholastic.co.uk

About the series

100 Maths Lessons is designed to enable you to provide clear teaching, with follow-up activities that are, in the main, practical activities for pairs of children to work on together. These activities are designed to encourage the children to use the mental strategies that they are learning and to check each other's calculations. Many of the activities are games that they will enjoy playing, and that encourage learning.

About the book

This book is divided into three termly sections. Each term begins with a **Medium-term plan** ('Termly planning grid') based on the National Numeracy Strategy's *Medium-term plans* and *Framework for teaching mathematics*. Each term's work is divided into a number of units of differentiated lessons on a specific subject.

   Note: Because the units in this book follow the structure of the National Numeracy Strategy's *Framework for teaching mathematics*, the units in each term jump from Unit 6 to Unit 8. The Strategy suggests you put aside the time for Unit 7 for Assess and review.

Finding your way around the lesson units

Each term is comprised of 11 to 13 units. Each unit contains:
- a short-term planning grid
- three to five lesson plans
- photocopiable activity sheets.

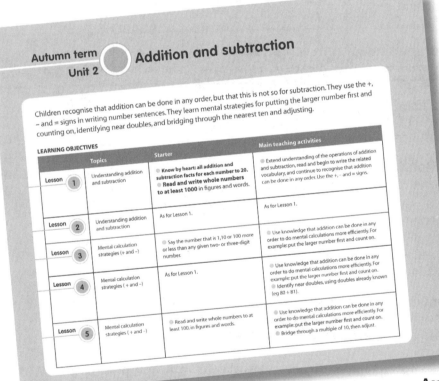

Short-term planning grids

The short-term planning grids ('Learning objectives') provide an overview of the objectives for each unit. The objectives come from the Medium-term plan and support clear progression through the year. Key objectives are shown in bold, as in the Yearly Teaching Programme in the NNS *Framework for teaching mathematics*.

Lesson plans

The lessons are structured on the basis of a daily maths lesson following the NNS's three-part lesson format: a ten-minute **Starter** of oral work and mental maths, a **Main teaching activities** session with interactive teaching time and/or group/individual work and a **Plenary** round-up including **Assessment** opportunities. In some lessons, differentiated tasks are supplied for more able and less able pupils.

   However, this structure has not been rigidly applied. Where it is appropriate to concentrate on whole-class teaching, for example, the lesson plan may not include a group-work session at all. The overall organisation of the lesson plan varies from unit to unit depending on the lesson content. In some units all the plans are separate, though they provide different levels of detail. Elsewhere you may find a bank of activities that you can set up as a 'circus', or instruction and support for an extended investigation, either of which the children will work through over the course of several days.

   Most units of work are supported with activity pages provided in the book, which can also be found on the accompanying CD. In addition to these core activity sheets, the CD contains differentiated versions for less able and more able ability levels. Some are available as blank templates, to allow you to make your own further differentiated versions.

How ICT is used

Ideas for using ICT are suggested wherever appropriate in *100 Maths Lessons*. We have assumed that you will have access to basic office applications, such as word-processing, and can email and research using the Internet. The QCA's *ICT Scheme of Work for Key Stages 1 and 2* has been used as an indicator of the skills the children will be developing formally from Year 1 and their progression in the primary years.

While some lessons use dataloggers or floor robots, we have avoided suggesting specific software, except for the games and interactive teaching programs (ITPs) provided by the NNS. If you do not already have them, these can be downloaded from the NNS website at: http://www.standards.dfes.gov.uk/numeracy

How to use the CD-ROM

System requirements

Minimum specification:
- PC with a CD-ROM drive and at least 32 MB RAM
- Pentium 166 MHz processor
- Microsoft Windows 98, NT, 2000 or XP
- SVGA screen display with at least 64K colours at a screen resolution of 800 x 600 pixels

***100 Maths Lessons* CD-ROMs are for PC use only.**

Setting up your computer for optimal use

On opening, the CD will alert you if changes are needed in order to operate the CD at its optimal use. There are two changes you may be advised to make:

Viewing resources at their maximum screen size

To see images at their maximum screen size, your screen display needs to be set to 800 x 600 pixels. In order to adjust your screen size you will first need to **Quit** the program.

If using a PC, select **Settings**, then **Control Panel** from the **Start** menu. Next, double click on the **Display** icon and then click on the **Settings** tab. Finally, adjust the **Screen area** scroll bar to 800 x 600 pixels. Click **OK** and then restart the program.

Adobe® Acrobat® Reader®

Acrobat® Reader® is required to view Portable Document Format (PDF) files. All of the unit resources are PDF files. It is not necessary to install **Acrobat® Reader®** on your PC. If you do not have it installed, the application will use a 'run-time' version for the CD, i.e. one which only works with the 100 Maths Lessons application.

However if you would like to install **Acrobat® Reader®**, version 6, can be downloaded from the CD-ROM.* To do this, right-click on the **Start** menu on your desktop and choose **Explore**. Click on the + sign to the left of the CD drive entitled '100 Maths Lessons' and open the folder called **Acrobat Reader Installer.** Run the program contained in this folder to install **Acrobat® Reader®**. If you experience any difficulties viewing the PDF files, try changing your **Acrobat® Reader®** preferences. Select **Edit**, then **Preferences**, within **Acrobat® Reader®**. You will then be able to change your viewing options.

(*Please note that **Acrobat® Reader®** version 6 is not compatible with some versions of Windows 98. To download version 5 or for further information about Adobe Acrobat Reader, visit the website at www.adobe.com.)

Getting started

The *100 Maths Lessons CD-ROM* program should auto run when you insert the CD-ROM into your CD drive. If it does not, use **My Computer** to browse the contents of the CD-ROM and click on the '100 Maths Lessons' icon.

From the start up screen there are three options: Click on **Credits** to view a list of acknowledgements. You must then read the **Terms and conditions**. If you agree to these terms then click **Next** to continue. **Continue** on the start up screen allows you to move to the Main menu.

Main menu

Each *100 Maths Lessons* CD contains:

- core activity sheets – with answers, where appropriate, that can be toggled by pressing the 'on' and 'off' buttons on the left of the screen
- differentiated activity sheets for more and less able pupils (though not necessarily both more and less able sheets in every instance)
- blank core activity sheets for selected core activity sheets – these allow you to make your own differentiated sheets by printing and annotating
- general resource sheets designed to support a number of activities.

You can access the printable pages on the CD by clicking:

- the chosen term ('Autumn', 'Spring' or 'Summer')
- the unit required (for example, 'Unit 2: Place value and ordering)
- the requisite activity page (for example, 'Numbers to 10'; 'Less able').

To help you manage the vast bank of printable pages on each CD, there is also an 'Assessment record sheet' provided on the CD that you can use to record which children have tackled which pages. This could be particularly useful if you would like less able children to work through two or three of the differentiated pages for a lesson or topic. The termly planning grids found on pages 6-7, 88-89 and 160-161 have also been supplied on the CD in both **PDF** and **Microsoft Word** formats to enable you to incorporate the 'All New 100 Maths Lessons' units into your planning or to adapt them as required.

CD navigation

- **Back**: click to return to the previous screen. Continue to move to the **Menu** or start up screens.
- **Quit**: click **Quit** to close the menu program. You are then provided with options to return to the start up menu or to exit the CD.
- **Help**: provides general background information and basic technical support. Click on the **Help** button to access. Click **Back** to return to the previous screen.
- **Alternative levels**: after you have accessed a CD page, you will see a small menu screen on the left-hand side of the screen. This allows you to access differentiated or template versions of the same activity.

Printing

There are two print options:

- The **Print** button on the bottom left of each activity screen allows you to print directly from the CD program.
- If you press the **View** button above the **Print** option, the sheet will open as a read-only page in **Acrobat® Reader®**. To print the selected resource from **Acrobat® Reader®**, select **File** and then **Print**. Once you have printed the resource, minimise or close the **Adobe®** screen using – or **x** in the top right-hand corner of the screen.

Viewing on an interactive whiteboard or data projector

The sheets can be viewed directly from the CD. To make viewing easier for a whole class, use a large monitor, data projector or interactive whiteboard.

About Year 3

In Year 3 children use the empty number line, together with mental methods, for calculating. They are encouraged to make jottings when calculating with longer, or more difficult, numbers. They are introduced to using a calculator, especially where they do not yet have an effective method for calculating , such as multiplication of larger numbers.

EVERY DAY: Practise and develop oral and mental skills (eg counting, mental strategies, rapid recall of +, –, × and ÷ facts)

- Read and write whole numbers to at least 1000.
- Say the number that is 1, 10 or 100 more or less than any given two- or three-digit number.
- Count on/back in 10s or 100s, starting from any two and three-digit number.
- **Know by heart: all addition and subtraction facts for each number to 20.**
- **Derive quickly doubles of all whole numbers to 15, and all the corresponding halves.**
- **Know by heart multiplication facts for the 2, 5 and 10 times-tables.**
- **Derive quickly: corresponding division facts.**

Units	Days	Topics	Objectives
1	3	Place value and ordering	• **Read and write whole numbers to 1000** in figures and words. • **Know what each digit represents**, and partition three-digit numbers into a multiple of 100, a multiple of ten, and ones (HTU).
		Estimating, rounding	• Give a sensible estimate of up to about 100 objects. Read and begin to write the vocabulary of estimation and approximation.
		Measures	• Read scales to the nearest division (labelled or unlabelled).
2–3	10	Understanding addition and subtraction	• Extend understanding of the operations of addition and subtraction, read and begin to write the related vocabulary, and continue to recognise that addition can be done in any order. Use the +, – and = signs.
		Mental calculation strategies (+ and –)	• Use knowledge that addition can be done in any order to do mental calculations more efficiently. For example: put the larger number first and count on. • Identify near doubles, using doubles already known (eg 80 + 81). • Bridge through a multiple of 10, then adjust.
		Problems involving 'real life', money and measures	• Solve word problems, including finding totals and giving change, and working out which coins to pay. • Recognise all coins and notes. **Understand and use £.p notation** (for example, know that £3.06 is £3 and 6p).
		Making decisions	• **Choose and use appropriate operations (including multiplication and division) to solve word problems**, and appropriate ways of calculating: mental, mental with jottings, pencil and paper.
		Checking results of calculations	• Check subtraction with addition.
4–6	13	Measures	• Read the time to 5 minutes on an analogue clock and a 12-hour digital clock, and use the notation 9.40. • Measure and compare using standard units (km, m, cm), including using a ruler to draw and measure lines to nearest half cm. • Read and begin to write the vocabulary related to length. • Suggest suitable units and measuring equipment to estimate or measure length. • Record estimates and measurements to the nearest whole or half unit (eg 'about 3.5kg'), or in mixed units (eg '3m and 20cm'). • Know the relationship between kilometres and metres, metres and centimetres. • Begin to use decimal notation for metres and centimetres. • Read scales to the nearest division (labelled or unlabelled).
		Shape and space	• Classify and describe 3-D and 2-D shapes including the hemisphere, prism, semicircle, quadrilateral... referring to properties such as reflective symmetry (2-D) the number or shapes of faces, the number of sides/edges and vertices, whether sides/edges are the same length, whether or not angles are right angles. • Read and begin to write the vocabulary of position, direction and movement: for example, describe and find position of a square on a grid of squares with the rows and columns labelled. • **Identify right angles** in 2-D shapes and in the environment.
		Reasoning about numbers or shapes	• Investigate a general statement about familiar numbers or shapes by finding examples that satisfy it.
7	2	Assess and review	

EVERY DAY: Practise and develop oral and mental skills (eg counting, mental strategies, rapid recall of + and – facts)

- Read and write whole numbers to at least 1000.
- Say the number that is 1, 10 or 100 more or less than any two- or three-digit number.
- Count on or back in tens or hundreds, starting from any two- or three-digit number.
- Say a subtraction statement corresponding to a given addition statement, and vice versa.
- Know by heart all addition and subtraction facts for each number up to 20.
- Derive quickly doubles of all whole numbers to 20, and all the corresponding halves.
- Identify near doubles, using doubles already known.
- Know by heart all pairs of multiples of 100 with a total of 1000.
- Recognise odd and even numbers to 100.
- Know by heart multiplication facts for the 2, 5 and 10 times-tables.
- Derive quickly: corresponding division facts.

Units	Days	Topics	Objectives
8	5	Counting, properties of numbers and number sequences	• **Count on or back in tens or hundreds, starting from any two- or three-digit number**. • Count on or back in twos, starting from any two-digit number and recognise odd and even numbers to at least 100.
		Reasoning about numbers or shapes	• Solve mathematical problems or puzzles, recognise simple patterns and relationships, generalise and predict. Suggest extensions by asking 'What if...?' • **Explain methods and reasoning** orally and, where appropriate, in writing.
9–10	10	Understanding × and ÷	• Understand multiplication as repeated addition. • Read and begin to write the related vocabulary. • Extend understanding that multiplication can be done in any order.
		Mental calculation strategies (× and ÷)	• To multiply by 10/100, shift the digits one/two places to the left.
		Problems involving 'real life', money and measures.	• Solve word problems involving numbers in 'real life', money and measures, using one or more steps, including finding totals and giving change, and working out which coins to pay. Explain how the problem was solved.
		Making decisions	• **Choose and use appropriate operations (including multiplication and division) to solve word problems,** and appropriate ways of calculating: mental, mental with jottings, pencil and paper.
		Checking results of calculations	• Check subtraction with addition, halving with doubling and division with multiplication. • Repeat addition or multiplication in a different order.
11	5	Fractions	• **Recognise unit fractions** 1/2, 1/3, 1/4, 1/5, 1/10, **and use them to find fractions of shapes and numbers.** • Begin to recognise simple fractions that are several parts of a whole 2/3, 3/4, or 3/10.
12	5	Understanding addition and subtraction	• Extend understanding that subtraction is the inverse of addition.
		Mental calculation strategies (+ and –)	• Say or write a subtraction statement corresponding to a given addition statement and vice versa. • Find a small difference by counting up from the smaller to the larger number.
		Measures	• Read and begin to write the vocabulary related to time. • **Use units of time and know the relationships between them (second, minute, hour, day, week, month, year).** • Use a calendar.
		Making decisions	• **Choose and use appropriate operations (including multiplication and addition) to solve word problems.**
		Checking results of calculations	• Check subtraction with addition, halving with doubling and division with multiplication.
13	5	Handling data	• **Solve a given problem by organising and interpreting numerical data in simple lists, tables, and graphs,** for example: – simple frequency tables – Carroll diagrams (one criterion).
14	2	Assess and review	

Autumn term
Unit 1
Reading and writing numbers, estimating and reading scales

Children read and write HTU numbers in figures and words, and begin to know what each digit represents. They give sensible estimates of up to about 100 objects. They read scales to the nearest division, and read and begin to write the vocabulary of estimation and approximation.

LEARNING OBJECTIVES

		Topics	Starter	Main teaching activities
Lesson	1	Place value and ordering	● **Count on or back in tens or hundreds, starting from any two- or three-digit number**.	● **Read and write whole numbers to 1000** in figures and words.
Lesson	2	Place value and ordering	As for Lesson 1.	● **Know what each digit represents,** and partition three-digit numbers into a multiple of 100, a multiple of ten, and ones (HTU).
Lesson	3	Estimating and rounding Measures	● **Read and write whole numbers to at least 1000.**	● Give a sensible estimate of up to about 100 objects. ● Read and begin to write the vocabulary of estimation and approximation. ● Read scales to the nearest division (labelled or unlabelled).

Lessons   overview

Preparation
Enlarge CD pages 'Three-digit numbers' and 'Three-digit number words' to A3 and cut out. Photocopy CD page 'HTU arrow cards' onto card and cut out the cards. Enlarge the core version of 'Paper abacus' to A3.

Learning objectives
Starter
● **Read and write whole numbers to at least 1000.**
Main teaching activity
● Read and write whole numbers to 1000 in figures and words.
● **Know what each digit represents** and partition three-digit numbers into a multiple of 100, a multiple of 10, and ones (HTU).
● Give a sensible estimate of up to about 100 objects.
● Read and begin to write the vocabulary of estimation and approximation.
● Read scales to the nearest division (labelled or unlabelled).

Vocabulary
number, zero, one, two, three… ten, eleven, twelve, thirteen… twenty, thirty, forty… one hundred, two hundred, three hundred… one thousand, digit, units, ones, tens, hundreds, one-/two-/three-digit number, larger, smaller, greater, place, place value, exchange, the same number as, as many as, equal to, before, after, next, between.

You will need:
Photocopiable pages
'Paper abacus' (page 12) enlarged to A3, one for each child.

CD pages
'Three digit numbers', 'Three-digit number words', 'HTU arrow cards' for each child (see General resources) and 'Paper abacus' less able and more able versions (see Autumn term, Unit 1).

Equipment
Blu-Tack; 13 small counters for each child.

Lesson

Starter

Review counting in tens from and back to any two-digit number. Say: *Start on 23. Count on in tens until I say 'Stop!' Then count back to the start number.* Repeat this several times with different start numbers, such as 17, 32, 26.

Now choose a larger two-digit start number, such as 87. This time ask the children to count back to as close to zero as they can go. Say: *Who can predict which number we shall stop on if we count back in tens? Yes, seven. Why do you think that?* Repeat this for other start numbers, such as 76, 99, 84.

Main teaching activities

Write '23' on the board and ask: *What does the 2 mean? What about the 3?* Write 'TU' above the digits. Now write up '123' and ask: *What does the one stand for? And the two? The three?* Write 'HTU' above the digits and explain that 'H' stands for 'hundreds'. Write the word 'hundreds' on the board. Now write up a different three-digit number, such as 253 and ask: *What number is this? Which is the tens/ hundreds/units digit?* Repeat this for other three-digit numbers.

Explain that you are going to hold up some three-digit numbers on cards. Ask the children to read each number as you show it to them. Show the cards from CD page 'Three-digit numbers' and ask the children to say each number. Now write on the board 'One hundred and thirty-four' and ask: *What number is this?* Ask a child to write the number again, this time in digits. Repeat this for other three-digit numbers. Use the cards from CD page 'Three-digit number words' and ask the children to read the words.

Group work: Provide each pair with a set of CD pages 'Three-digit numbers' and 'Three-digit number words'. Ask them to shuffle the cards together, and play either Snap or Pelmanism with them so that they have practice in matching words and numerals for hundreds numbers. Give the children about ten minutes to do this. Then ask the children to shuffle their cards again, and to take turns to take the top card. Without showing their partner, they say the number (whether in words or numerals) and their partner writes the number down, both as a numeral and in words. They check each other's work.

Differentiation

Less able: Decide whether to just provide numeral cards at this stage, so that the children can concentrate on reading these. If so, ask the children to work in pairs and to take turns to read out the number from the card for their partner to write down using numerals.

More able: Challenge the children to choose two of their cards then to write at least five numbers which fit between them, so that the numbers are ordered from least to most. They can repeat this for different pairs of numbers.

Plenary & assessment

Ask a pair of the more able children to write up a set of numbers on the board, but out of order. Invite the rest of the class to read these numbers, then ask individual children to write the numbers again, this time in words. Ask questions such as:
- *Which is the hundreds/tens/units/digit?*
- *How can you tell?*

Repeat this with several different sets of numbers. If you have time, invite the children to order the numbers, starting with the smallest.

Lesson

Starter

Repeat the Starter from Lesson 1, but this time invite the children to count across the hundreds 'bridge'. For example, count on from 94 to 194 and back again; count down from 187 to 87 and back again, and so on.

Main teaching activities

Write the headings 'Hundreds', 'Tens' and 'Units' on the board. With Blu-Tack, stick the 100-card from CD page 'HTU arrow cards' onto the board under the hundreds heading. Now put the 10-card under the tens heading and the 1-card under the units heading. Ask the children to read each card. Combine the cards to make 111 and ask the children to read this. Write 100 + 10 + 1 = 111. Repeat for randomly chosen arrow cards, each time making the complete number.

Erase what is written on the board. Now write up 415 and ask: *What does the four/one/five represent? What is this number? Who can write it as words for me?* Invite the children to jot down another number which uses all three of the digits 1, 4, 5. Ask: *What number did you write?* Invite a child to write this on the board for you, and ask what each digit represents.

Group work: Provide each child with activity sheet 'Paper abacus' and several small counters. Ask them to use the three digits on their sheet to make as many HTU numbers as they can, modelling each number using the counters on the abacus. They write the numbers as hundreds add tens add units, as an HTU number, and in words.

Differentiation

Less able: Decide whether to use the version of 'Paper abacus' which asks the children to make TU numbers.

More able: There is a version of the sheet which asks the children to order their sets of numbers from largest to smallest.

Plenary & assessment

Review the core version of 'Paper abacus', using the A3 version pinned to the board. Ask: *How did you decide where to put your counters?* Invite a child to write the first set of numbers in order, from smallest to largest. Ask: *Which number is the smallest? How can you tell? So which is the largest?* Write another set of three digits onto the board, and challenge the children to say which numbers can be made from these. Encourage them to think about which would be the smallest, and which the largest numbers that they can make.

Lesson overview

Preparation:
Make an OHT from CD page 'Reading scales' and enlarge a few copies of 'Measuring scales' to A3.

Learning objectives
Starter
- Read and write whole numbers to at least 1000.

Main teaching activity
- Give a sensible estimate of up to about 100 objects.
- Read and begin to write the vocabulary of estimation and approximation.
- Read scales to the nearest division.

Vocabulary
guess how many, estimate, nearly, roughly, close to, approximate, approximately, too many, too few, enough, not enough

You will need:
Photocopiable pages
'Measuring scales' (page 13) for each child with some copies enlarged to A3.

CD pages
'Reading scales', copied onto an OHT for the teacher's/LSA's reference (see General resources).

Equipment
Metre stick marked in decades; OHP; jars with different quantities of cubes in, from about 50 to 100; counting stick; individual whiteboards and pens.

Lesson ③

Starter

Explain that you will give a fact about a three-digit number. Ask the children to write a number that fits that fact onto the whiteboard and to hold it up when you say 'Show me'. Say, for example: *Write a number that has a seven as a hundreds/tens/units digit. Write a number that is even/odd. Use the same digits as the number on your board; don't rub it out; now write the number that has the largest digit in the hundreds/tens/units space.*

Main teaching activities

Whole class: Show the children the jar of cubes and ask: *How many cubes do you think there are here?* Invite a child to open the jar and count the cubes. Discuss how these can be counted most efficiently, such as counting in twos or fives. Repeat for another jar.

Group work: Provide each group of four children with a jar of cubes to estimate, then check by counting.

Whole class: Invite the children to say how close their estimate was to their count. Ask: *How did you count the cubes?* Praise those children who grouped the cubes for ease of counting.

On the board draw a line and label one end '0' and the other '100'. Explain that you would like the children to estimate what should go at points on the line. Point to the mid-point of the line and ask: *Which number do you think will go here?* Invite a child to write in their answer. Repeat for other positions along the line, working in approximate decades. Draw another line like the first one. This time mark positions which are not quite decades. Invite the children to explain how they made their decisions.

Use a metre stick which is marked in 10cm increments. Point to positions on the metre stick, at first to decade markings, then to positions that are not 'exact' decades. Ask the children to give an estimate of what the reading would be. Put up the OHT of CD page 'Reading scales'. Invite the children to look at the ruler. With a washable (whiteboard) pen, put an arrow above the 15cm position and invite the children to say what the reading is, and why. Repeat for other positions. Repeat this for the dial scale, then for the litre jug. Each time invite a child to explain how they made their reading.

Group work: Provide each child with a copy of activity sheet 'Measuring scales'. Ask the children to look carefully at each picture and to write in their estimate of the reading from the scale. Explain that for the dial scales they can write their answer as, for example, '1kg and 500 g' or '1½ kg'.

Differentiation

Less able: Decide whether to work with these children as a group. Use an enlarged version of the 'Measuring scales' and discuss each picture so that the children have the opportunity to take turns to make their reading.

More able: When the children have finished the 'Measuring scales' sheet, ask them to work with a partner. They take turns to draw a line and mark the beginning and end of it with numbers, then mark a point on the line. Their partner estimates the reading on the scale.

Plenary & assessment

Show the children a counting stick and label the ends of the stick, for example, '0' to '100'. Ask the children to estimate the number at the point where you touch the stick. At first point to the decades, then point between the decades, and challenge the children to decide what to estimate and to explain their thinking. Extend this, by re-labelling the ends of the stick '0' to '1000', so that the intermediate points are in hundreds. Ask: *What number do you think this point is? Why do you think that? Write that number onto the board for me.*

Name	Date

Paper abacus

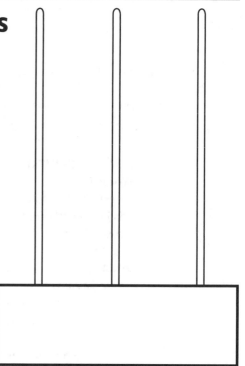

You will need 13 counters.

Use the counters to make three-digit numbers on the abacus.

Each number must have the digits 2, 5 and 6.

How many different numbers can you make?

Write the value of the numbers that you make in the table below.

Hundreds	Tens	Units	The number

Now write your numbers again, in words here.

_____

_____

_____

_____

_____

_____

| Name | Date |

Measuring scales

Look at the arrows on these scales.

Write in your estimate of the measurement in the first answer box.

Write what length is shown between the arrows in the second answer box.

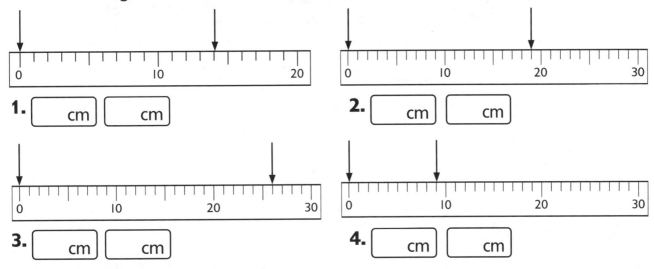

1. [cm] [cm]

2. [cm] [cm]

3. [cm] [cm]

4. [cm] [cm]

Write the weight.

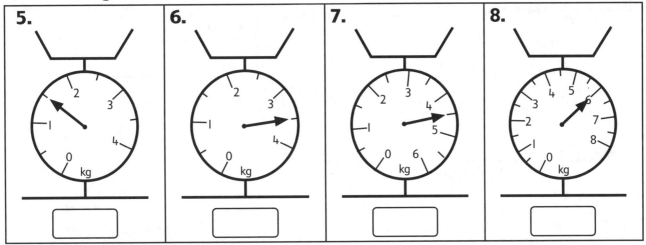

5.

6.

7.

8.

Write how much water is in the jug.

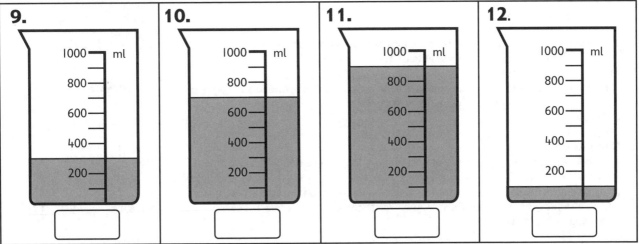

9.

10.

11.

12.

Addition and subtraction

Children recognise that addition can be done in any order, but that this is not so for subtraction. They use the +, – and = signs in writing number sentences. They learn mental strategies for putting the larger number first and counting on, identifying near doubles, and bridging through the nearest ten and adjusting.

LEARNING OBJECTIVES

		Topics	Starter	Main teaching activities
Lesson	1	Understanding addition and subtraction	● **Know by heart: all addition and subtraction facts for each number to 20.** ● **Read and write whole numbers to at least 1000** in figures and words.	● Extend understanding of the operations of addition and subtraction, read and begin to write the related vocabulary, and continue to recognise that addition can be done in any order. Use the +, – and = signs.
Lesson	2	Understanding addition and subtraction	As for Lesson 1.	As for Lesson 1.
Lesson	3	Mental calculation strategies (+ and –)	● Say the number that is 1,10 or 100 more or less than any given two- or three-digit number.	● Use knowledge that addition can be done in any order to do mental calculations more efficiently. For example: put the larger number first and count on.
Lesson	4	Mental calculation strategies (+ and –)	As for Lesson 1.	● Use knowledge that addition can be done in any order to do mental calculations more efficiently. For example: put the larger number first and count on. ● Identify near doubles, using doubles already known (eg 80 + 81).
Lesson	5	Mental calculation strategies (+ and –)	● **Read and write whole numbers to at least 1000** in figures and words.	● Use knowledge that addition can be done in any order to do mental calculations more efficiently. For example: put the larger number first and count on. ● Bridge through a multiple of 10, then adjust.

Lesson   overview

Preparation
Enlarge CD page 'Numeral cards 0 to 20' to A3, photocopy onto card and cut out to make a teaching set of numeral cards. Photocopy CD page 'Number fans' onto card. Ask the children to cut these out and fix the 'petals' together with a paper fastener. Enlarge CD page 'Number lines' to A3 and photocopy.

Learning objectives
Starter
● **Know by heart: all addition and subtraction facts for each number to 20**.
● **Read and write whole numbers to at least 1000** in figures and words.
Main teaching activity
● Extend understanding of the operations of addition and subtraction, read and begin to write the related vocabulary, and continue to recognise that addition can be done in any order. Use +, – and = signs.

Vocabulary
add, addition, more, plus, make, sum, total, altogether, double, near double, one more, two more, ten more… one hundred more, subtract, take away, minus, leave, how many are left/left over? difference between, one less, ten less… one hundred less, above, below, before, after, left, right, up, down, higher, lower, next to, listen, recite, think, remember, start at, read, write, write in figures, start at

You will need:
CD pages
'Numeral cards 0 to 20', 'Number fans', 'Number lines', all enlarged to A3 for the teacher's/LSA's reference and one for each child (see General resources).

Equipment
Paper fasteners; Blu-Tack; pens.

Lesson ①

Starter

Explain to the children that you will show them a numeral card, from 0 to 10 to begin with. Ask them to use their number fans to show you what must be added to the number on the card to total 10. Keep the pace of this sharp as you want to encourage rapid recall. Extend this to complements for 20 by asking the children to show the number that must be added to the one that you show to total 20.

Main teaching activities

Whole class: Fasten CD page 'Number lines' onto the board with Blu-Tack. Explain to the class that you would like them to use the number line to help them to add. On the board, write an addition sentence, such as 65 + 10 and ask: *How could we use the number line to work this out?*

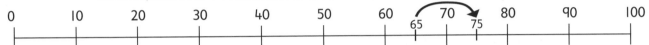

Children may suggest 60 + 10 + 5, or 65 and count on 10. Both are acceptable. Model these and write up the answer: 65 + 10 = 75. Now say: *If 65 + 10 = 75, what would 75 subtract 10 equal? How did you work that out? What other addition and subtraction sentences can you make from the numbers 65, 10 and 75?* Write up the children's suggestions of 10 + 65 = 75 and 75 – 65 = 10. Repeat this for other addition and subtraction sentences, such as 27 + 30. Encourage children to work mentally where possible, by counting along a mental number line to add/subtract 30.

Group work: Write some addition sentences onto the board which involve addition of a decade number, such as: 54 + 10, 82 + 10, 37 + 30, 59 + 40. Keep the total to less than 100. Ask the children to calculate the totals and to write three more sentences: one for addition and two for subtraction for each original number sentence. Remind them that the three numbers that they have must each be used in these number sentences. Provide blank copies of CD page 'Number lines' which the children can use to help them.

Differentiation

Less able: If the children find counting on in steps of ten difficult, work with this group and complete the first two number sentences together. Model how to count along the line. Ask the children to work in pairs to complete the next two sentences, then work together as a group again to check that they have understood.

More able: Suggest that the children work using a mental number line in order to add and subtract.

Plenary & assessment

Review some of the number sentences together. Invite children to explain how they worked out the answer. Ask: *If I know that 37 add 30 is 67, what other addition and subtraction facts can I work out?* Repeat this for some new examples, such as 56 + 40 or 35 + 60.

Lesson ②

Starter

Repeat the Starter for Lesson 1. This time include all of the 0 to 20 cards from CD page 'Numeral cards 0 to 20' to find complements for 20.

Main teaching activities

Whole class: Write the numbers 46 and 27 onto the board and ask: *What is 46 subtract 27?* Invite suggestions of how to work this out. Children may find it useful to either count back from 46 or on from 27 along a number line if they cannot calculate this mentally. Write 46 – 27 = 19 on the board. Ask: *What other addition and subtraction sentences can we write from these numbers?* Write up the suggestions: 46 – 19 = 27; 27 + 19 = 46; 19 + 27 = 46. Remind the children that if one fact is known there are three other facts that can be derived. Now write up 19 – 46 and ask: *Is this the same as 46 – 19? Why not? How do you know that?* Explain that, for example, 27 + 19 = 19 + 27 = 46 but that 46 – 19 is not the same as 19 – 46.

Group work: Explain to the children that you would like them to work in pairs to respond to some written number sentences. Ask them to answer each one, then to explain to each other how they worked out the answer. Suggest that where they disagree they should think about how they could check the answer, for example, using the fact that there are four addition and subtraction facts that use the same numbers. Write some facts on the board such as:

1. 67 add 20.
2. 25 take away 9.
3. 40 plus 50.
4. 34 subtract 20.
5. What is the difference between 33 and 28?
6. What must I add to 6 to make 24?
7. 9 added to a number is 59. What is the number?
8. I think of a number. I add 35. The answer is 70. What is my number?
9. Subtract 30 from 95.
10. Find pairs of numbers with a difference of 20.

Differentiation
Less able: Provide CD page 'Number lines' for the children to use if they need further support.
More able: Set the children a further challenge: to use the number range 0 to 70. Find pairs of numbers with a difference of 17. Work systematically and order the answers.

Plenary & assessment
Review the work that the children have done. Invite them to explain the calculation methods that they chose. Ask questions such as: *How did you work this out? Who chose a different way?* Ask the children who respond to model how they calculated. Set another question for the children, such as 'How many less is 13 than 37?' Ask: *How would you work this out?* Children may count up from 13 to 37. Model this on the board: 13 + **7** = 20; 20 + **10** = 30; 30 + **7** = 37, so 7 + 10 + 7 = 24, or 37 – 13 = 30 – 10 + 7 – 3 = 20 + 4 = 24. Remind the children that in order to calculate some subtraction sentences they may find it easier to count up, or add on from the lower to the higher number.

Lesson overview

Preparation
Have ready two sets of 0 to 9 numeral cards from CD page 'Numeral cards 0 to 20' for each pair.

Learning objectives
Starter
● Say the number that is 1, 10 or 100 more or less than any two- or three-digit number.
● **Know by heart: all addition and subtraction facts for each number to 20.**
● **Read and write whole numbers to at least 1000** in figures and words.
Main teaching activity
● Use knowledge that addition can be done in any order to do mental calculations more efficiently. For example: put the larger number first and count on.
● Identify near doubles, using doubles already known (eg 80 + 81).
● Bridge through a multiple of 10, then adjust.

Vocabulary
add, subtract, double, sum, total, hundred, ten, unit

You will need:
Photocopiable pages
'Using mental strategies' (page 19) and 'Working mentally' (page 20) for each child.

CD pages
'Using mental strategies' and 'Working mentally', less able and more able versions (see Autumn term, Unit 2); two sets of 0 to 9 numeral cards (from CD page 'Numeral cards 0 to 20') for each pair (see General resources).

Lesson ③

Starter

On the board draw this table:

Number	+ 1	– 1	+ 10	– 10	+ 100	– 100

Write a three-digit number into the first column, such as 236, and ask the children to say the answer for each column as you point along the table. Repeat this for other three-digit numbers. Keep the pace sharp so that the children have to think quickly in order to respond. You may wish to ask individual children to respond to particular parts of the table, to check that they can add/subtract 1, 10 or 100.

Main teaching activities:

Whole class: Explain that today the children will use the mental strategy of putting the larger number first in order to count on. On the board, write 5 + 126 and ask: *How should we begin to do this mentally?* Accept the suggestion of rewriting the sentence as 126 + 5. You may find it helpful to use an empty number line:

+5
126   131

When the children have understood the modelling using an empty number line, provide further examples of adding a single digit to an HTU number, such as 7 + 238.

Now write up 30 + 53 and explain that the same method can be used to calculate this. Draw an empty number line:

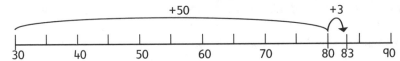

Explain that this can be calculated by starting at 53 and counting on three tens. Show this on the number line by marking in the three tens.

Now ask children to try this counting along a mental number line. Say: *What is 40 + 57?* Invite children to explain how they calculated: 57 + 10 is 67; add 10 is 77; add 10 is 87; add 10 is 97. So 40 + 57 is the same as 57 + 40 which is 97.

Group work:

Ask the children to work in pairs. Give each pair two sets of 0 to 9 numeral cards and ask them to shuffle the cards together. One of them takes three cards, generates an HTU number; the other takes a single card. They write an addition sentence, putting the larger number first and counting on mentally to find the answer. Ask them to generate ten such questions, shuffling the cards after each one. Then they take turns to take two cards to make a TU number and take one more card, to which they add a zero to make a decade number. Again, they write the addition sentence and calculate mentally. Again, ask them to generate ten such questions.

Differentiation

Less able: Suggest to the children that they make TU add U sentences, and draw a blank number line if they need help.
More able: Challenge these children to calculate HTU add decade numbers.

Plenary & assessment

Invite children from each ability group to write up one of their number sentences, without the answer onto the board. Ask the class: *How can we solve this?* Invite the children to explain how they calculated the answer.

Lesson 4

Repeat the Starter from Lesson 2. This time maintain a quick pace to ensure that the children are using rapid recall. For the whole-class work, ask the children to calculate doubles, such as 35 + 35. Now ask them to calculate 36 + 35 and discuss how this can be seen as double 35 + 1. Repeat for other examples, such as 40 + 50 (double 40 + 10); 17 + 19 (double 20 −1 − 3). Provide activity sheet 'Using mental strategies', which is available in differentiated formats. During the 'Plenary & assessment', ask further near doubles questions, challenging the children to explain how they worked these out. Not everyone will use the same method, which will give good talking points. Discuss which method was easier and more efficient, and why.

Lesson 5

Starter

Shuffle together three sets of 0 to 9 cards. Explain that you will hold up three cards at a time to make an HTU number. Ask the children to say the number. Repeat this several times, keeping the pace sharp. Now invite individual children to write the number words onto the board, for example for the less able you might choose 57; for the more able you might choose 307 or 370, and ask questions such as: *What does the zero represent?*

Main teaching activities

Whole class: Explain to the class that today they will be adding and subtracting to/from a two-digit number, crossing the tens boundary. Begin with subtracting a single-digit number from a teens number, such as 16 – 7. Explain that this can be done in two steps: 16 – 6 – 1, so that the calculation could be written as 16 – 6 – 1 = 10 – 1 = 9. Repeat this for other examples, such as 13 – 7, 15 – 8, 14 – 9. Now ask the children to respond to questions that you write on the board such as: 14 – 8 = ☐; 14 – ☐ = 6; ☐ – 8 = 6. Discuss how if you know one fact, others can be found.

Now write on the board: 57 + 6 = and explain that this can be calculated by crossing the tens boundary like this: 57 + 6 = 57 + 3 + 3 = 60 + 3 = 63. Repeat for further examples, such as 45 + 8, asking the children to work mentally and to explain what they did. Write the mental calculation onto the board for everyone to see. Repeat this for subtraction, such as 53 – 8. Then ask the children to work mentally to complete questions that you write on the board: 47 + 6 = ☐; 47 + ☐ = 53; ☐ + 6 = 53; and 74 – 7 = ☐; 74 – ☐ = 67; ☐ – 7 = 67.

Individual work: Provide each child with a copy of activity sheet 'Working mentally' to complete. This covers the work for today and recaps on Lessons 3 and 4 of this unit.

Differentiation

Less able: Decide whether to use the differentiated version of the activity sheet for this group, which contains addition and subtraction for crossing 10 and 20.
More able: You may like to use the version of the activity sheet which includes some examples of crossing hundreds.

Plenary & assessment

Divide the class into two teams and choose captains. Ask the captains to come to the front. Explain that each team will, in turn, be given a number question to solve, and that the captain will decide who answers. However, the captain must ask a different person each time! Keep a score on the board for correct answers, and the first team to score ten points wins. Ask questions such as: *What is 15 subtract 7? What is 67 + 8? 92 – 5? 54 – 8?* When one team has gained ten points, ask: *What strategies did you find helpful to work out the answers?*

Name	Date

Using mental strategies

There are some near-double questions in the cloud, and the answers are on the birds.

Join the questions to the answer.

Use the mental strategy of doubling and adjusting to find the answers.

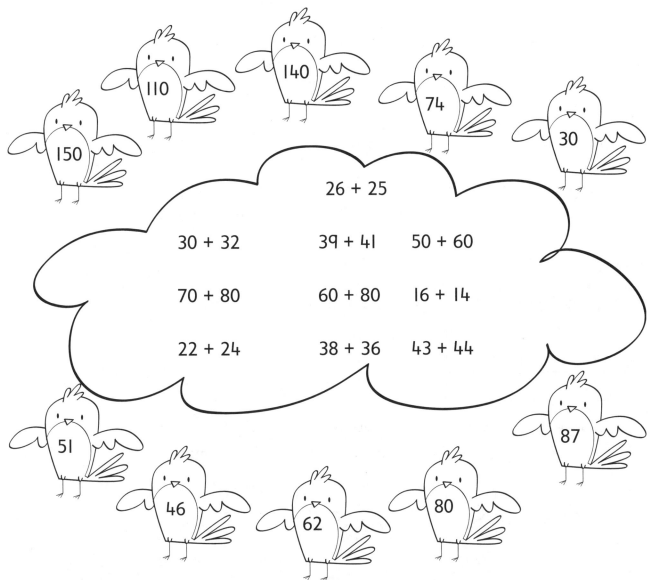

Now write the answers to these.

Write a number sentence for each one to show how you worked out the answer.

46 + 45 _____

70 + 80 _____

17 + 19 _____

_____

Name	Date

Working mentally

Write the answers to the number sentences.

1. 16 – 8 = ☐   **2.** 15 – 6 = ☐

3. 17 – 9 = ☐   **4.** 16 – 9 = ☐

5. 35 + 7 = ☐   **6.** 47 + 8 = ☐

7. 64 + 7 = ☐   **8.** 73 + 9 = ☐

9. 65 – 8 = ☐   **10.** 72 – 9 = ☐

11. 56 – 8 = ☐   **12.** 87 – 8 = ☐

Write the answer to this number sentence.

Then write three more number sentences using the same numbers.

64 + 6 = ☐

☐ + ☐ = ☐

☐ – ☐ = ☐

☐ – ☐ = ☐

Now choose your own two-digit number and a single-digit number.

Write four number sentences like the ones you have just done.

☐ + ☐ = ☐

☐ – ☐ = ☐

☐ – ☐ = ☐

Decide how to work this out.

Write the answer and a sentence to show how you worked out the answer.

_____

45 + 46 = ☐   _____

_____

Money, solving problems and making decisions

Children learn to record money using the decimal point. They solve word problems concerning money, choose appropriate operations, find totals and give change. They check addition with subtraction, and subtraction with addition.

LEARNING OBJECTIVES

	Topics	Starter	Main teaching activities
Lesson 1	Problems involving 'real life', money and measures	● **Know by heart: multiplication facts for the 2, 5, and 10 times-tables.**	● Solve word problems, including finding totals and giving change, and working out which coins to pay. ● Recognise all coins and notes. **Understand and use £.p notation** (for example, know that £3.06 is £3 and 6p).
Lesson 2	Problems involving 'real life', money and measures	● **Know by heart multiplication facts for the 2, 5, and 10 times-tables.** ● Derive quickly: division facts corresponding to the 2, 5 and 10 times-tables. ● **Read and write whole numbers to at least 1000** in figures and words.	As for Lesson 1.
Lesson 3	Problems involving 'real life', money and measures	● **Know by heart: all addition and subtraction facts for each number to 20.**	As for Lesson 1.
Lesson 4	Making decisions	As for Lesson 3.	● **Choose and use appropriate operations (including multiplication and division) to solve word problems,** and appropriate ways of calculating: mental, mental with jottings, pencil and paper.
Lesson 5	Checking results of calculations Making decisions	● **Know by heart: all addition and subtraction facts for each number to 20.** ● **Read and write whole numbers to at least 1000** in figures and words.	● Check subtraction with addition. ● **Choose and use appropriate operations (including multiplication and division) to solve word problems,** and appropriate ways of calculating: mental, mental with jottings, pencil and paper.

Lesson   overview

Preparation
Enlarge 'Multiplication facts for 2, 5 and 10 times-tables' and 'Price tags' to A3 and photocopy onto card to make teaching sets.

Learning objectives
Starter
● **Know by heart: multiplication facts for the 2, 5, and 10 times-tables.**
● Derive quickly: division facts corresponding to the 2, 5 and 10 times-tables.
● **Read and write whole numbers to at least 1000** in figures and words.
Main teaching activity
● Solve word problems, including finding totals and giving change, and working out which coins to pay.
● Recognise all coins and notes. **Understand and use £.p notation** (for example, now that £3.06 is £3 and 6p).

Vocabulary
coin, pound, £, pence, price, cost, cheaper, pay, change, total, how much? note, value, more/less expensive, collect, use, make, name, pick out, discuss

You will need:
CD pages
'Multiplication facts for 2, 5 and 10 times-tables', 'Number fans' and 'Price tags' for each child (see General resources).

Equipment
Large sheets of sugar paper and pens; pots of coins containing 5p, 10p, 20p, 50p, £1 and £2 coins; £5 and £10 notes.

Lesson ①

Starter

Explain to the children that you will hold up a card which has a 2, 5 or 10 times-table fact on it. Ask the children to use their number fans to show the answer when you say 'Show me'. Keep the pace sharp as this is an opportunity for children to recall rapidly these facts.

Main teaching activities

Whole class: Provide each group with a pot of coins and ask the children to use the coins to make £2 in different ways. They can make a group record of what they have done by writing addition money sentences onto large sheets of paper to make posters. Give the children about five minutes to do this and impress on them the need to work quickly but accurately. Now ask one of the groups to show their poster to the rest of the class. Invite a child to 'prove' that one of the money sentences is correct by holding up and counting the coins, using the shopkeeper's method, for example: *50p and 50p is a pound, and a £1 coin makes £2.* Repeat this for other suggestions from other groups. Now ask: *How much is £2 and 50p? How would this be written on a price tag?* Invite a child to write on the board £2.50. Explain that the dot separates the pounds from the pence and that it must be included otherwise this would be £250! Repeat for other amounts, including pence, such as £5.45 and £6.25. Each time, ask a child to count out coins to make the amount and another child to write the amount on the board. Ask questions such as: *How many pence are there in £1? So how many pence are there in £6? How many pence are there in £6.25? How would you write 356p in pounds and pence?*

Group work: Ask the children to work in groups of four. They will need a pot of coins which also includes 5p pieces. Write some amounts of money onto the board, such as: £3.50; £5.60; £7.75, up to £10. Ask the children to find three different ways of paying each amount and to record these as addition money sentences on large sheets of paper.

Differentiation

Less able: If the children are unsure about larger amounts of money, decide whether to limit them to finding amounts to £1. Alternatively, suggest that they find ways of paying whole pounds: £1, £2, using the coins in their pots, and finding three different ways each time.
More able: Challenge the children to find the way which uses least coins each time as one of their three ways.

Plenary & assessment

Review what the children have done. Invite each group to present one of their suggestions. Ask the more able children to show how they would use the fewest number of coins for each example. Ask questions such as: *How would I write the total of three £1 coins and five 5p coins? How would I write the total of six 50p coins and three 20p coins? How many pennies are there in £6.90? £8.05?*

Lesson ②

Starter

Repeat the Starter from Lesson 1, this time reading out the facts you choose as division rather than multiplication. For example, for a card that reads 3 × 2, you might say 'What is 6 divided by 2?' Keep the pace sharp, asking the children to show their answers using number fans.

Main teaching activities

Whole class: Explain that today the children will be finding totals and giving change. Provide them with pots of coins and notes so that they can model the questions. Show the children the £5 note and explain that it is worth £5, before asking them to work quickly in their groups to find different ways of making £5. Repeat this for the £10 note. Now ask all the children, apart from the less able ones, to put the coins and notes away so that they work mentally. Say: *You have £5 to spend. Here is a price tag for £3.50. How much change would you receive? How can you work this out?* Invite suggestions, such as counting up to £4 then adding £1. Model this with the children. Draw an empty number line on the board and put on £3.50, £4 and £5. Count up: *£3.50 and 50p makes £4 and £1 makes £5. 50p and £1 is £1.50 so the change from £5 is £1.50.* Repeat this for other examples, such as £4.60 and £6.85.

Paired work: Provide each pair with a set of price tags from CD page 'Price tags'. Ask them to take turns to take a tag and work out the change from £10. Remind them that they can use the empty number line to help them to count up if they find this difficult to do mentally.

Differentiation
Less able: there are blank tags available. These can be used with this group with smaller prices and a starting sum of money such as £2.
More able: Decide whether to use the blank tags and write in more challenging amounts, such as £6.87.

Plenary & assessment
Invite pairs to model one of their responses. Ask them to explain how they worked out the change. Ask: *Who did it this way? Did anyone use a different method? Which do you think is better? Why do you think that?* Now set a challenge for all the children to try, writing it on the board as you explain. *You have £5 to spend. There are three CDs that you would like but you can only afford to buy two. The prices are £3.15, £2.60 and £1.75. Which two would you choose? How much would they cost in total? How much change would you have?* Give the children about five minutes to solve this. Then ask: *Which did you choose? How did you work out your answers?*

Lesson ③④⑤ overview

Preparation
Make an OHT of 'Reading and writing numbers'.

Learning objectives
Starter
● **Know by heart: all addition and subtraction facts for each number to 20.**
● **Read and write whole numbers to at least 1000** in figures and words.
Main teaching activity
● Solve word problems, including finding totals and giving change, and working out which coins to pay.
● Recognise all coins and notes. **Understand and use £.p notation** (for example, know that £3.06 is £3 and 6p).
● **Choose and use appropriate operations (including multiplication and division) to solve word problems**, and appropriate ways of calculating: mental, mental with jottings.
● Check subtraction with addition.
● **Choose and use appropriate operations (including multiplication and division) to solve word problems,** and appropriate ways of calculating: mental, mental with jottings, pencil and paper.

Vocabulary
number facts, number bonds, number pairs, operation, number sentence, jotting, mental calculation, calculate, answer, explain your method, explain how you got your answer, give an example of… show how you… show your working

You will need:
Photocopiable pages
'Money problems' (page 25) and 'Checking answers' (page 26) for each child.

CD pages
'Money problems' and 'Checking answers' less able and more able versions (see Autumn term, Unit 3); 'Reading and writing numbers' for each child (see General resources).

Equipment
Pots of coins; Blu-Tack.

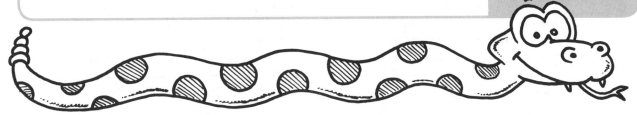

Lesson ③

Starter
Ask the children to call out the complement of 20 to random numbers you give from one to 20. For example, if you say *Eighteen*, the children reply *Two*. Keep the pace sharp.

Main teaching activities
Whole class: Explain that today the children will be solving word money problems. Say: *Cal buys three packets of crisps and the crisps cost 35p per packet. How much did he pay altogether? How much change did he get from a £2 coin?* Ask the children to suggest how much they estimate the three packets of crisps will cost and write their estimates on the board. Now ask: *How can you work out the cost of three packets of crisps?* Children may suggest doubling 35p to 70p and adding on 35p. Invite suggestions for finding the change. If children are unsure about working mentally to count up, draw an empty number line on the board and demonstrate the counting up method again (see Lesson 2).
Paired work: Ask the children to work in pairs to solve the following problem: *Paul sends six letters. Each letter costs 30p to send. How much do the letters cost to send in total? How much change does Paul get from £2?* Provide coins for the less able to model the problem.
Individual work: Provide each child with a copy of activity sheet 'Money problems'. Ask them to record how they worked out the problems as well as their answers.

Differentiation
Less able: There is a differentiated version of 'Money problems' with totals up to £5.
More able: You may prefer to use the activity sheet with change from up to £20 with this group.

Plenary & assessment
Review together the problems on the core 'Money problems' sheet. Invite children to explain the methods that they chose.

Lesson ④

Repeat the Starter from Lesson 3. This time divide the children into two groups, each with a captain. As you ask for complements the captain decides who should answer, but must choose a different child each time. Keep score. The first team to score 10 correct answers wins. Explain that you would like the children to solve a problem. On the board write: *Some toys cost £2.80, £1.70, £1.50, £1.30, £2.10 and £1.40. You have £5. Which three toys could you buy?* Invite the children to suggest some ways of solving this. Now ask the children to work in pairs to solve the problem. Ask them to keep a careful record of what they do, and to write money number sentences to show their answers. Challenge them to find different ways of spending the £5. Provide some coins to help the less able children. During the 'Plenary & assessment', invite pairs to show how the £5 could be spent.

Lesson ⑤

Using an OHT of CD page 'Reading and writing numbers', ask children to mark the three-digit numbers/the two-digit numbers/numbers greater than... Then write up a problem: *Kit Ling gave £1.20 of her pocket money to her brother. She had £2.30 left. How much pocket money did Kit Ling have left?* Invite the class they might solve this before asking a child to write it as a money number sentence, such as £1.20 + £2.30 = £3.50. *How can we check this using subtraction?* Write up £3.50 – £2.30 = ☐ and invite an answer. Then provide the differentiated activity sheet 'Checking answers' for the children to complete. During the Plenary & assessment, write 56p + 8p on the board and ask: *How can we work out the answer?* Children may suggest: 56p + 4p + 4p = 60p + 4p = 64p. Now ask: *How could we check our answer?* Children may suggest: 64p – 8p = 64p – 4p – 4p = 60p – 4p = 56p.

Name	Date

Money problems

Read the problem.

Decide how you will solve it.

Then write some money sentences to show how you worked out the answer.

1. Gilly eats 10 firelighters. Each firelighter costs 25p.

How much did Gilly spend?

What change did she have from £5.00?

2. Gilly eats 5 gritty cakes that cost 40p each.

How much does she spend?

What is her change from £5.00?

3. Gilly buys an enormous spider for £2.50, a frog for £1.75 and a juicy toad for £2.25.

How much did she spend in total?

What change did she have from £10.00?

Name	Date

Checking answers

Solve these problems.

Write a money sentence to show how you solved each problem.

Then write a check sentence to show how you checked your answer.

1. Mark bought a torch for £2.50 and a battery for £1.70.

How much did he spend? ☐

What change did he receive from £5? ☐

I checked my answers by:

£2.50

£1.70

2. Dillip had £10 in his pocket to spend. He bought two CDs at £4.65 each.

How much did he spend? ☐

How much change did he receive? ☐

I checked my answers by:

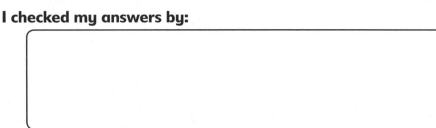
£4.65
£4.65

3. In a sale, Lily bought some shorts for £3.55 and a T-shirt for £4.85.

How much did she spend in total? ☐ She had £1.60 left.

How much money did she have to start with? ☐

I checked my answers by:

£4.85
£3.55

Autumn term
Unit 4

Time and length

Children learn to read the time in five-minute intervals using both analogue and digital clocks. They read and begin to write the vocabulary of length, suggest suitable unit and measuring equipment, and record to the nearest half centimetre. They use rulers to measure lines and to make lines of a given measurement.

LEARNING OBJECTIVES

	Topics	Starter	Main teaching activities
Lesson 1	Measures	● **Know by heart multiplication facts for the 2, 5, and 10 times-tables**.	● Read the time to 5 minutes on an analogue clock and a 12-hour digital clock, and use the notation 9.40.
Lesson 2	Measures	● **Know by heart multiplication facts for the 2, 5, and 10 times-tables.** ● Derive quickly: division facts corresponding to the 2, 5 and 10 times-tables.	● Measure and compare using standard units (km, m, cm), including using a ruler to draw and measure lines to nearest half centimetre.
Lesson 3	Rapid recall of multiplication and division facts Measures	● Derive quickly: doubles of all whole numbers to at least 20, and all the corresponding halves.	● Read and begin to write the vocabulary related to length. ● Suggest suitable units and measuring equipment to estimate or measure length.
Lesson 4	Measures	● **Read and write whole numbers to at least 1000** in figures and words.	● Know the relationship between kilometres and metres, metres and centimetres. ● Begin to use decimal notation for metres and centimetres. ● Record estimates and measurements to the nearest whole or mixed units (eg 1g and 20cm). ● Read scales to the nearest division (labelled or unlabelled).
Lesson 5	Measures	● Derive quickly: division facts corresponding to the 2, 5 and 10 times-tables. ● Derive quickly: doubles of all whole numbers to at least 20, and all the corresponding halves. ● **Read and write whole numbers to at least 1000** in figures and words.	As for Lesson 4.

Lesson overview

Preparation
Photocopy CD page 'Analogue clock face' onto card. Ask the children to cut these out and make up their clock faces using paper fasteners to fit the hands.

Learning objectives
Starter
● **Know by heart multiplication facts for the two, five and ten times-tables.**
Main teaching activity
● Read the time to 5 minutes on an analogue clock and a 12-hour digital clock, and use the notation 9.40.

Vocabulary
time, hour, minute, o'clock, half past, quarter to, quarter past, clock, watch, hands, digital, am, pm

You will need:

Photocopiable pages
'Digital times' (page 32) for each child.

CD pages
'Analogue clock face' for each child (see General resources).

Equipment
Teaching analogue and teaching digital clocks; individual whiteboards and pens.

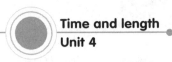

Lesson ①

Starter

Explain that you will say a number, such as 15, which is an answer to a multiple of five. Ask the children to write down the multiples (3 × 5) on their whiteboards and, when you say 'Show me', to hold these up. Repeat this for multiples of two, then multiples of ten.

Main teaching activities

Whole class: Show an analogue teaching clock. Ask: *How many minutes are there in an hour?* Move the minute hand forward from 12 and encourage the children to count in leaps of five up to 60. Now set the hands of the clock to, for example, ten past five and ask: *What time does the clock show? Where does the hour hand point? And the minute hand? So how do you know that the minute hand shows ten minutes past the hour?* Repeat this for other five-minute intervals, such as 5.20, 7.15, 8.45. Now discuss how to read 'minutes to the hour', such as 8.40. Explain that this is 20 minutes to the next hour, nine. Repeat this for all of the five-minute intervals to the next hour.

On the board write a digital time such as 7.30 and ask: *What time is this?* Elicit the responses of both 7.30 and half past seven. Repeat this for quarter past and quarter to times. Now introduce the other five-minute intervals written as digital time, such as 4.05, 2.10, 7.40, 9.50. Explain that the way in which we write time is the same way in which digital clocks and watches show digital time. Children who have their own digital watch could show this to a neighbour at this point, if you wish.

Using the analogue teaching clock, set the times to five-minute intervals of your choice, such as 2.05 or 6.20. Then invite the children to use their whiteboards to write down the digital time, and to hold up their boards when you say 'Show me'.

Group work: Provide each child with the activity sheet 'Digital times', which asks them to write the digital equivalent for different analogue times.

Differentiation

Less able: Work with this group. Provide each child with an individual clock face so that they can set the time shown on the activity sheet. If they are unsure of the 'minutes to' times, count from half past: 30, 25… to the clock minute hand, to find the minutes, then agree what the next hour would be. Ask the children to count around the clock in five-minute intervals in order to find the digital time.

More able: When the children have completed the activity sheet, ask them to write down their favourite TV programmes. They should draw or stamp two clock faces next to each other, and show the start and finish times as analogue time, then write underneath the digital times.

Plenary & assessment

Ask children to work in pairs to write a digital time (using multiples of five minutes only) that would appear before midday, for example 9:05. One child of each pair comes out and holds up time for the class to see. Those children still sitting direct you to move children until they are standing in time order, with earliest time on left to latest on right. Ask the children:

● *What helped you to sort this out?*
● *How many minutes are there in every hour?*
● *What other facts do you know now from this lesson that might help at another time?*

Use a large digital clock face. Set the digital clock in turn to these times:
10:15   08:20   12:45   06:50
Now ask the children to set their individual clock faces to these times. When you say 'Show me', for each time they hold up their clock face for you to check.

If you have time, invite the more able children to say their favourite TV programmes and to set both the analogue and digital clock faces to start and finish times for the other children to read. Challenge the more able and, where appropriate, the other children, to state how long each programme lasts.

Lesson overview

Preparation
Cut the string into 1.5m, 1m, 50cm, 2m and 5m lengths.

Learning objectives
Starter
● **Know by heart multiplication facts for the 2, 5 and 10 times-tables.**
● Derive quickly: division facts corresponding to the 2, 5 and 10 times-tables.

Main teaching activity
● Measure and compare using standard units (km, m, cm) including using a ruler to draw and measure lines to nearest half centimetre.

Vocabulary
metre, centimetre, distance apart, length, further, furthest, ruler, metre stick, tape measure

You will need:
CD pages
'Lines to measure' for each child (see General resources).

Equipment
String; tape measure; rulers marked in cm and half cm; clear plastic ruler to use with the OHP; OHP; OHT pen; 2-D shape templates.

Lesson

Starter
Write on the board three numbers that make a multiplication or division fact in the 2 times-table, such as 2, 5, 10. Ask the children to put up their hands to give you one of the facts and write this on the board. Repeat this until all four facts have been written. Continue with other sets of three numbers, for the 2, 5 and 10 times-tables. Keep the pace sharp.

Main teaching activities
Whole class: Hold up a piece of string that measures approximately 1.5 metres and ask: *How long do you think this string is?* Invite some suggestions and write these on the board. Now invite suggestions of which measuring equipment would be best for measuring the string, such as a tape measure. Invite two children to come to the front and measure the string. Ask: *How long is it? How close was this to our estimate? How will you record this?* On the board write '3 metres 50 centimetres' and explain that this can be written in another way. Write '3.5 metres'. Explain that the decimal point separates the whole metres from parts of a metre, and that the .5 represents 50cm, or half of a metre. Repeat this for the other lengths of string. Each time, invite a child to record the measurement on the board.

Now show how to measure with reasonable accuracy using a ruler. Explain that the measurement begins at the beginning of the marks on the ruler, not at the edge of the ruler. Using the OHT of CD page 'Lines to measure' and a clear plastic ruler, demonstrate how to measure. Show where the ruler is placed against the line and how to read the measurement. Repeat for the other lines on the sheet, asking a child to make the measurement this time and explain, where necessary, that halfway between two centimetres is .5 of a centimetre, or 5 millimetres. Write a measurement on the board, such as 5.5cm and 5cm 5mm. Record each measurement against the line using an OHT pen.

Now, using a fresh, blank OHT sheet, demonstrate how to draw a line of a given length, such as 6cm. Repeat this, this time inviting a child to demonstrate.

Individual work: Ask the children to draw lines in their book of the following lengths: 10cm, 5cm, 8cm, 13cm, 9.5cm and 3.5cm. Check that everyone is using the ruler appropriately. Now ask the children to swap books with the person sitting next to them to check the lengths of the lines by measuring.

Paired work: Ask the children each to draw a line on a sheet of paper. They swap papers with their partners, measure the line and write its measurement, then their partner checks that they agree.

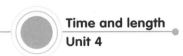

Time and length

Unit 4

Ask them to do this six times, each drawing three lines which are whole centimetres in length, and three lines which have a half centimetre in the length, such as 8.5cm.

Differentiation:

Less able: Check that the children understand how to use the ruler appropriately. If they are unsure, simplify the task by providing rulers marked just in centimetres to begin with, so that they measure and draw lines of whole centimetres in length.

More able: Invite the children to draw around a shape template, such as a rectangle or pentagon. Ask them to estimate first the total length around the shape, then to measure each side and to calculate the total length.

Plenary & assessment

Draw a line, for example 9.5cm in length, on a fresh, blank OHT and invite a child to measure it. Ask the other children to watch carefully and to check where the ruler is placed against the line, and what they think the length is. Ask the child to record the length on the board. Now invite the children to explain the following:

- *Which part of the ruler is not used for measuring? Why is that?*
- *Where do we place the ruler against the line?*
- *How would we record six and a half centimetres?*
- *What is another way to say .5 of a centimetre?*

Lesson   overview

Learning objectives

Starter
- Derive quickly: doubles of all whole numbers to at least 20, and all the corresponding halves.
- **Read and write whole numbers to at least 1000** in figures and words.

Main teaching activities
- Read and begin to write the vocabulary related to length.
- Suggest suitable units and measuring equipment to estimate or measure length.
- Know the relationship between kilometres and metres, metres and centimetres.
- Begin to use decimal notation for metres and centimetres.
- Record estimates and measurements to the nearest whole mixed unit (eg 1g and 20cm).
- Read scales to the nearest division (labelled or unlabelled).

Vocabulary
distance apart… between… to… from… kilometre, metre, centimetre

You will need:

Photocopiable pages
'Measuring lengths' (page 33) for each child.

CD pages
'Number fans', 'Three-digit numbers', 'Three-digit number words' for each child (see General resources).

Equipment
For each group a tray with items measuring less than, more than and about 20cm, such as pens, pencils, strips of card, ribbon; rulers; measuring tapes; individual whiteboards and pens.

Lesson

For the Starter explain that you will say a number and that you would like the children to show you the double of that number using their number fans. Use numbers between 1 and 15. For the Main teaching activity, write on the board '1 kilometre', and ask: *How many metres in a kilometre?* Repeat this for centimetres in metres, and millimetres in centimetres. Invite the children to work in groups of four and to write lists of what could they measure in: kilometres; metres, centimetres and millimetres. During the 'Plenary & assessment', review their lists, invite others to say whether they agree with suggestions and to explain their thinking. Explain that in the United Kingdom we still measure road distances in miles, but in Europe they use kilometres, and that a kilometre is just over half a mile in length.

Lesson 4

Starter

Explain that you will hold up a card with a number on it. Ask the children to read the number aloud. Use cards from CD pages 'Three-digit numbers' and 'Three-digit number words' so that the children practise reading three-digit numbers and number words.

Main teaching activities

Whole class: Explain that today and tomorrow you would like the children to solve some measurement problems. Begin by asking the children to work in small groups of about four to look at the items on the tray and to decide which of these measure more than 20cm, which measure less, and which measure about 20 cm. Suggest that they make a group list to show their estimates. Review the sorting that the children have done and ask: *How did you decide which items you estimated were more than/less than/about 20cm?* Encourage the children to explain their thinking. Now ask the children to use rulers to check their sorting. Ask: *Did you make a good estimate?*

Paired work: Working in pairs, ask the children to begin with the first of these measuring activities, and to try the second one if time allows.

1. Choose a measuring device to estimate and measure the handspan, around the wrist, and arm length of a partner. Measure and record to the nearest half centimetre. Decide which of the partners has the wider handspan, longer arm, larger wrist.

2. Find ten things in the classroom that are estimated to be about 30cm in length. Check by measuring and record each measure to the nearest half centimetre.

Differentiation

Less able: Decide whether to work as a group at this activity, and check the children's measuring skills for reasonable accuracy.

More able: Encourage the children to work quickly but accurately, and to complete both activities.

Plenary & assessment

Review the measuring of wrists, etc. Ask: *Who had the longer arm? Did this match your estimate?* Ask each pair to compare their results with another pair and to order the results for handspan from widest to narrowest. Invite a group of four to write up the handspan measurements, in order, on the board and ask the other children to check that they agree with the ordering. If children have found items of about 30cm in length, invite individuals to measure one of their choices to show how close their estimate was.

Lesson 5

For the Starter, ask the children to record on their whiteboard the three-digit numbers that you suggest. Say whether you would like the children to record their answer in numerals or words. Review recording to the nearest half centimetre and how to write this as a decimal fraction of a centimetre. Ask the children to complete the activity sheet 'Measuring lengths' individually. This is not differentiated and so you may wish to work with the less able children as a group. During the Plenary ask questions such as:

● *Which measurement do we use to measure distances in the United Kingdom? In Europe?*
● *How would you write the measurement eight and a half centimetres?*
● *So how do you think you would record three and a half metres?*
● *How much, in centimetres, is 3.5 metres?*
● *How many centimetres do you think there are in 3.05 metres?* (If necessary, explain that the .05 means five centimetres, or five out of 100 centimetres.)

Name	Date

Digital times

Look at the clocks below. Write the time they show as digital time. The first one has been done for you.

Remember, the clock is a 12-hour clock only.

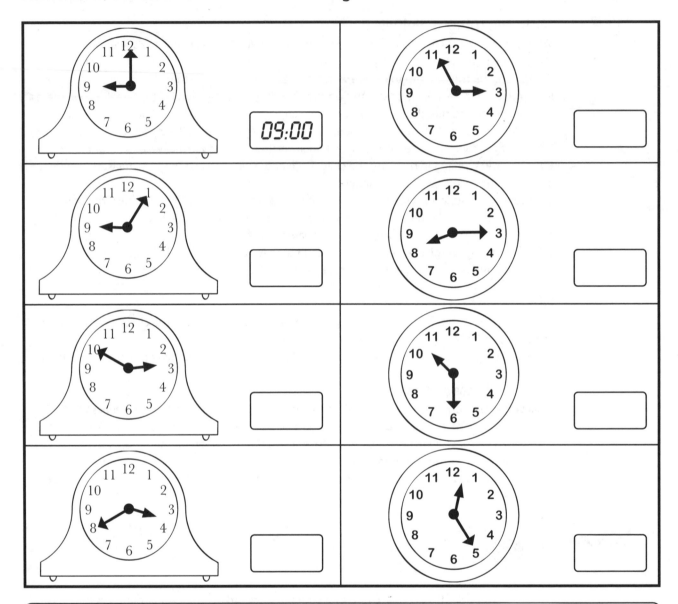

Now draw and write your own analogue and matching digital time.

Name	Date

Measuring lengths

Use a ruler to measure these lines to the nearest half centimetre.

Write their measurement in centimetres.

1.

2.

3.

4.

5.

6.

You will need a large sheet of paper.

Draw these lines as accurately as you can.

7.   6cm

8.   12cm

9.   5.5cm

10.   13.5cm

Children learn to classify and describe 3-D and 2-D shapes. They identify right angles. They learn about position, direction and movement.

LEARNING OBJECTIVES

	Topics	Starter	Main teaching activities
Lesson 1	Shape and space	● Derive quickly doubles of all whole numbers to at least 20, and all the corresponding halves.	● Classify and describe 3-D and 2-D shapes, referring to properties such as reflective symmetry (2-D), the number or shapes of faces, the number of sides/edges and vertices, whether sides are the same length, whether or not angles are right angles. ● **Identify right angles** in 2-D shapes and the environment.
Lesson 2	Shape and space	As for Lesson 1.	As for Lesson 1.
Lesson 3	Shape and space	As for Lesson 1.	As for Lesson 1.
Lesson 4	Shape and space	● **Know by heart multiplication facts for the 2, 5, and 10 times-tables.** ● Derive quickly: division facts corresponding to the 2, 5 and 10 times-tables.	● Read and begin to write the vocabulary of position, direction and movement: for example, describe and find the position of a square on a grid of squares with the rows and columns labelled.
Lesson 5	Shape and space	As for Lesson 4.	As for Lesson 4.

Lesson   overview

Learning objectives
Starter
● Derive quickly doubles of all whole numbers to at least 20, and all the corresponding halves.
Main teaching activity
● Classify and describe 3-D and 2-D shapes, referring to properties such as (2-D), the number or shapes of faces, the number of sides/edges and vertices, whether sides are the same length, whether or not angles are right angles.
● **Identify right angles** in 2-D shapes and the environment.

Vocabulary
cube, cuboid, pyramid, sphere, hemisphere, cone, cylinder, prism, flat, curved, straight, two-dimensional (2-D), three-dimensional (3-D), quadrilateral

You will need:
Photocopiable pages
'Shape descriptions' (page 38) for each child.

Equipment
Individual whiteboards and pens; a tray for each group with 3-D shapes; A2 sheets of sugar paper; trays of 2-D shape tiles.

Lesson

Starter

Explain that you will say a number between 1 and 15. Ask the children to write the double of the number on their whiteboards and, when you say 'Show me', they hold up their boards for you to see. Keep the pace sharp.

Main teaching activities

Whole class: Provide each group with a tray of 3-D shapes and have a collection of these shapes for yourself. Ask the children to check that they can name each shape: hold up each shape in turn, ask the children to find it on their tray and then to volunteer its name. Write the name of each shape name on the board. Some may know the name of the hemisphere, but give this name and write it on the board. Ask: *How can you describe a hemisphere? What is special about it?* Encourage the children to use the vocabulary of 3-D and 2-D shape to do this, for example: *It is round; it has a circle as a base.* Repeat this for the triangular prism. Discuss right angles, and where children can see these, for example on a triangular prism.

Now explain that some of the shapes can be classified as prisms. Write 'prism' onto the board. Say: *If you cut a prism along its length it always has the same face. The end faces of a prism are identical.* Ask the children to sort the shapes into prisms (cubes, cuboids, triangular prisms) and not prisms (spheres, hemispheres, cones, pyramids, cylinders). Note that prisms have end faces which are polygons, and circles are not classified as polygons – so that the cylinder is not a prism.

Point to one of the vertices of the cube and say: *This is one of its vertices.* Write 'vertex' and 'vertices' on the board and say: *A vertex is the point where two lines or edges meet. Two or more are called vertices.* Invite the children to identify the vertices on the shapes in front of them. Explain that both two-dimensional and three-dimensional shapes have vertices, and write 'two-dimensional' and 'three-dimensional' on the board.

Paired work: In pairs, using sheets of A2 sugar paper and felt pens, ask the children to write three clear statements that describe a 3-D shape. It should read like a large description tag: 'Our shape is three-dimensional. It has four faces. Each face forms an equilateral triangle'. Remind the children that they can refer to 2-D shapes when describing 3-D ones, such as: *The shape has a circle as its base.* Ask the children to write statements for three different 3-D shapes.

Differentiation

Less able: Decide whether to complete the task as a group. This will give the children the opportunity to hear and use the vocabulary of shape.
More able: Challenge the children to write an extra statement for each shape that they choose.

Plenary & assessment

Invite pairs from each ability group to give statements for one of their shapes. Ask all the children: *Do you agree with this statement? What other statements could be made about this shape?*

Lesson ②

Repeat the Starter from Lesson 1, this time asking the children to write half of the number you say, within the range 2 to 30. One at a time, hold up the shapes from the tray for Lesson 1 and ask the children to give a description of the shape. Encourage them to refer to the 2-D faces, such as: *It has square faces.* Provide each child with a copy of 'Shape descriptions'. Ask them to read the description and to sketch how they think the shape would look. The less able children will find it helpful to have a selection of both 2-D and 3-D shapes in front of them. Challenge the more able children to draw another shape for each description, where possible. During the 'Plenary & assessment', review what the children have done. Invite children to show their shapes that they drew, and discuss the range of different shapes that fit the description. For example, the 2-D shape with four sides and a right angle does not have to be a square or rectangle!

Lesson ③

Starter

Use a combination of Lesson 1 and 2 Starters so that children practise both doubling and halving.

Main teaching activities

Whole class: Explain that a quadrilateral is any flat shape with four straight sides. Write 'quadrilateral' on the board. Now ask the children to use their whiteboard to sketch a quadrilateral for you that has a mathematical name. They will probably sketch a square or rectangle, but perhaps some more able children might sketch a parallelogram or trapezium. Provide each group with a tray of 2-D shapes and explain that you will describe a shape and you want them to hold up any shape that fits the description.

- *Hold up a quadrilateral. What shape are you holding?*
- *Hold up any shape that has a right angle.*
- *Hold up the shape that is half of a circle. What is this shape called?* (Write 'semicircle' on the board.)
- *Hold up any shape that has five equal sides and five vertices.*
- *Hold up any shape with a line of symmetry.*

Discuss symmetry in 2-D shapes, and which shapes do have a line of symmetry. Challenge your more able children identify shapes with more than one line of symmetry.

Paired work: Ask the children to sort out their set of flat shapes. They should write the names of the shapes into a Carroll diagram on large sheets of paper, with the following headings: 'Has straight sides'; 'Does not have straight sides'; 'Has at least one right angle'; 'Does not have at least one right angle'. Then ask the children to sort their shapes into those with a line of symmetry and those without. They can record these as lists.

Differentiation

Less able: Decide whether to limit the children to sorting by one property into a simplified Carroll diagram, such as 'Has straight sides'; 'Does not have straight sides'; or 'Has at least one right angle'; 'Does not have at least one right angle'.

More able: Challenge the children to suggest their own properties for sorting and to make another four-region Carroll diagram for sorting the shapes.

Plenary & assessment

Invite the more able children to set their challenge for the other children. Ask them to give one of their sorting properties, and invite the others to sort out the shapes that fit. Ask questions such as: *Which shapes fit this property? Which shapes do not fit that property? What other sorting properties can you think of? Which shapes would fit that property?*

Lesson   overview

Preparation
Photocopy CD page 'Grid coordinates' onto acetate to make an OHT and decide which squares will have words in them and make a note of this. Pin up the sheets of paper with 'North','South','East' and 'West' written on them appropriately in the classroom. Copy activity page 'Find the treasure' onto acetate.

Learning objectives
Starter
- **Know by heart multiplication facts for the 2, 5, and 10 times-tables.**
- Derive quickly: division facts corresponding to the 2, 5 and 10 times-tables.

Main teaching activity
- Read and begin to write the vocabulary of position, direction and movement: for example, describe and find the position of a square on a grid of squares with the rows and columns labelled.

Vocabulary
position, corner, direction, route, grid, column, row, North, South, West, East, whole turn, half turn, quarter turn, right angle, compass point

You will need:
Photocopiable pages
'Find the treasure' (page 39) for each child.

CD pages
'Multiplication facts for 2, 5 and 10 times-tables', 'Number fans' and 'Grid coordinates' for each child (see General resources).

Equipment
OHP; sheets of paper with 'North','South','East' and 'West' written on them; Roamer or PIP.

Lesson ④

Starter

Explain to the class that you will hold up multiplication fact cards for the 2, 5 and 10 times-tables (from the CD page). Ask the children to hold up their number fans to show the answer when you say 'Show me'. Keep the pace sharp so that the children use rapid recall to answer.

Main teaching activities

Whole class: Explain that today the children will be learning about the four compass directions. Show the children the sheets pinned up on the wall and ask them to point to each one as you say its name. On the board, write 'North', 'South', 'East' and 'West' and their shortened form of 'N', 'S', 'E' and 'W'. Now explain that you would like children to take turns to programme Roamer to move towards whichever compass direction you say. Explain that to programme Roamer to turn through one right angle it is necessary to input the number 90. Invite children to take turns to programme Roamer to move towards each of north, south, east and west.

Show the children how to read coordinates from a grid using an OHT of CD page 'Grid coordinates'. Explain that the convention is to read along the horizontal axis first and then up the vertical axis. Demonstrate this to show that the word 'cat' is at E5 (for example). Now explain that hidden on the grid there are some more words. Divide the class into two teams, each with a captain who will choose someone to suggest the coordinates of a square. If a correct square is chosen, write in a word into that square and award that team a point. Continue until one team has won five points.

Paired work: Give each pair of children several copies of 'Grid coordinates' and explain how to play 'Hunt the cat'. Explain that each of them draws in a cat and four mice on their own grids, but does not show their partner what they have done. They take turns to say a coordinate for a square. Their partner either says 'Found cat', 'Mouse' or 'Miss!' The children should mark in which squares they choose with a cross, and mark in cat or mouse when they find one of those squares. The winner is the one who finds all of his/her partner's cat and mice first.

Differentiation

Less able: Group the children in fours so one pair makes the choices and one pair checks the correct finds.
More able: Challenge this group by suggesting that they draw in the cat and mice, but to extend beyond one square each time. Now they need to find all the squares which contain each animal.

Plenary & assessment

Show the children the OHT of 'Grid coordinates' again. Mark a square with a cross and a different square with a circle. Invite children to suggest how they can move from one square to another by describing the route as, for example, 'Two squares west and two squares north'. Repeat this for other pairs of squares, using the vocabulary of both compass points and of coordinates.

Lesson ⑤

Repeat the Starter from Lesson 4, this time asking for division facts for the 2, 5 and 10 times-tables, and review coordinates and compass point directions. Provide each pair with a copy of activity page 'Find the treasure'. Ask them to write a list of movements to get from the ship to the treasure on the island. Remind the children that they should give the direction using compass directions and the square to move to using coordinates. Challenge the more able children to draw their own treasure island on squared paper, and to write how to find the treasure using both coordinates and compass points. Work with the less able to complete the task. During the 'Plenary & assessment' use an acetate of 'Find the treasure' and mark the treasure in a different position. Invite individual children to say the moves and to use an OHT pen to mark in the moves on the acetate to assess their understanding of both coordinates and compass points.

Name	Date

Shape descriptions

Read each description of a mathematical shape.

Sketch the shape in the space and write its name.

1. This shape is two-dimensional (2-D). It has four straight sides and at least one right angle. What could it look like?

_____

2. This shape is two-dimensional (2-D). It has three straight sides. No side is the same length. What could it look like?

_____

3. This shape is three-dimensional (3-D). It has six faces. Each face is a rectangle. What could it look like?

_____

4. This shape rolls easily along the floor. It is the same shape used for a football. It is 3-D. What could it look like?

Name	Date

Find the treasure

Find a route from the ship to the treasure.

Write down your moves using coordinates and compass point directions.

Now put a cross elsewhere on the island.

This is where more treasure is buried.

Write the moves again.

Children investigate general statements about numbers and shapes. They provide examples that fit the statements.

LEARNING OBJECTIVES

	Topics	Starter	Main teaching activities
Lesson 1	Reasoning about numbers or shapes	● Say the number that is 1, 10 or 100 more or less than any two- or three-digit number.	● Investigate a general statement about familiar numbers or shapes by finding examples that satisfy it.
Lesson 2	Reasoning about numbers or shapes	● **Know by heart: all addition and subtraction facts for each number to 20.**	As for Lesson 1.
Lesson 3	Reasoning about numbers or shapes	● **Read and write whole numbers to at least 1000** in figures and words.	As for Lesson 1.

Lesson   overview

Preparation
Draw a large rectangle onto card (about 120cm × 50cm) and cut out. Draw and cut out two equilateral triangles onto acetate. Photocopy CD page 'Hundred square' to make multiple copies.

Learning objectives
Starter
● Say the number that is 1, 10 or 100 more or less than any two- or three-digit number.
● **Know by heart: all addition and subtraction facts for each number to 20.**
● **Read and write whole numbers to at least 1000** in figures and words.
Main teaching activity
● Investigate a general statement about familiar numbers or shapes by finding examples that satisfy it.

Vocabulary
pattern, right, correct, wrong, what could we try next? rectangle, rectangular, square, line of symmetry, symmetrical, quadrilateral, triangle, triangular, hexagon, hexagonal, octagon, octagonal, describe the rule, investigate, explain

You will need:
Photocopiable pages
'Rectangles' (page 43) and 'Equilateral triangles' (page 44) for each child.

CD pages
'Hundred square' for each child (see General resources).

Equipment
2-D large rectangular shape cut from cardboard; plastic equilateral triangles; rulers; individual whiteboards and pens; OHP; sheets of A3 paper; hundred squares or number lines.

Lesson ①

Starter

Explain that you will say a number and how many more than that number you would like the children to write on their whiteboards. When you say 'Show me', the children hold up their boards for you to check. Say:

● *Write the number that is one more/less than 3, 15, 73, 99, 200, 501.*
● *Write the number that is ten more/less than 14, 25, 76, 98, 400, 721.*
● *Write the number that is 100 more/less than 100, 258, 803.*

Main teaching activities

Whole class: Explain that you are going to investigate some true/false statements using some simple shapes. On the OHP, place a rectangle at an angle so none of the sides are parallel to the edge of the illuminated screen.

Ask the children what they can already tell you about this shape and gather as many facts as possible. What do the children think would happen if you cut the shape in half? Ask:

● *Will both shapes have anything in common?*
● *Will the space the two shapes occupy (the area) remain the same or not?*
● *What sorts of angles will both shapes have?*
● *What do your answers depend upon?* (Whether the cuts are horizontal, vertical or diagonal.)

● Cut the shape in half to form two rectangles and replace onto the OHP. What can the children say now about both shapes? Emphasise their identical size and the symmetrical nature after cutting.

Paired work: Ask the children to work in pairs to investigate the statement 'When you cut any rectangle exactly in half, you will always get two rectangles'. They should sketch their findings. Hopefully someone will use a diagonal cut so you can say 'No' to the statement posed initially (if necessary, prompt this solution with direction). Now eliminate the use of diagonal cuts and ask the children to try cutting lots of rectangles from the activity sheet 'Rectangles' before asking: *When you cut any rectangle in half without diagonal cuts, will you always get two rectangles?* Be prepared for the question: 'Is a square a rectangle?' (Yes) Ask the children to measure their rectangles with a ruler. Encourage them to record their work systematically.

Differentiation

Less able: Work with this group once they have some findings. Help them to say a sentence each about what they have found out, so that they can contribute to the Plenary.
More able: Set the challenge: 'When you make a horizontal and vertical cut through a rectangle to make quarters, will all the quarters be rectangles?'

Plenary & assessment

Ask the children to make true or false statements to you, for example: 'All my cut shapes had four sides.' 'All my cut shapes had four lines of symmetry.' 'All my shapes had sides longer than 6cm.' Let all the children help show whether the statements are true or false.

Discuss with the children:
● *What have you learned today?* (One child might feel more confident in recognising that a square is a special rectangle.)
● *Can you see the relevance in doing this work?* (Knowing how to cut or fold a rectangle to make two smaller rectangles, and knowing the properties of both shapes are identical, can help predict what might happen when cutting other regular shapes up.)
● *When might an adult use this knowledge?* (When cutting up carpet tiles for laying, for example.) Emphasise that making a general statement about shapes helps us to understand the properties of shapes.

Lesson ②

Starter

Explain that you will ask an addition question and would like the children to work quickly mentally to answer. Ask, for example: *What must I add to 7 to give 12?* Write the addition sentence $7 + 5 = 12$ on the board, then ask the children to give you another addition and two subtraction sentences which use these numbers.

Main teaching activities

Whole class: Ask the children to close their eyes and visualise a triangle. Invite them to sketch what they picture on their whiteboards. (Most children will draw an equilateral triangle.)

Discuss the properties of a triangle, drawing examples of scalene, isosceles and right-angle triangles on the board. Check that the children recognise all of these as forms of triangles.

Now ask the children to visualise two equilateral triangles sliding together so one of the sides touches fully. They should sketch what they visualise on their whiteboards before showing this happening on the OHP. *What shapes can be made? Will the shapes always have four sides if we insist on two sides touching?* (Yes)

Group work: The children use activity sheet 'Equilateral triangles'. Explain that equilateral triangles are special and that their sides are all the same length. Ask the children to investigate the statement: 'If two equilateral triangles join so that one side of one triangle always touches a side of the other triangle, the new shape will always have four sides.'

Differentiation

Less able: Provide this group with plastic equilateral triangles as colour can help the children keep track of what they have tried.

More able: What if there were three triangles? How could the children write down their ideas without the cut-out shapes? Distribute the activity sheet 'Equilateral triangles' to the group. Explore with them the idea of using correct mathematical vocabulary to describe what they see. Write all their statements on A2 paper. Cut out the statements into strips and reassemble in order of clarity.

Plenary & assessment

Invite children from each ability group to show their sketches and to say a sentence to explain their results.

Lesson ③

For the Starter, ask the children to write a three-digit number on their whiteboards. In groups of four, the children line up, showing their whiteboards from the smallest to the largest numbers. Continue adding groups until the whole class is standing in a semicircle with all the numbers in the correct order. Now say: *The multiplication table for 2 is always even.* Ask the children to discuss this in pairs for about a minute and to find examples that match this statement. Talk about their ideas before challenging pairs to investigate the statement: 'The multiplication table for four is always even.' Ask the children to record their work systematically. For Plenary & assessment, invite children from each ability group to explain what they have found out and to give examples which show that the statement is true.

Name   Date

Rectangles

Work with a partner.

Cut out the rectangles.

Investigate the statement: 'When you cut any rectangle in half without diagonal cuts, you always get two rectangles.'

Make some sketches and write some sentences to explain what you find out.

Name	Date

Equilateral triangles

Cut out the triangles at the bottom of this sheet.

Join them together as your teacher described.

Continue to join them together.

Sketch your results here.

Write a sentence to explain your results.

_____

_____

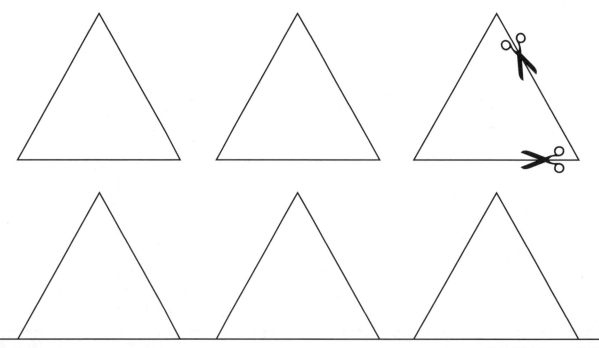

Counting in 10s and 100s and solving problems

Children count on and back in 10s and 100s, and develop their understanding of odd and even two-digit numbers. They solve problems using patterns and relationships, and make generalisations and predictions. They record orally or in writing.

LEARNING OBJECTIVES

	Topics	Starter	Main teaching activities
Lesson **1**	Counting, properties of numbers and number sequences	● Say or write a subtraction statement corresponding to a given addition statement, and vice versa.	● **Count on or back in tens or hundreds, starting from any two- or three-digit number.** ● Count on or back in twos, starting from any two-digit number and recognise odd and even numbers to at least 100.
Lesson **2**	Counting, properties of numbers and number sequences	As for Lesson 1.	● **Count on or back in tens or hundreds, starting from any two- or three-digit number.** ● Count on or back in twos, starting from any two-digit number and recognise odd and even numbers to at least 100. ● Count larger collections by grouping them: for example in tens, then other numbers.
Lesson **3**	Reasoning about numbers or shapes	● **Know by heart multiplication facts for the 2, 5 and 10 times-tables.** ● Derive quickly: division facts corresponding to the 2, 5 and 10 times-tables.	● Solve mathematical problems or puzzles, recognise simple patterns and relationships, generalise and predict. Suggest extensions by asking 'What if…?' ● **Explain methods and reasoning** orally and, where appropriate in writing.
Lesson **4**	Counting, properties of numbers and number sequences	● Identify near doubles, using doubles already known.	As for Lesson 3.
Lesson **5**	Reasoning about numbers or shapes	As for Lesson 3.	As for Lesson 3.

Lesson   overview

Preparation
Fill sets of three containers with objects and label 'A', 'B' and 'C', one set for each group.

Learning objectives
Starter
● Say or write a subtraction statement corresponding to a given addition statement, and vice versa.
Main teaching activity
● **Count on or back in tens or hundreds, starting from any two- or three-digit number.**
● Count on or back in twos, starting from any two-digit number and recognise odd and even numbers to at least 100.
● Count larger collections by grouping them: for example in tens, then other numbers.

Vocabulary
odd, even, multiple of, sequence, continue, predict, pair, relationship.

You will need:
Photocopiable pages
'Counting larger groups of numbers' (page 50) for each child.

CD pages
'Counting larger groups of numbers' more able version (see Autumn term, Unit 8) (see General resources).

Equipment
Counting stick; interlocking cubes; sets of three different-sized transparent pots marked 'A', 'B' and 'C' and filled with up to 100 different resources (such as conkers, marbles, paperclips – one set of three pots per group of four children); paper cups.

Lesson ①

Starter

Explain that you will say an addition or subtraction fact and ask the children to write the answer onto their whiteboards. They hold up their boards when you say 'Show me'. Use a variety of vocabulary for this, such as: *8 add 7, 9 plus 4, 17 subtract 11, What is 5 less than 12? What is 8 more than 6? What is the difference between… and…? How many more should I add to… to make…?* and so on. Keep the pace sharp to encourage rapid recall and check who responds accurately and who will need further help with recall.

Main teaching activities

Whole class: Practise counting sequences, which cross the hundreds boundaries, with the children by chanting, pointing to the numbers on a counting stick as you do so, eg 29, 39, 49… 99, 109, 119, 129. Lead the children both in sequence but also by hopping your finger around the stick. If you hold the stick in one hand with a thumb at the centre point of the stick this will give the children a visual clue of where which numbers come on the stick. Try using these numbers:

- Jumping in tens from 9, 28 and 32.
- Jumping in tens from 120, 222 and 314.
- Jumping in hundreds from 30, 100, 58 and 247.

Include chanting backwards with the counting sequences.

Now ask: *How can we tell if a number is odd or even?* If the children are unsure, make a tower of ten cubes and ask: *Is this odd or even?* Invite a child to break the tower into two and to note that the two smaller towers are the same height. Repeat for an odd number of cubes. Explain that even numbers will halve exactly; odd numbers will always have one left over. Invite the children to list all the single-digit even numbers and the odd numbers. These can be written on the board as two ordered lists. Then ask: *Is 12 even or odd? What about 17? 39? 124?* Elicit from the children that if the units digit is even then it is an even number, and if it is odd, then it is an odd number.

Group work: Ask the children to work in pairs. They take turns to say a three-digit start number less than 900, then count on in tens, stopping after saying ten numbers and writing down the numbers that they say. They decide whether their numbers are odd or even. Ask the pairs to generate at least five even number patterns and five odd number patterns.

Differentiation

Less able: Decide whether the children should start their counting patterns with a two-digit number between 70 and 99 so that they cross the first hundreds boundary in their counting.
More able: Challenge the children to find counting patterns which cross the thousands boundary.

Plenary and assessment

Invite children from each group to give one of their counting patterns. The other children can join in the chant, forwards and back again. Ask: *Is this an odd or an even pattern? How can you tell?* Ask the children to count in tens from, say, 178. Ask questions such as: *Is this an odd or even pattern? How can you tell? But the starting number tens digit is odd and so is the hundreds digit. Doesn't that make a difference? Can you explain why not?*

Lesson ②

Starter

Repeat the Starter from Lesson 1 using different numbers in similar number questions. Ensure that the pace is sharp to encourage rapid recall.

Main teaching activities

Whole class: Repeat the counting stick activity from Lesson 1, this time counting in twos, tens and hundreds. Now invite the children to look at the jar of cubes. Ask: *How many do you think there are in the jar?* Write the estimates on the board. Ask: *How can we check how many?* If children suggest counting in ones, say that this will take a long time and that you would like them to check quickly. Children may suggest counting in twos, fives or tens. Invite a child to count in tens before discussing how efficient this was. Talk about how it can sometimes be easier to count in twos or fives, depending upon what it is that you are counting. Compare the estimates with the count.

Group work: This task will help the children to practise their estimating skills. Display the sets of pots labelled 'A', 'B' and 'C' where each group can see them. Give the children the activity sheet 'Counting larger groups of numbers'. Tell them that they should answer the questions by estimating how many objects are in each container, before counting them as instructed on the sheet.

Differentiation

Less able: Put no more than 50 objects in each pot for this group. This group will also benefit from working in mixed-ability pairings for the counting. Provide paper cups to be used as counting pots.

More able: Decide whether to provide the differentiated sheet for this group which includes writing explanations of how the children found the answers.

Plenary and assessment

Using pot A, take out a handful of the objects. Ask the children to estimate how many handfuls (your hands, not theirs) there are in total in the jar. Let the children see how many objects you can pick up in one handful.

Ask what strategies they could use to work out how many handfuls there are. For example, using knowledge of how many objects are in one handful multiplied by how many handfuls they think are in the pot to find a total near to the number of objects in the pot discovered during the lesson.

Lesson   overview

Learning objectives

Starter
- **Know by heart multiplication facts for the 2, 5 and 10 times-tables.**
- Derive quickly: division facts corresponding to the 2, 5 and 10 times-tables.
- Identify near doubles, using doubles already known.

Main teaching activity
- Solve mathematical problems or puzzles, recognise simple patterns and relationships, generalise and predict. Suggest extensions by asking 'What if…?'
- **Explain methods and reasoning** orally and, where appropriate in writing.

Vocabulary

carry on, continue, repeat, what comes next? predict, describe the pattern, find, find all, find different

You will need:

Photocopiable pages
'Guess my rule' (page 51) for each child.

CD pages
'Guess my rule' less able and more able versions (see Autumn term, Unit 8).

Equipment
Individual whiteboards and pens, teacher's whiteboard; giant dominoes; interlocking cubes; OHP.

Lesson

Starter

Explain that you will ask multiplication facts for the 2, 5 and 10 times-tables. Invite the children to respond by saying the answers quietly. You can hold up your hand for the answer, giving the children a few seconds thinking time. Ask, for example, *What is… multiplied by 2? 5? 10? How many is… times…?* Keep the pace sharp.

Main teaching activities

Whole class: Play a Going on Holiday game, during which the class has to try to work out what rule you are following. Say that you are taking sunglasses on holiday but not flipflops, a swimming costume but not goggles. The children (working in pairs) join in and have a turn at choosing what to say/take. If they give any object that fits with your rule (in this case anything that starts with an 's') they can join you. Note: this game is for pairs only as it can be very isolating if children cannot work out the rule.

Group work: Explain to the children that they are going to try to spot mathematical groups which follow a rule, such as that a wasp, dragonfly and bird are all creatures that can fly. Hand out activity sheet 'Guess my rule' for the children to complete.

Differentiation

Less able: This group's sheet 'Guess my rule' has less challenging groups to add a drawing to.
More able: This group is asked to add an item to the groups, explaining their choices.

Plenary & assessment

Consider whether most children are able to explain the groupings on their sheet. Note that there may be more than one possibility, for example, 'slippers, dressing gown, pyjamas'. These could be classified as items we can wear/items related to night-time/items worn inside the house, all of which would be correct.

Lesson ④

Starter

Extend the Starter from Lesson 3 to include division facts as well as multiplication facts. Say, for example: *What is… divided by 2? 5? 10? How many… are there in…?* Again, keep the pace sharp.

Main teaching activities

Whole class: Introduce the vocabulary for the Lesson, and use with a function machine example on the large whiteboard. Ensure that all the class appreciate that ⟶ represents 'maps on to' and is a mathematical convention. Try the same idea but using other items. Ask:
● *What if we applied a doubling rule to a quarter piece of pizza? What would the pattern be?* (One quarter followed by one half followed by one whole, etc.)
● *What if a halving rule was applied to 100cm of string? How long would it be before there was nothing much to see?*

Group work: Working in pairs, children choose a rule to investigate from a list you give. Write these numbers on the board: 2, 8, 3, 6, 5, 9, 4, 7; and some rules:

2 ⟶ 6
3 ⟶ 9
4 ⟶ 12
(multiplying by three each time)

● Add 4 to each number.
● Double each number.
● Multiply each number by 10 and then halve each answer.
● Add 8 to each number.
● Subtract 2 from each number.
Also write up lists of numbers like these: 2, 8, 3, 6, 5, 9, 4, 7.

Differentiation

Less able: Suggest that this group selects the rule 'Add 4 to each number'.
More able: Encourage this group to reason about their answers. For example, 'All my answers will be less than 20 if I add 8 because my largest number is 9'. Use these reasonings for the Plenary.

Plenary & assessment

Take each rule in turn and check the children's responses by asking volunteers to give the answers. The children can 'mark' their own answers. Can the class make reasoned statements relating to each rule? Look for:

● *If I add four to each number, this would have the same effect as adding six and subtracting two.*
● *If I double each number, then odd numbers will map onto even answers and even numbers will still become even numbers.*

Lesson ⑤

Starter

Tell the children that they are going to identify near doubles. Spread out some near doubles and doubles giant dominoes. Can the children identify which is which? If they know that the three-dot/four-dot domino is an example of a near double, can they write other near doubles (eg 13-dot/14-dot) on their whiteboards? How many examples can they write within 100? Discuss how they would calculate adding these numbers mentally. Now give each child (or pair) their own domino.

Challenge the class to add up all the doubles and near doubles in the domino set. Discuss useful approaches to doing this, perhaps starting with all the doubles first.

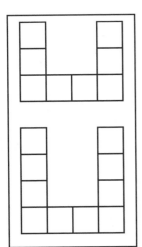

Main teaching activities

Whole class: Place a shape like this made from interlocking cubes onto the OHP and ask the children to describe the shape. Rotate the shape through 90° and ask: *Is this the same shape? How would you describe it now?* Now add a cube to each side like this. Ask: *What shape do you think would come next? And next? Why do you think that?* Invite the children to sketch the shapes on their whiteboards.

Group work: Ask the children to work in small groups of three or four. They use seven cubes to make a starting shape, then decide how to make the next three shapes in their pattern, for example by adding/subtracting two cubes each time. Challenge the children to think of rules for adding/subtracting cubes to their shapes. The results can be used in the Plenary.

Differentiation

Less able: Give this group a rule to start with, such as: 'Subtract one cube each time' from a shape that they make with the seven cubes.
More able: Challenge this group to introduce positional vocabulary into their rule, for example, 'My shapes also turn through a quarter turn each time'.

Plenary & assessment

Use three of the children's cube sequences to show the class. For each example, ask the class to make the next in the sequence. Compare how, although some people may have chosen the same starting shape, their sequences are different because they have chosen a different rule.

Remind the children that over the last week they have been reasoning, generalising and predicting in their activities. Explain that you are interested in how well they can now explain and justify their reasons. Try the following number examples, assessing which children are able to explain their thoughts clearly:
● *Darius saved 20p every week for eight weeks. How much did he save in total? Explain why it couldn't have been 90p.*
● *Lisa said 27 does not appear in the four times-table or the two times-table. Is she right? Explain your thinking, using sketches to help.*
● *What if I say all the answers of the 2 times-table are odd. Do you agree? How would you convince someone that I am wrong?*

| Name | Date |

Counting larger groups of numbers

Answer these questions about pots A, B and C.

Pot A

1. Estimate how many _____ are in the pot. ☐

2. Will the total be odd or even? ☐

3. Now count the amount accurately into groups of 10.

How many groups of 10 can you make? ☐

4. Are there any left over? If so, how many? ☐

5. Now practise grouping in fives.

How many groups of 5 can you make? ☐

Pot B

1. Estimate how many _____ are in the pot. ☐

2. Will the total be odd or even? ☐

3. Now count the amount accurately into groups of 10.

How many groups of 10 can you make? ☐

4. Are there any left over? If so, how many? ☐

5. Now practise grouping in fives.

How many groups of 5 can you make? ☐

Pot C

1. Estimate how many _____ are in the pot. ☐

2. Will the total be odd or even? ☐

3. Now count the amount accurately into groups of 10.

How many groups of 10 can you make? ☐

4. Are there any left over? If so, how many? ☐

5. Now practise grouping in fives.

How many groups of 5 can you make? ☐

Name	Date

Guess my rule

Write the rule for each of these groups.

1. spoon, fork, teaspoon, chopsticks

The rule is _____

2. trainers, flipflops, boots, socks

The rule is _____

3. pencil, eraser, sharpener, stapler

The rule is _____

4. sheet, pillow, mattress, bunk bed

The rule is _____

5. flannel, soap, toothbrush, brush

The rule is _____

6. float, dingy, snorkel, swimsuit

The rule is _____

7. spade, hoe, hosepipe, watering can

The rule is _____

Autumn term
Unit 9 — Multiplication

Children explore multiplication as repeated addition and as arrays. They read and begin to write the vocabulary of multiplication. They understand that multiplication can be done in any order and learn to multiply by 10 or 100 by shifting the digits to the left.

LEARNING OBJECTIVES

	Topics	Starter	Main teaching activities
Lesson 1	Understanding multiplication and division	● **Know by heart multiplication facts for the 2, 5 and 10 times-tables.** ● Derive quickly: division facts corresponding to the 2, 5 and 10 times-tables.	● Understand multiplication as repeated addition. ● Read and begin to write related vocabulary.
Lesson 2	Understanding multiplication and division	As for Lesson 1.	● Understand multiplication as repeated addition. ● Read and begin to write related vocabulary. ● Extend understanding that multiplication can be done in any order.
Lesson 3	Understanding multiplication and division Mental calculation strategies (× and ÷)	● Recognise odd and even numbers to 100.	● Read and begin to write related vocabulary. ● Extend understanding that multiplication can be done in any order. ● To multiply by 10/100, shift the digits one/two places to the left.
Lesson 4	Understanding multiplication and division Mental calculation strategies (× and ÷)	● Derive quickly doubles of all whole numbers to at least 20, and all the corresponding halves.	As for Lesson 3.
Lesson 5	Understanding × and ÷ Mental calculation strategies (× and ÷)	As for Lesson 4.	As for Lesson 3.

Lesson overview

Preparation
Copy CD page 'Blank hundred square', once onto an OHT and one set onto card. Cut out the squares from the card hundred square to make 100 tiles that fit the OHT grid exactly.

Learning objectives
Starter
● **Know by heart multiplication facts for the 2, 5 and 10 times-tables.**
● Derive quickly: division facts corresponding to the 2, 5 and 10 times-tables.
Main teaching activity
● Understand multiplication as repeated addition.
● Read and begin to write related vocabulary.
● Extend understanding that multiplication can be done in any order.

Vocabulary
double, times, multiply, multiplied by, product, multiple of, array, lots of, groups of, repeated addition, present, represent, trace, copy, complete, finish

You will need:
Photocopiable pages
'Multiplying or dividing' (page 57) for each child.

CD pages
'Blank hundred square', one copied onto an OHT for the teacher's/LSA's reference and one set copied onto card; '2, 4, 5 and 10 times-tables' for each child; 'Multiplying or dividing' less able and more able versions (see Autumn term, Unit 9) (see General resources).

Equipment
Individual whiteboards and pens; calculators; OHP calculator and OHP; Multilink, strings of 100 beads; an empty number line (ENL).

Lesson ①

Starter

Ask the children to sit in a circle. Taking turns, one child chooses a multiplication fact from the 2, 5 or 10 times-tables (eg $2 \times 10 = 20$). The next child then says a related fact and a completely different fact from the 2, 5 or 10 times-tables, for example $10 \times 2 = 20$ for the related fact followed by $5 \times 3 = 15$ as an unrelated fact. The third child might then say $15 \div 3 = 5$ for the related fact and $7 \times 5 = 35$ for the unrelated fact.

When the children understand the activity, split the class into three separate groups to continue the activity. This will give each child more opportunities to speak and help to keep the pace sharp.

Main teaching activities

Whole class: Explain to the children that this lesson is about making arrays and repeated addition to represent multiplication facts. Ask them to arrange some of the card tiles from CD page 'Blank hundred square' onto the OHT of the hundred square to show some multiplication facts. For example, if you asked a child to come and show 2 multiplied by 5 and 5 multiplied by 2, it could be shown in two ways.

$5 \times 2 =$ ▭▭▭▭▭ Invite the children to check the calculation by totalling.
For example, for 2×5 this is $2 + 2 + 2 + 2 + 2 = 10$ and 5×2 is $5 + 5 = 10$.
Also try 3×5, 5×3; 2×7, 7×2; 3×8 and 8×3.

$2 \times 5 =$ ▭ Then relate division facts from the known multiplication facts, such as
$3 \times 5 = 15$, $5 \times 3 = 15$, $15 \div 3 = 5$ and $15 \div 5 = 3$.

Paired work: Provide CD page '2, 4, 5 and 10 times-tables' and ask the children to complete the missing table facts. They should show the fact using the empty hundred grid and cards, then write in the answer onto the sheet. If they do not 'know' the answer, then suggest that they use repeated addition to work out the total.

Differentiation

Less able: Decide whether to limit the table facts to those for 2 and 5 times-tables.
More able: Challenge the children to find all the facts for the 3 times-table, modelling these in the same way.

Plenary and assessment

Ask the children to draw arrays on their individual whiteboards using dots for 3×6 and ask: *What other multiplication uses these numbers? Yes, 6×3. Now try 4×2* in the same way. Then invite the children to write the calculation for this story: *A farmer sells three boxes of half dozen eggs. How many eggs does he sell? How many eggs does he sell if he doubles his sales?* Repeat for other multiplication stories.

Lesson ②

Starter

Show the children the following triangle of facts:

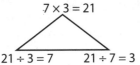

Working in groups of four, ask the children to choose any multiplication fact they know. The children then work round their foursome: child one chooses the start multiplication fact, child two says the related multiplication fact, child three suggests a division fact and child four the related division. Challenge the groups to perform their calculations for the class by saying them rapidly in sequence. Ask each group to prepare for performance three different multiplication facts and the related facts.

Main teaching activities

Whole class: Explain that today's lesson continues the work begun yesterday. Write on the board 5 × 6 and ask: *How can we work this out?* Children may suggest making arrays or using repeated addition. Invite a child to draw some dots on the board to represent 5 × 6 as an array. Now, using the OHP and an OHP calculator set to perform repeated addition (usually, number then ++= will set this, but check the manufacturer's instructions as some calculators operate differently), input 5, then press =. This should give 10. Repeat this, and ask the children to predict the next output each time until 30 is reached (5 × 6). Repeat this for a different multiplication, such as 8 × 6. Ask the children to keep count of how many eights are added until six of them are totalled.

Provide pairs with a calculator between them. Ask them to try these for themselves: 4 × 6, 9 × 6, 5 × 4 and 8 × 3. Then ask the children to feed back the answers.

Now write on the board: 24 ÷ 3 = □ and ask: *How can we work this out?* Children may suggest counting in threes to find how many are needed to reach 24. Do this together, then show how 24 can be placed in three rows using dots on the board. Ask *How many dots are there in each row?* Repeat this for another example, such as 18 ÷ 6 = □.

Individual work: Provide each child with a copy of activity page 'Multiplying and dividing' and ask them to complete the sheet individually.

Differentiation

Less able: Give the children the activity sheet version that uses multiples of 3 only. Assist this group by relating all their questions to concrete materials, eg Multilink or bead chains.

More able: Give the children the activity sheet with multiples of 6. Ask the children to write out the 6 times-table by doubling the 3 times-table. Show the group jumps of 6 on an empty number line:

Plenary and assessment

Ask questions such as: *Ten times what equals 80? What times five equals 30?*

Now ask: *What multiplication sentences could give the answer 60?* Invite the children to write their responses on the board, such as 12 × 5, 6 × 10 and 30 × 2, and so on. Using the OHP and the calculator set to repeated addition, check the children's suggestions so that they can all follow these multiplications.

Lesson overview

Preparation
Cut out the numbers from CD page 'Doubles'. Photocopy CD page 'Multiplication vocabulary' to A3 and make an A3 enlargement of the 'Word problems' activity sheet.

Learning objectives
Starter
● Recognise odd and even numbers to 100.
● Derive quickly doubles of all whole numbers to at least 20, and all the corresponding halves.
● Extend understanding that multiplication can be done in any order.
● To multiply by 10/100, shify the digits one/two places to the left.
Main teaching activity
● Read and begin to write related vocabulary.
● Extend understanding that multiplication can be done in any order.
● To multiply by 10/100, shift the digits one/two places to the left.

Vocabulary
count in tens, hundreds, thousands, rule, one more/less, ten more/less, one hundred more/less, none, as many as

You will need:
Photocopiable pages
'Missing numbers' (page 58) for each child; 'Word problems' (page 59) for each child and one copied to A3 for class display.

CD pages
'Doubles', one copy for the teacher's/LSA's reference and one copy for each child; 'HTU arrow cards' for each child; 'Multiplication vocabulary', for the teacher's/LSA's reference; 'Missing numbers' and 'Word problems' less able and more able versions (see Autumn term, Unit 9) (see General resources).

Equipment
Calculators; individual whiteboards and pens; Post-It Notes; washing line and pegs; stopwatch; scissors; empty box to put 'brainteaser' questions in.

Lesson ③

Starter

Play the Buzz game. The children stand in a circle and each child says a number in sequence ascending from any three-digit number. Each time a child says an odd number they should also say 'Buzz'. Encourage the children to do this at speed. Repeat the game counting backwards from any three-digit number.

Main teaching activities

Whole class: On the board write 5×10 and ask: *What is 5 multiplied by 10?* Write 50. Repeat this for other ×10 of single-digit numbers. Ask: *What happens when you multiply by 10?* Write TU headings above 5, then 50, 6 and 60 and so on. Elicit understanding that when multiplying by ten the digits shift one place to the left. Now ask: *What is the value of 5 in 5? 50?*

Then introduce the concept of dividing by ten by writing on the board $40 \div 10 = 4$. Ask:

- *What is 30 divided by ten?*
- *What is 500 divided by ten?*
- *What is 1000 divided by ten?*

Discuss how the digits move when multiplying and dividing by ten, then when multiplying and dividing by 100.

Invite the children to come up with three questions they can ask the rest of the class to solve, such as: What is six multiplied by ten? Use some of the children's questions with the whole class. Encourage the more able children to ask, and answer multiples of 100 questions.

Group work: The children complete activity page 'Missing numbers', which contains calculations such as $2 \times 10 \div 10 = 2$.

Differentiation

Less able: This group multiples and divides by ten only using the differentiated activity page 'Missing numbers'.

More able: Distribute the more challenging differentiated activity page. This group has to follow two functions being used, eg $\square \times 10$, then $\div 10$. This emphasises the inverse nature of multiplication and division. The group should also have access to a calculator to check and to assist with the investigation of $\square \times \square \times \square = 300$. (Two possible likely solutions are $3 \times 10 \times 10$ or $5 \times 6 \times 10$.) Tell the children that you would like them to suggest answers to this question in the plenary and to explain their thinking.

Ask the children whether the order they put their calculation in the calculator makes any difference to the product.

Plenary and assessment

Ask the more able children to give answers to $\square \times \square \times \square = 300$. They can write their responses onto the board. For each response, using the OHP calculator, demonstrate the multiplication for others to see. Now ask questions such as:

- *What is five multiplied by ten? By 100?*
- *What happens to the digits when you multiply by ten? By 100?*
- *What is 500 divided by ten? By 100?*
- *What happens to the digits when you divide by ten? By 100?*

For each question write the number sentence and answer onto the board, so that the answer and the reasoning are clear.

Lesson ④

Starter

This Starter has an element of problem solving to it and can appear very easy until you try it! Children will need to develop their own approach to solving the problem at speed.

Peg the numbers from CD page 'Doubles' on a washing line in random order. Then select two children to reorder the numbers in ascending order from left to right. Time how long they take with a stopwatch.

● Give each pair of children in the class their 'Doubles' page to repeat the activity at their tables. (They should place the cards in a line on the table, in random order, before reordering.) Ask:

● Is it better to pick up all the numbers and start again, or move the numbers one by one? What might be the fewest possible number of moves before the numbers are all in order?

Main teaching activities

Whole class: Ask questions such as: *What is 30 multiplied by ten, then divided by 100, and then multiplied by ten?* Encourage the children to follow your maths 'journey' and make aide memoir jottings if they wish. Everyone says the answer at the same time. Ask: *What is happening to the numbers?* Invite explanations. Repeat for other 'journeys' such as $50 \times 10 \div 100$ and so on.

Group work: Ask the children to work in pairs to generate three maths 'journeys' for another pair to solve. The children need to write the questions and check the answer with a calculator. After about 15 minutes, swap the sheets of paper for another pair to try and solve.

Differentiation

Less able: Lead this group by acting as scribe but prompt use of multiplication/division so the children do not move outside the numbers on the 'Doubles' CD page. For example: *Start with ten, then multiply by two. Next, halve this answer. Now multiply this number by ten. Your answer is this number divided by 100. The answer is one.*

More able: Allow the children to move on quickly to write more challenging extension questions on separate sheets, for example: *300 multiplied by ten, then double this answer and divide by 100.* (The answer is 60.) These can be put in a 'brainteaser box' and used by those who so wish.

Plenary & assessment

Display CD page 'Multiplication vocabulary', pointing at words such as 'count in tens' to ask questions, such as: *What is 30 multiplied by ten? How many hundreds must we count to reach 800? What is 100 divided by ten?*

Assess whether the majority of children can solve the following problem: *Darren sells his games console for ten times less than he paid for it. He received £20. How much did he pay for it?* Encourage the children to reflect on what they have learned. Explain that you intend them to improve their ability to multiply and divide by ten. Does the majority feel they have achieved this? Consider who has exceeded your expectations and who needs more practice or a different teaching approach.

Lesson ⑤

Begin the Starter as Lesson 4, but this time organise teams to play against each other. The fastest team wins a point. Splitting the class into six teams where the winners play the winners and the losers play the losers can work well in a Starter that lasts about 15 minutes. Now ask a word problem: *Seema has four hair ties. Sharon has twice as many. How many hair ties does Sharon have?* Invite children to suggest how to solve this problem, and which calculation they would choose. Repeat this for another problem. Provide copies of activity page 'Word problems', which is differentiated, and ask the children to complete the page working individually. During the Plenary, review the core activity page, using an A3 copy for all to read. Invite children to explain how they worked out the answers. Discuss each one, and encourage the children to explain their reasons for choosing particular mathematics.

Name	Date

Multiplying or dividing

1. Circle the multiples of 6.

  3   18   12   14   25   24

2. Fill in the missing numbers.

  [ ] x 3 = 18   6 x [ ] = 30   24 ÷ [ ] = 3   21 ÷ 7 = [ ]

  5 x [ ] = 25   [ ] x 4 = 4   45 ÷ 5 = [ ]   6 x [ ] = 36

3. Write the calculation needed to solve this problem.
   Vicky bought 3 tubes of chocolate buttons. Each tube cost 25p.
   How much did she spend? [ ]

My calculation

Name	Date

Missing numbers

Work out the missing numbers and then check your answers with a calculator.

1. 2 × 10 = 20

2 × 10 × 10 = ☐

2. 4 × 10 = 40

4 × 10 × 10 = ☐

3. 6 × 10 = ☐

6 × 10 × 10 = ☐

4. 200 ÷ 10 = ☐

20 ÷ 10 = ☐

5. 400 ÷ 10 = 40

40 ÷ 10 = ☐

6. 600 ÷ 10= ☐

60 ÷ 10 = ☐

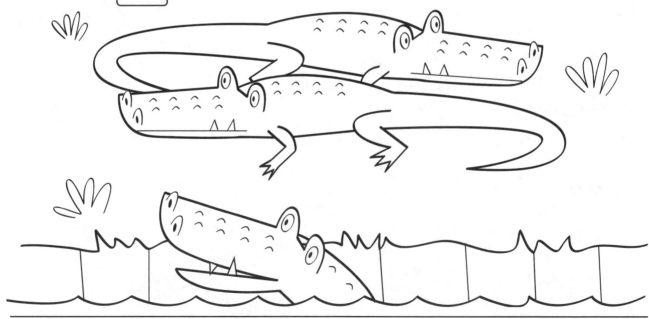

Name	Date

Word problems

Answer the following problems. Draw pictures to help.

1. Sue buys 2 boxes of eggs. There are 6 eggs in each box. How many eggs does she buy?

2. Ola has 3 stickers. Sonia has 5 times as many stickers as Ola. How many stickers does Sonia have?

3. Mei Mei walks 6km, which is twice as far as Paul. How far does Paul walk?

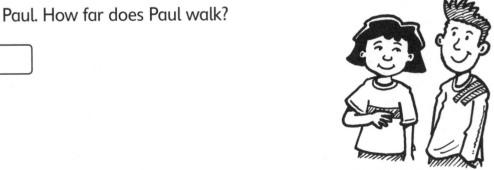

4. Joolz makes 18 cakes. Mark eats half of them. How many cakes are left?

Solving word problems

Children solve word problems using one or more steps, and explain how they solved the problem. They choose and use appropriate operations and calculation methods. They check the results of calculations, repeating addition or multiplication in a different order.

LEARNING OBJECTIVES

	Topics	Starter	Main teaching activity
Lesson 1	Problems involving 'real life', money and measures	● Say or write a subtraction statement corresponding to a given addition statement, and vice versa.	● Solve word problems involving numbers in 'real life', money and measures, using one or more steps, including finding totals and giving change, and working out which coins to pay. Explain how the problem was solved.
Lesson 2	Problems involving 'real life', money and measures	● **Know by heart:** all pairs of multiples of 100 with a total of 1000.	As for Lesson 1.
Lesson 3	Making decisions	As for Lesson 2	● **Choose and use appropriate operations (including multiplication and division) to solve word problems,** and appropriate ways of calculating: mental, mental with jottings, pencil and paper.
Lesson 4	Making decisions	As for Lesson 2.	As for Lesson 3.
Lesson 5	Checking results of calculations	As for Lesson 1.	● Check subtraction with addition, halving with doubling and division with multiplication. ● Repeat addition in a different order.

Lessons   overview

Preparation
Copy 'Inside the Post Office' to A3 and display where the whole class can see it.

Learning objectives
Starter
● Say or write a subtraction statement corresponding to a given addition statement, and vice versa.
● **Know by heart:** all pairs of multiples of 100 with a total of 1000.
Main teaching activity
● Solve word problems involving numbers in 'real life', money and measures, using one or more steps, including finding totals and giving change, and working out which coins to pay. Explain how the problem was solved.

Vocabulary
money, note, penny, buy, bought, sell, sold, spend, spent, dear, costs more, most expensive, least expensive, how many, amount

You will need:
Photocopiable pages
'Post Office problems' (page 66) for each child.

CD pages
'Inside the Post Office', copied to A3, for the teacher's/ LSA's reference; 'Post Office problems' less able and more able versions (see Autumn term, Unit 10) (see General resources).

Equipment
Teacher's whiteboard and pens; OHP, pens and calculator; individual whiteboards and pens.

Lesson ①

Starter

Provide the children with individual whiteboards and pens and ask them to work in pairs. Explain that you will write a number trio onto the board, which, when placed into an addition or subtraction sentence, will make a true statement. For example, 6, 4, 2 makes $2 + 4 = 6$, $6 - 2 = 4$, and so on. Ask the children to write two addition and two subtraction sentences for each number trio. When you say 'Show me' they hold up their boards to show what they have written. Ask the pairs to swap over each time, so that they take turns writing addition or subtraction sentences. Write trios such as: 23, 36, 59; 19, 31, 50; 32, 35, 67; 64, 28, 36.

Main teaching activities

Whole class: Talk briefly about why people use post offices – to collect pensions, send parcels, pick up passport forms, car tax and so on. Share CD page 'Inside the Post Office' with the class, covering the word problem at the end of the sheet. This shows that stamps are 30p and that a 500g parcel would be 70p to send. Ask:

- *How much would three stamps cost?*
- *How much would it cost to send two parcels each weighing 500 grams? Explain how you worked it out.*

Make jottings on a whiteboard to accompany the children's explanations, for example: Three stamps would be $30p + 30p + 30p = 90p$. One child might have jotted 60p and then 90p, as if keeping a running addition record. Point out that the child is using repeated addition. An alternative might be thinking $3 \times 30p = 90p$.

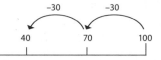

Move on to explaining repeated subtraction for the following problem:
- Mia buys two 30p stamps using a pound coin. (Tell the children to think of £1 as 100p when using the empty number line.) She thinks that is $100p - 30p - 30p = 40p$

Show the class how to make an empty number line (ENL) to show their thinking.

Alternatively, the children might say they worked the answer out by multiplying $30p \times 2$ to equal 60p, and then subtracting 60p from one pound. This could be expressed as working out the difference between 60p and 100p (see diagram 1) or as 100p, jump backwards 60p to reach 40p. Both responses are acceptable.

Refer again to CD page 'Inside the Post Office' and ask the children:

- *What information have we not used on the picture so far?* (The date is visible.)
- *What units are the problems likely to be in?* (Pounds and pence, grams and kilograms and so on.)
- *Looking at the picture, what do you anticipate the problems might be about?* (Money)
- *What operations do you think you might be using, and why?*

Uncover the word problem on the OHT 'Inside the Post Office'. The problem is: *Melinda went to the Post Office to buy a set of six special edition stamps. The stamps were all the same price – 50p each. How much did she spend? How much change did she get from £5?* Invite the children to explain in their own words what is to be calculated, and how. They may suggest multiplication ($6 \times 50p$) or repeated addition, perhaps using an empty number line. Both methods are acceptable.

Individual work: Ask the children to complete the word problems on activity page 'Post Office problems'.

Differentiation

Less able: This group can work on activity page in pairs to solve simpler problems. They calculate a total, then choose which coin/s to pay with from a selection.

More able: This group work on two-step operations on activity page 'Post Office problems', which have challenging mathematical expressions such as 'three times the amount'. Provide calculators for the final part of the sheet, where children invent their own problem.

Plenary & assessment

Explain that you will ask another word problem about money. Say: *Glenn pays 90p for some stamps. Each stamp costs 30p. How many stamps did he buy? How much change did he get from £1?* (Three stamps, 10p change) *How did you work that out? Who did this a different way?* Now, using the information in the Inside the post office sheet, ask the children what question they made up. Invite a child from each ability group to read out their question for the others to solve. Ask each time: *What mathematics do you need to use? Is there another way to answer this? Which way do you think is better? Why do you think that?* so that the children consider methods for efficiency and effectiveness.

Lesson ②

Starter

Write on the board the following numbers: 5, 8, 2, 1, 9. Ask the children to multiply each digit by 100 mentally. Write these answers down as a class. Now ask the children to work in pairs to find the complement to 1000 for each multiple of 100, for example, 300 + 700 = 1000. Suggest that they begin with 100, and write their addition sentences as an ordered list.

Main teaching activity

Whole class: On the board write: 9 o'clock, 1 o'clock, 2 o'clock, 6 o'clock. Explain that these times are on the door of a shop. Ask: *What do you think these times mean?* Children may well suggest that these are to do with when the post office is open. Now ask questions such as: *The shop opens at 9 o'clock and shuts at 1 o'clock for lunch. How long is it open? Now it opens again at 2 o'clock and shuts at 6 o'clock. How long is the shop open during the whole day?* Invite the children to explain how they worked out the answer. Repeat this for another time question, such as: *It is the shop manager's birthday today. He decides to open the shop at 9.30 in the morning, take a break of half an hour for lunch, then shut in the afternoon at 4.30. How long is the shop open today? How much less time is this than normal?* Ask: *Is all the information useful? What do I not need to know in order to solve the problem? Yes, that it is the manager's birthday.* Now ask the children to solve the problem and invite individuals to explain how they did this, and whether they needed to make any jottings. Some children may find it useful to draw a simple clock face to mark in the passage of time. This problem needs more than one step to solve it: find out how long the shop is open (some children may do this in two steps; morning opening and afternoon opening); then find the difference between that time and the previous day's opening hours.

Group work: Ask the children to work in groups of four. Explain that you would like them to invent some problems to do with time for others to solve. Ask each group to invent two time problems. Suggest that these should also include some information that is not needed to solve the problem. This part of the lesson should not take more than about ten minutes.

Differentiation

Less able: Decide whether to work with these children as a group. You may act as scribe. Encourage the children to explain how they would solve each problem.

More able: Ask the children to invent some more complex time problems, which involve more than one step in order to answer them.

Plenary and assessment

Invite each group to set one of their problems for the others to solve. Children will find it useful to have paper and pencils handy in order to make jottings as they work. Ask questions such as:
- *Which information do we need?*
- *Which information will not help us to solve the problem?*
- *How many steps will you need to solve this? What are the steps?*
- *Who can think of a different way to solve the problem?*

Lessons overview

Preparation
Enlarge CD pages 'How shall I calculate?' and 'Jack's story' to A3, laminate and display.

Learning objectives
Starter
● **Know by heart:** all pairs of multiples of 100 with a total of 1000.
Main teaching activity
● **Choose and use appropriate operations (including multiplication and division) to solve word problems**, and appropriate ways of calculating: mental, mental with jottings, pencil and paper.

You will need:
Photocopiable pages
'Jack's bean in trouble again!' (page 67) and 'Mrs Wishy Washy's launderette' (page 68) one for each child.

CD pages
'How shall I calculate?' and 'Jack's story' copied to A3, for the teacher's/LSA's reference; 'Jack Bean's in trouble again!' less able and more able versions (see Autumn term, Unit 10) (see General resources).

Equipment
1–6 dice; individual and teacher whiteboards and pens; Easiteach computer software, or similar (optional); a selection of all coins.

Lesson

Starter
Roll a dice to generate a number. Ask the children to multiply this number by 100 mentally and then write down the complement of this number to 1000 on their whiteboards. For example, $6 \times 100 = 600$, so the written complement would be 400. Ask the children to work out which complements arise during this dice activity. ($100 + 900$; $200 + 800$; $300 + 700$; $400 + 600$; $500 + 500$; $600 + 400$)

Main teaching activities
Whole class: Introduce CD page 'How shall I calculate', which shows ways of calculating mentally (M), mentally with jottings (MJ) and using the calculator (C). Explain to the class that you want them to think about the appropriate use of these different methods as they work on this lesson. Calculators have been included as, by now, the children should be selecting when to use them appropriately following the coverage of other units. Formal written procedures have not been used as this is not relevant until the final term of Year 3.

Read aloud the story on CD page 'Jack's story' without stopping for the questions. Reread the story and pause, stage by stage, to allow the children time to decide on the calculation and whether to do it mentally, mentally with jottings or with a calculator. Now revisit the story, each time stopping to ask: *What sort of calculation did you choose? Why did you make that choice?* Where children differed, ask them to justify their choice.

Group work: Jack's story continues on activity page 'Jack's bean in trouble again!', and he still needs help with some calculations. Ask the children to decide on the calculations needed in the version of the differentiated page you select for them. Emphasise that you are interested in their choice of M, MJ or C, and that each calculation they do needs one of these letters circled at the side to show which they chose.

Differentiation
Less able: This version of the activity on activity page 'Jack's bean in trouble again!' has more prompts for the children to choose the correct calculation, rather than write it themselves.
More able: This activity requires more complex decision-making on activity page 'Jack's bean in trouble again!'

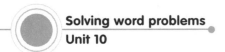
Plenary & assessment

Ask one child from each group to read out their activity sheet. Start with the less able, then the more able and finish with the core group, having checked all are correct. The story should flow from beginning to end.

If possible, as the story unfolds, write the calculations on the board (or use Easiteach or similar to generate empty number line calculations electronically) so all the class can see what each child did. Discuss other ways of doing some of the calculations, such as where repeated subtraction, addition, multiplication or division could have been used.

Lesson

Starter

Repeat as for Lesson 2, but extend the activity to using multiples of 50 and not just 100, for example, $350 + 650 = 1000$. Ask a child to pick a number from 1 to 9. Then everyone multiples the chosen number by 100, adds 50 and works out that number's complement to 1000. Invite individual children to explain how they worked out the complement.

Main teaching activities

Whole class: Explain to the children that today the focus is on keeping track of their thinking for all the calculations they do. The children are expected to model each answer using an empty number line (ENL) each time. Practise using the ENL to help the children explain their thinking out loud. Say: *Aladdin had three bags of washing for Mrs Wishy Washy. Each bag cost 20p to wash. How much did it all cost?* Draw an ENL on the board and ask a child to volunteer to draw in the jumps along the line. Ask: *What numbers will you write on the line?*

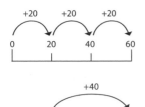

Discuss how the ENL can be used to show their thinking and to help with calculating. Say together: *20p add 20p add 20p is 60p.* Now ask: *How much change did Aladdin get from £1?* Again, invite a volunteer to show this using an ENL, this time showing 60p and counting up to £1. Discuss how £1 can be thought of as 100p.

Encourage the use of complements of decade numbers to 100 here, that is $60 + 40 = 100$.

Group work: There are some calculations to complete using the theme of Mrs Wishy Washy on activity page 'Mrs Wishy Washy's launderette'.

Differentiation

Less able: Use real coins to complete the calculations orally.

More able: Encourage these children to add an extra calculation to the question that would warrant the use of a calculator, for example: *If Mrs Wishy Washy washed 5 bags of washing every day for 2 weeks, then how many bags would she have washed?* ($5 \times 14 = 70$) *How much would the washing have cost?* Ask the children what would they need to put in the calculator. What would they estimate the answers to be first?

While the children are working, select three interesting uses of the ENL to show during the Plenary. If you have Easiteach or similar, ask some children to work on the interactive whiteboard so the examples are ready for the Plenary immediately.

Plenary & assessment

Ask three children, in turn, to write up their ENL workings out (or use the interactive examples). The rest of the class can then work out which question from the sheet the working relates to. Ask: *Why do you think that? What clues were there on the ENL to help you? Do you think that the answer is correct? Why/Why not?*

Ask the class for suggestions for solving the problems they have completed, such as 'Draw your own sketch of what the question is asking of you'. You may like to make a poster of the helpful suggestions for the children to refer to.

Lessons overview

Preparation
Check how your calculator uses the CE or C button so that you can demonstrate how to remove the last entry.

Learning objectives
Starter
● Say or write a subtraction statement corresponding to a given addition statement, and vice versa.
Main teaching activity
● Check subtraction with addition, halving with doubling and division with multiplication.
● Repeat addition in a different order.

Vocabulary
order, sequence, explain your method, tick, circle, cross, rearrange, change, change over

You will need:
Photocopiable pages
'Aladdin's adding' (page 69) for each child.

CD pages
'Aladdin's adding' less able and more able versions (see Autumn term, Unit 10) (see General resources).

Equipment
Individual whiteboards and pens.

Lesson

Starter
Repeat the Starter from Lesson 1. This time explain that you would like the children, in pairs, to find their own two-digit number trios. Give them a couple of minutes to find two sets of number trios. Now invite each pair to give one of their trios to the other children who write, as before, the number sentences onto their whiteboards. Keep the pace of this sharp.

Main teaching activities
Whole class: Explain to the children that by the end of this lesson they should be able to re-order the numbers in their calculations so that they can check they have the correct answer. Point out that this is more helpful than just redoing a calculation in the same order as it is easy to repeat a mistake. Write the following calculation on the board: $2 + 5 + 16 + 4 = \square$. Ask the children how many different ways they could do this mentally. Choose one child's suggestion, for example: $16 + 4 = 20, 5 + 2 = 7, 20 + 7 = 27$

Discuss how helpful it is to search for pairs of numbers to make a ten ($16 + 4 = 20$). Explain that when checking addition it is helpful to add again, this time adding the numbers in a different order, and consider another child's method. Repeat this for another addition such as $7 + 19 + 3 + 8$ ($7 + 3 = 10$ and $19 + 8 = 20 + 8 - 1$).

Group work: The children work on marking Aladdin's homework (activity sheet 'Aladdin's adding') as if they were teachers. Give the children 20 minutes to see how many questions they can check properly using re-ordering mental methods.

Differentiation
Less able: Ask the children to work on the differentiated activity sheet in pairs. Suggest that they may find using an empty number line helpful when calculating mentally.
More able: Decide whether to use the more challenging version of the sheet for these children.

Plenary & assessment
Write on the board: $9 + 13 + 11 + 7$ and ask: *How could you work this out mentally?* Responses may include: $9 + 11 + 13 + 7$, so that children look for two 'tens'. Now ask: *How could you check this?* Encourage the children to suggest other ways of ordering, such as adding the tens, then totalling the units: $10 + 10 + 9 + 1 + 3 + 7$. Repeat this for other examples.

Name	Date

Post Office problems

The prices that you need are in the picture.
Write your calculations in the box provided.

1. Cal spent 90p on stamps. How many stamps did he get?

2. Eleanor spent twice as much as Cal on stamps. How much did she spend?

How many stamps did she get?

3. How much would it cost to send one 500g parcel and two letters?

4. It costs 70p to send a 500g parcel. How much will it cost to send a 2kg parcel?
How much change would you get from £3.00?

5. How much does a parcel weigh if it cost £3.50 to post?

6. What is the difference in cost between a stamp and a 500g parcel?

Now, using the data in the picture, write your own problem here, and work out the answer. You may want to make some jottings on some spare paper to remind you how you worked this out.

_____

_____

Name	Date

Jack's bean in trouble again!

Put a tick by the right answer then circle mentally (M), mentally with jottings (MJ) or using a calculator (C) to show how you worked out the answer.

1. When Jack fell he cut both knees in three places on each leg. How many cuts was that altogether?	$2 \times 3 = 8$ ☐ 2 knees × 3 cuts each = 6 cuts altogether ☐	**M** **MJ** **C**
2. "Serve you right," thought Daisy the cow. She carried on munching grass in the field. Daisy chomped 200g of grass every 15 minutes. How much did she eat in one hour?	$200g + 200g + 200g + 200g = 900g$ ☐ $4 \times 200g = 800g$ ☐	**M** **MJ** **C**
3. Jack remembered he had to sell Daisy. He asked for £10 but had to have a half-price sale when no one wanted her. How much was he asking for Daisy?	£10 divided by 2 = £5000 ☐ $£10 \times 2 = £20$ ☐ Half of £10 = £5 ☐	**M** **MJ** **C**
4. Still no one wanted Daisy. Then an elf appeared and gave him three magic beans. Each bean weighed just 15 grams. What did all that magic weigh together?	$3 \times 15g = 44g$ ☐ $15g \times 3 = 45g$ ☐ $15g + 15g + 15g = 450g$ ☐	**M** **MJ** **C**

But Jack's troubles were only just starting!

Name	Date

Mrs Wishy Washy's laundrette

Show how much these cost.

Draw jumps on the number line and write in the numbers.

1. Two bags of washing. ☐

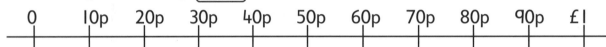

2. Three bags of washing and one box of powder. ☐

3. One suit, one bag of washing. ☐

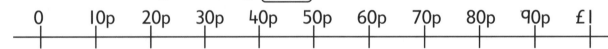

Now can you work out the change from £1 for each question? Draw your answer on the empty number lines below.

1. ☐

2. ☐

3. ☐

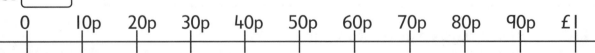

Name	Date

Aladdin's adding

Put X or ✔ next to the answer then write what you did mentally to check.

The first one has been done for you.

Aladdin's calculation and answer.	Is he right? Use a tick or cross.	How you checked it.
2 + 3 + 15 + 2 = 11	X	15 + 2 + 3 + 2 = 22
3 + 4 + 15 + 1 = 23		
6 + 3 + 12 + 4 = 26		
7 + 13 + 5 + 1 = 29		
8 + 4 + 6 + 1 = 19		
2 + 3 + 15 + 2 = 11		
3 + 3 + 15 + 1 = 22		
6 + 14 + 2 + 1 = 26		
7 + 13 + 5 + 3 = 29		
8 + 14 + 2 + 1 = 26		

Fractions

Children recognise unit fractions and find fractions of shapes and numbers. They begin to recognise fractions that are several parts of a whole, and solve problems involving fractions.

LEARNING OBJECTIVES

	Topics	Starter	Main teaching activity
Lesson 1	Fractions	● **Read and write whole numbers up to 1000** in figures and words.	● **Recognise unit fractions 1/2, 1/3, 1/4, 1/5, 1/10 and use them to find fractions of shapes and numbers.**
Lesson 2	Fractions	As for Lesson 1.	As for Lesson 1.
Lesson 3	Fractions	● Recognise odd and even numbers to 100.	● Begin to recognise simple fractions that are several parts of a whole, such as 3/4, 2/3 or 3/10.
Lesson 4	Fractions	● Derive quickly doubles of all whole numbers to at least 20, and all the corresponding halves.	As for Lesson 3.
Lesson 5	Fractions	As for Lesson 4.	● Begin to recognise simple fractions that are several parts of a whole, such as 3/4, 2/3 or 3/10.

Lessons overview

Learning objectives
Starter
● **Read and write whole numbers up to 1000** in figures and words.
Main teaching activity
● **Recognise unit fractions 1/2, 1/3, 1/4, 1/5, 1/10 and use them to find fractions of shapes and numbers.**

Vocabulary
part, fraction, whole, one half, two halves, one quarter, two/three/four quarters, one third, two thirds, one tenth

You will need:
Equipment
Interlocking cubes in red and blue; individual whiteboards and pens; strips of card; elastic bands; squared paper; paperclips.

Lesson ①

Starter

Provide each child with a strip of card with nothing on it apart from an elastic band. Explain that one end represents 0 and the other 10. Say: *Move your band to where you think 6/9 would be. Show me.* Now ask the children to imagine that the scale goes from 0 to 100. Ask: *Where would 50 be? How do you know? What helps you to work this out?* Repeat with the scale 0 to 1000. *Where would 500 be?* Then prompt the children, working in pairs, to think of a different three-digit number and ask their partner to adjust their paperclip to where they think that would be. Do they agree on the position? Repeat for other choices of three-digit numbers.

Main teaching activities

Whole class: Ask the children to suggest fraction vocabulary, and write down their suggestions. Now ask the children to sketch, on their whiteboards, what they think one half looks like. Use some of their examples to illustrate that a half can be half of any shape (circles very likely to be drawn). Consider with the children that 'half' can also represent part of a number greater than/less than one:

● *I can place all of the numbers on a number line:*   0   1/2   1   1½   2…

Ask the children to use their card strips and elastic bands from the Starter to show 'halfway between' for the following examples: 0 and 1 (1/2), 0 and 10 (5), 0 and 20 (10), 30 and 50 (40). Then prompt the children to think of 0 to 10 and then put the elastic band where they think 5 would be. Then ask where 5½ would be, noting that 5½ is between 5 and 6. Consolidate all the half numbers between zero and 10. Emphasise that fractions are numbers too and that they are always there on the number line having their own place.

Now provide each table with some interlocking cubes. Ask the children to count out given quantities. Say, for example: *Count out 6 cubes. How many will half of 6 be? How many would 1/3 be?* Write the fraction and the quantity onto the board so that the children see how the unit fraction is written each time. Repeat this for different quantities and fractions, to include 1/2, 1/5 and 1/10.

Group work: Ask the children to work in pairs. They count out 20 cubes. Ask them to find out what 1/2, 1/4, 1/5, 1/10 of 20 would be. Now ask them to find if it is possible to make exactly 1/3 of 20, and if not, to find a number near to 20 where it is possible to find exactly 1/3. Ask the children to decide for themselves how to record their work.

Differentiation

Less able: Decide whether to work with this group and record each fraction onto the board, and how many.

More able: Challenge this group to explore the quantity 60 in the same way, and to report back what they discover during the Plenary.

Plenary and assessment

Invite the children to report their findings for the number 20. Ask *Can you find exactly 1/3 of 20? Why not?* Children may well have found 1/3 of 21 or 18. Invite the more able children to report their findings for the number 60. Encourage them to explain why it is possible to find all of the fractions of 60. (They will need to realise that 60 can be divided exactly by 2, 3, 4, 5 and 10).

Lesson ②

Starter

Repeat the Starter from Lesson 1, but use these more challenging numbers for the children to work out what the number would be at the halfway point on their strip of paper: 30 to 40, 50 to 100, 100 to 200, 60 to 80, 44 to 54, 89 to 90. Ask them to write the number onto their whiteboards and show you each time.

Main teaching activity

Write the number 30 on the board. Ask: *What is half of 30? How did you work that out? What is half of 20? And what is half of 10? Explain that 5 is 1/4 of 20.*

Write on the board: 1/2 + 1/2 = 1/4 . Now draw a rectangle on the board and divide it into three unequal parts. Ask: *Are these sections thirds? Why not?* Discuss how fractions are always about equal parts. Repeat with a rectangle divided into four unequal parts so that children recognise that fractions refer to equal parts of a whole.

Group work: Ask the children to work in pairs. Provide them with squared paper. Ask them to find different ways of colouring in a rectangle made from 20 squares: 1/2 red and 1/2 blue; 1/4 red, 1/2 blue and 1/2 yellow. Invite them to find five different ways of showing each of these fraction colourings.

Differentiation

Less able: Decide whether to reduce the number of squares to be coloured to eight or 12 in order to increase the opportunities of successfully making the fractions.

More able: Challenge the children to make a rectangle of 24 squares. Ask them to find different ways of colouring 1/3 in blue (eight squares) and 1/4 in red (six squares).

Plenary and assessment

Ask: *How can we find, say 1/2 of a number? Or 1/4 or 1/3?* Invite the children to suggest ways of doing this such as dividing by 2, 3, or 4. Now invite a pair to show their set of colouring for 1/2 red and 1/2 blue. Ask: *Do all of these show half? How can you check?* Repeat this for 1/4. If there is time, invite the more able to show their colourings of 1/3 and 1/4 of 24.

Lessons overview

Preparation

Copy CD 'Smiley hundred square 1' onto an OHT and 'Smiley hundred square 2' onto card. Cut out the L-shapes from the card. Set up the classroom for two main activities during the group work of Lessons 3 and 4, putting capacity resources in one area and length resources in another.

Learning objectives
Starter
- Recognise odd and even numbers to 100.
- Derive quickly doubles of all whole numbers to at least 20, and all the corresponding halves.

Main teaching activity
- Begin to recognise simple fractions that are several parts of a whole such as 3/4, 2/3 or 3/10.

Vocabulary
part, fraction, one whole, one half, two halves, one quarter, two/three/four quarters, one third, two thirds, one tenth

You will need:

CD pages
'Smiley hundred square 1' copied onto an OHT and 'Smiley hundred square 2' copied onto card, for the teacher's/LSA's reference (see General resources).

Equipment
OHP; bean bags; five or more 1-litre measuring jugs marked in millilitres, 20 or more empty plastic containers of different shapes but all geared to hold 1 litre, coloured water, ten or more empty transparent cola bottles holding one litre, containers that hold 250ml, 500ml and 750ml; metre rule, metre sticks marked in cm; interlocking cubes, counting stick, sticky labels and black pens, metre length strips of paper.

Lesson

Starter

Using the OHT of CD page 'Smiley hundred square 1' and the L-shaped card, cover up 37 faces, leaving the remainder 'clear'. Ask the children to calculate the number of faces that are covered. Ask: *How did you work out how many are covered? Is the number odd or even? How can you tell? What about the uncovered faces – is this an odd or even number?* The children should begin to notice that when the total of covered faces is even/odd, the other total of uncovered faces (the complement) is also even/odd. Repeat, using the other L-shapes from the sheet.

Main teaching activities

Whole class: Invite the children to explain how many smiley faces would be in half the hundred square. Ask:

- *How many faces would be in a quarter?*
- *What about in a third? Why is this difficult?* (To be exact, one face would need to be split into three parts or the answer could be 33r1 whole faces.)
- *What if you had 90 smiley faces, what would 1/3 be then? What helps you to work this out?* (Knowing that $3 \times 3 = 9$, so $3 \times 30 = 90$)
- *How could we calculate 2/3 of the faces?*

Explain that fractions can be 2/3, 3/4 and so on. This means 'two equal parts out of three, three equal parts out of four'. Ask the children for their thoughts, before sharing out six bean bags between three children. Write on the board '1/3 of 6 equals 2'. Calculate with the children what 2/3 of six would be.

Explain to the children that during the group work over the next two lessons, they are going to consider fractions in terms of measures (capacity and length). Split the class into two main groups for the next two lessons.

Group work: Capacity: Ask the children to estimate how much they think each plastic container would hold in terms of litres and fractions of a litre, such as 1/2, 1/4… They use the measuring jugs to check their estimates. The water from each jug can then be poured into litre cola bottles for display and labelled by the children with the correct amount. Challenge the children to display the fractions in order of size.

Length: Provide strips of paper and metre sticks. Ask the children to mark the following fractions onto a strip of paper: 1/2 metre, 1/4 metre, 3/4 metre. Then ask them to think about how they might do the same for the fractions 1/3 metre and 2/3 metre. If time, they can repeat this for the fractions 1/5 metre, 2/5 metre, 4/5 metre.

Differentiation

Less able: This group would benefit from working with an adult for both activities. The adult should encourage the children to use appropriate language of measures and fractions as they explain their work.

More able: This group use fractions of one tenth and multiples of this for the capacity activity. Challenge them to find more complex fractions of length, such as 1/8, 2/8, 3/8 of a metre.

Plenary and assessment

For the capacity activity ask questions such as:

- *What do you need to add to half a litre to get one whole litre?*
- *How many half litres are in two litres?*

Invite the children to explain how they worked out their answers.

For the length activity, invite children to explain how they found the fractions of length. Ask:

- *How many centimetres are there in 1/2 of a metre? What about 1/4? 1/5?*
- *How close did you get to finding 1/3 of a metre?*
- *What about 1/5, 2/5 of a metre? How did you discover this?*

Discuss how children recorded their findings on the strips of paper.

Fractions
Unit 11

Lesson ④

Use the Starter from Lesson 3 but extend by expecting the children to improve their ability to predict the evenness or oddness of the answer each time. Invite children to use the OHP of CD page 'Smiley hundred square 1' and the L-shaped cards to show other combination of numbers to 100. For the main part of the lesson, provide the children with 30cm rulers, and ask them to calculate one-half, one-third, two-thirds and one-tenth of their 30cm ruler.

Swap over the capacity and length groups from Lesson 3, using the same differentiation. For the Plenary review the ordering of the cola bottles, and discuss the fraction of a litre that each one shows. Show a 2- or 3-litre cola bottle and ask: *How many times would the litre bottle fill this?* Show a 1/2 litre bottle. Ask the children to estimate where half of the half-litre bottle liquid would rise to in the litre bottle. Demonstrate this. How far out were the children? Remind the class that a litre of liquid does not fill the litre bottle. Ask why they think this is.

Lesson ⑤

Starter

Write a list of numbers on the board, such as 20, 7, 4, 9, 15, 6 and 2. Ask: *Which of these numbers can be halved to make a whole number? How can you tell?* Now say any number between 1 and 20 and ask the children to say its double. Repeat this for any even number between 2 and 20 and ask the children to say its half.

Main teaching activities

Whole class: Explain that today children will continue to think about fractions that are several parts of a whole, this time using quantities of counting apparatus. Invite a child to count out 30 cubes and ask: *What would 1/3 of the cubes be? How can you tell? So what fraction would 20 cubes be?* Discuss how the children can divide by three in order to find 1/3. Explain that if they find 1/3, then 2/3 would be 10 × 2. Repeat for 20 cubes and finding 1/5, 2/5 and so on.

Group activities: Provide each pair with some counting apparatus. Ask them to count out 36 cubes and find the following fractions: 1/2, 1/4; 1/3, 2/3. They decide how to record what they find. They can repeat this for 50 cubes and finding 1/5, 2/5, 4/5 and 1/10, 2/10, 9/10.

Differentiation

Less able: Decide whether to reduce the number of cubes to 24, then 30.
More able: Challenge the children to work mentally to find the solutions, rather than by counting cubes. They should prepare to report back during the Plenary on how they did this.

Plenary and assessment

Invite the more able children to explain how they worked mentally. Discuss the strategies that they used, which may include, division, multiplication, repeated addition, and so on. You may find it helpful to model what the children report back with cubes. Ask questions such as:
● *What is 1/2 of 12?*
● *So what would 2/4 be?*
● *How did you work that out?*
● *What would 4/4 be?*

Subtraction and time

Children extend their understanding that subtraction is the inverse of addition. They find small differences by counting up from the smaller number. They use calendars in order to develop their understanding of time vocabulary.

LEARNING OBJECTIVES

	Topics	Starter	Main teaching activities
Lesson 1	Understanding addition and subtraction Mental calculation strategies (+ and –)	Count on or back in tens or hundreds starting from any two- and three-digit number.	Extend understanding that subtraction is the inverse of addition. Say or write a subtraction statement corresponding to an addition statement and vice versa. Find a small difference by counting up from the smaller to the larger number.
Lesson 2	Mental calculation strategies (+ and –)	Say the number that is 1, 10 or 100 more or less than any given two- or three-digit number.	Find a small difference by counting up from the smaller to the larger number. Say or write a subtraction statement corresponding to an addition statement and vice versa.
Lesson 3	Measures	Know by heart multiplication facts for the 2, 5 and 10 times-tables. Derive quickly: division facts corresponding to the 2, 5 and 10 times-tables.	Read and begin to write the vocabulary related to time. Use units of time and know the relationship between them (second, minute, hour, day, week, month, year). Use a calendar.
Lesson 4	Measures	Know by heart multiplication facts for the 2, 5 and 10 times-tables. Derive quickly: division facts corresponding to the 2, 5 and 10 times-tables.	Use units of time and know the relationship between them (second, minute, hour, day, week, month, year).
Lesson 5	Making decisions Checking results of calculations	Derive quickly: doubles of all whole numbers to at least 20, and all the corresponding halves.	Choose and use appropriate operations (including multiplication and division) to solve word problems. Check subtraction with addition, halving with doubling and division with multiplication.

Lesson overview

Preparation
Make a tower of 12 and a tower of 15 with the interlocking cubes. Make an OHT of CD page 'Hundred square'.

Learning objectives
Starter
Count on or back in tens or hundreds starting from any two- and three-digit number.
Say the number that is 1, 10 or 100 more or less than any given two- or three-digit number.
Main teaching activity
Extend understanding that subtraction is the inverse of addition.
Say or write a subtraction statement corresponding to an addition statement and vice versa.
Find a small difference by counting up from the smaller to the larger number.

Vocabulary
how many more to make? how many sore is? than? equals? sign, how many fewer is? more, less, fewer, count on, count back, how many? size, compare, difference between, count on

You will need:
CD pages
'Three digit numbers', 'Two-digit numbers' and 'Hundred square' for each child (see General resources).

Equipment
Interlocking cubes; OHP; individual whiteboards and pens.

Lesson ①

Starter

Choose a card from CD page 'Three digit numbers' as the start number. Ask the children to count forwards from the number that you show them in tens, until you say 'Back', at which point they count back in tens to where they started. Repeat this for counting back from the start number until you say 'Forward', when they count forward to the start number again. Repeat this for different start numbers, and then for counting forwards and backwards in hundreds.

Main teaching activities

Whole class: Explain that in this and the next lesson the children will be considering the relationship between addition and subtraction. On the board write: 42 – 36 and ask the children to say the answer. Ask: *How did you work this out?* Some may have counted up from 36 to 40 (4) then 40 to 42 (2) to make 6. Remind the children that they can use an empty number line if they need help with calculations. Now ask the children to suggest another subtraction sentence that uses the numbers 36, 42 and 6. Write up 42 – 6 = 36. Ask the children to suggest two addition sentences which also use these numbers. Write these on the board: 6 + 36 = 42 and 36 + 6 = 42. Discuss how, with addition it does not matter in which order the addition is carried out, i.e. 6 + 36 or 36 + 6, but that for subtraction the order does matter and that 42 – 36 is different from 36 – 42, and that the latter would give an answer with a number less than zero.

Group work: Ask the children to work in pairs using two sets of 0 to 10 number cards. Ask them to shuffle the cards and take turns to take three cards to make a two-digit number, and a single-digit number, such as 4, 9, 7 and 49 and 7. They use their cards to make an addition sentence, for example: 49 + 7 = 56. They then make another addition and two subtraction sentences: 7 + 49 = 56, 56 – 7 = 49 and 56 – 49 = 7. Challenge the children to write ten sets of four number sentences. Suggest that they use an empty number line if they need help with their mental calculations.

Differentiation

Less able: Decide whether to limit the number range to addition and subtraction of teen numbers and single-digit numbers.
More able: Challenge the children to take four cards and make two two-digit numbers each time to use in their number sentences.

Plenary and assessment

Invite pairs of children to write up one of their pairs of numbers on the board and challenge the other children to work mentally in order to calculate two addition and two subtraction sentences. Ask questions such as:
● *Does the order in which you add matter?*
● *What about the order in which you subtract? Is 12 – 36 the same as 36 – 12?*

Lesson ②

Starter

Explain that you will hold up a two-digit number (from CD page 'Two-digit numbers') and ask the children to write on their whiteboards the number that is 1, 10 or 100 more or less. Give a few seconds each time for the children to respond, before asking them to show you their board, then move swiftly on to the next number in order to keep the pace sharp.

Main teaching activities

Whole class: Explain that today's lesson is about small differences. Show the children the two towers of interlocking cubes. Ask them to describe what difference they see – that is, a difference of three cubes. Now turn the towers so they appear on a horizontal axis. Point to the difference between them and count on from 12 to 15. Break off the three cubes and say 'The difference between 15 and 12 is 3'. Now write a number sentence to show this: 15 – 12 = 3. Show this with an empty number line drawn on the board and explain that you can use an empty number line to count on from the lower to higher number to find a difference.

Provide each child with CD page 'Hundred square' and ask the children to find 12 on their square, then 15, and to note that there is a difference of 3 between the two numbers. Repeat this, modelling with cubes, an empty number line, and the hundred square for another small difference, such as 18 and 14.

Paired work: Using the hundred square, challenge the children to write a list of 20 pairs of numbers with a difference of 3. Give the children ten minutes only on this task. Then ask the children to find ten pairs of numbers with a difference of 4. This time they should use an empty number line in order to check. Suggest that if they are unsure, they could start with any two-digit number, then count on 4 to find two numbers with a difference of 4.

Differentiation

Less able: Decide whether to limit the children to numbers to 30. Alternately, work with these children as a group and use the OHT of CD page 'Hundred square' and then the board to model an empty number line.

More able: Challenge the children to find differences of 4 with pairs of three-digit numbers, such as 321 and 317.

Plenary and assessment

Using the OHT hundred square, invite children from each ability group to demonstrate numbers with a difference of 3. Repeat this for differences of 4, using the empty number line. Now set a challenge. Ask the children to use the empty number line and their whiteboards and to find a number which has a difference of 5 with the number 46. (They should answer either 41 or 51.) Repeat this for other starting numbers and finding numbers that have single-digit differences. By viewing all the whiteboards each time, you will be able to assess who has understood this lesson and who needs further help and experience. Now ask the children to count on mentally to find a small difference. Say, for example: *What is the difference between 56 and 63? 87 and 91? 99 and 101? 386 and 391?*

Lesson   overview

Preparation
Make an OHT of CD page 'Time vocabulary' and, perhaps, an A3 copy for the less able group.

Learning objectives
Starter
● **Know by heart multiplication facts for the 2, 5 and 10 times-tables.**
● Derive quickly: division facts corresponding to the 2, 5 and 10 times-tables
Main teaching activity
● Read and begin to write the vocabulary related to time.
● **Use units of time and know the relationship between them (second, minute, hour, day, week, month, year).**
● Use a calendar.

Vocabulary
Monday, Tuesday… Sunday, January, February… December, Spring… Winter, day, week, fortnight, month, year, century, weekend, calendar, date

You will need:
Photocopiable pages
'Calendar days' (page 80) and 'Measuring time' (page 81) for each child.

CD pages
'Multiplication facts for 2, 5 and 10 times-tables' and 'Time vocabulary' for the teacher's/LSA's reference (see General resources).

Equipment
OHP.

Lesson ③

Starter
Put the children into two teams, each with a captain. Explain that you will hold up a multiplication card from the 2, 5 or 10 times-table from CD page 'Multiplication facts for 2, 5 and 10 times-tables'. Ask the team captains to take turns to choose a child to say the answer to the multiplication. The captains must ask each child in their team only once so that everyone has a turn. Keep a score on the board for each team. Keep the pace sharp, so that the child to answer must give the answer straight away. The winning team is the one with the most correct answers when all of the cards from the CD page have been used.

Main teaching activities

Whole class: Show the OHT of CD page 'Time vocabulary'. Point to the first word on the list, read it together, then say: *Please think of a sentence where you would use 'Monday'.* Repeat this for other vocabulary words, concentrating particularly on the meanings of the words in the calendar days list, especially any vocabulary that the children are unsure about. You may need to give a sentence for words such as 'century' to help the children understand its meaning, such as: *Mrs Brown was 100 this year. She has lived for a century.*

Now focus on the 'Calendar' section of the OHT. Show the children how to read the dates and point out that the days of the week along the top row for each month refer to all the days in the appropriate column. Choose one month and ask questions such as: *What day is third? Twenty-fourth? What is the last day in this month? What date is that?* Remind the children that different months have different quantities of days. Make a list on the board of the months with 28, 30 and 31 days. Now ask: *Which month comes before/after…? How many months in a year? In ten years? In a century? How did you work that out? How many days in a year? In a leap year?* Show the children how to write the date, and ask them to write their birthday to demonstrate that they understand how to do this.
Individual work: Provide a copy of activity page 'Calendar days' for each child. Ask the children to use the calendar for March on the sheet to help them to answer the questions.

Differentiation

Less able: Decide whether to work as a group, with an A3 enlargement of the activity sheet. Use the enlarged calendar from CD page 'Time vocabulary' to show how the days/dates are found.
More able: When the children have completed the activity sheet, set a challenge. Based on the calendar for March, ask them to work out what day of the week April 15 would be (Friday).

Plenary and assessment

Show again the OHT Calendar. Ask questions such as *On what day would Christmas day be on this calendar? How many Fridays are there in … month? Which months have 31… 30… 28 days?* Check that the children understand how to find the days/dates using the calendar.

Lesson ④

Repeat the Starter from Lesson 3, this time saying a division question for each multiplication fact. Discuss with the children which units of time (seconds, minutes, hours, days, weeks) they would use to measure how long it takes to, for example, read a book, eat a meal, clean their teeth… Provide the children with a copy of activity page 'Measuring time', perhaps working in mixed-ability pairs to complete the sheet. In this case, check that the less able children are contributing to the discussion. During the Plenary, invite children from each ability group to give examples of what they put in each section of the table at the end of the sheet. Check that others agree, and if not ask for explanations. This could lead to a lively discussion! This will enable you to check whether the children understand about how to choose suitable units of time for measuring particular events.

Lesson overview

Learning objectives

Starter
● Derive quickly doubles of all whole numbers to at least 20, and all the corresponding halves.

Main teaching activity
● **Choose and use appropriate operations (including multiplication and addition) to solve word problems.**
● Check subtraction with addition, halving with doubling and division with multiplication.

Vocabulary
sign, method, half, halve, twice, four times, divide, share equally

You will need:

Photocopiable pages
'Solving Dr Checkmate's problems' (page 82) for each child.

CD pages
'Solving Dr Checkmate's problems' less able and more able versions (see Autumn term, Unit 12) (see General resources).

Equipment
Pack of playing cards with the picture cards removed.

Lesson

Starter
Ask the children to double the value of every playing card or playing card pairs you stick randomly on the board. Give them one minute thinking time, then point to a card(s) and ask them to chant the double. Look at the card again. Ask which ones would have a whole number when halved. Ask targeted individual questions to elicit children's ability to double and halve small numbers.

Main teaching activities
Whole class: Explain that today's lesson is about choosing appropriate mathematics to solve problems and checking answers. Say: *Doctor Checkmate buys some stick-on spots. Ten spots cost £1.20. How much did each spot cost?* Ask: *What do we need to find out? Which operation do we need to find the answer? Can we do this mentally or do we need some apparatus to help us?* Review the children's responses. Some may see that £1.20 is the same as 120p and that this can be divided by ten mentally by shifting the digits to the right, so that the answer is 12p. Explain that the answer can be checked by multiplying: 12p × 10 = 120p or £1.20. Now say: *Dr Checkmate does 25 operations each day. How many operations does he do in two days?* Again, invite responses using the questions above. Explain that you would like the children to solve some problems where they choose the operation to use, then check their answer: multiplication with division; division with multiplication; addition with subtraction; subtraction with addition; halving with doubling; doubling with halving.
Paired work: Provide activity page 'Solving Dr Checkmates problems' for each child. This sheet has a space for solving the problem, for recording how it was solved, and for a check calculation.

Differentiation
Less able: Decide whether to use the activity sheet with lower numbers for this group.
More able: Decide whether to use the activity sheet with more challenging numbers for this group.

Plenary and assessment
Using the core version of 'Solving Dr Checkmate's problems', invite individual children to explain how they solved the problem and how they checked their calculation. Where children used different methods encourage discussion of how efficient each method was. Ask: *Which operation would you use to check addition/subtraction/multiplication/division/halving/doubling?*

Now invite some of the children to set their own problem for others to solve. Discuss how the problems should be solved, and how the answers can be checked.

Name	Date

Calendar days

Use this calendar for March to help you to answer the questions.

MARCH

Monday	Tuesday	Wednesday	Thursday	Friday	Saturday	Sunday
	1	2	3	4	5	6
7	8	9	10	11	12	13
14	15	16	17	18	19	20
21	22	23	24	25	26	27
28	29	30	31			

1. What day of the week is 4th March? _____

2. How many Mondays are there in March? _____

3. What are the dates of all the Saturdays in March? _____

4. Peter is going on holiday for a fortnight. He goes away on Saturday 5th March. What date will he come home? _____

5. Peter likes to go to football practice on a Sunday morning. Which Sundays will he be able to go to football practice in March? (Don't forget his holiday!)

_____

6. Ying Sum always goes dancing on Wednesdays. Which dates will she go dancing in March? _____

Name	Date

Measuring time

Decide how you would measure the time for each of these.

Join the picture to the units of time that you would use.

Picture	Caption	Unit
	Tying a shoe lace	minutes
	The Smith family is going on holiday	hours
	Plane flying from London to New York	days
	Lunchtime at school	seconds

Think of some things that you do.

Decide which units of time you would use to measure how long you take.

Write the things by the headings in this table.

Seconds	
Minutes	
Hours	
Days	
Weeks	

Name	Date

Solving Dr Checkmate's problems

Read the problem. Decide how you will solve it.

Write a number sentence to show the operation you used.

Now write a number sentence to show how you checked your answer.

1. All the patients go out to the seaside for the day. Dr Checkmate leaves half of the patients behind by mistake. If 30 went, how many came back? [ ]

My calculation:	My check:

2. Dr Checkmate bought 45 bottles of medicine. He then gave 21 bottles of medicine to his patients. How many bottles of medicine did he have left? [ ]

My calculation:	My check:

3. A bottle of medicine costs 30p. How much would 5 bottles of medicine cost? [ ]

My calculation:	My check:

4. Dr Checkmate eats 5 large chicken legs every day. How many chicken legs does he eat in a week? [ ]

My calculation:	My check:

Now invent your own problem about Dr Checkmate.

Write it here. Ask a friend to solve it. _____

_____

My calculation:	My check:

Autumn term
Unit 13
Handling data

Children begin this unit by considering lists of data, how they are presented, how they can be improved, and how the data can be used. They learn how to construct and interpret the data in frequency tables and two-region Carroll diagrams.

LEARNING OBJECTIVES

	Topics	Starter	Main teaching activities
Lesson 1	Organising and using data	● **Know by heart multiplication facts for the 2, 5 and 10 times-tables.** ● Derive quickly: division facts corresponding to the 2, 5 and 10 times-tables.	● **Solve a given problem by organising and interpreting numerical data in simple lists, tables, and graphs.**
Lesson 2	Organising and using data	As for Lesson 1.	● **Solve a given problem by organising and interpreting numerical data in simple lists, tables, and graphs,** for example: Carroll diagrams (one criterion).
Lesson 3	Organising and using data	● Say the number that is 1, 10 or 100 more or less than any given two- or three-digit number.	● **Solve a given problem by organising and interpreting numerical data in simple lists, tables, and graphs,** for example: simple frequency tables.
Lesson 4	Organising and using data	● **Know by heart:** all pairs of multiples of 100 with a total of 1000.	● **Solve a given problem by organising and interpreting numerical data in simple lists, tables, and graphs,** for example: simple frequency tables; Carroll diagrams (one criterion).
Lesson 5	Organising and using data	As for Lesson 4.	As for Lesson 4.

Lesson overview

Preparation
Prepare an OHT of CD page 'Fishy business menu'.

Starter
● **Know by heart multiplication facts for the 2, 5 and 10 times-tables.**
● Derive quickly: division facts corresponding to the 2, 5 and 10 times-tables.
● Say the number that is 1, 10 or 100 more or less than any given two- or three-digit number.
● **Know by heart:** all pairs of multiples of 100 with a total of 1000.

Main teaching activity
● **Solve a given problem by organising and interpreting numerical data in simple lists, tables, and graphs,** for example: simple frequency tables; Carroll diagrams (one criterion).

Vocabulary
count, tally, sort, vote, graph, block graph, pictogram, represent, list, chart, frequency table, Carroll diagram, most popular/least popular

You will need:
Photocopiable pages
'Fishy business!' (page 87) for each child.

CD pages
'Multiplication facts for 2, 5 and 10 times-tables' and 'Fishy business menu' for the teacher's/LSA's reference; 'Fishy business!' more able and less able version (Autumn term, Unit 13); 'Numeral cards 0 to 20' for each child (see General resources).

Equipment
OHT; sugar paper; pens; individual whiteboards and pens; boxes of assorted 2-D shapes; squared paper; Blu-tack.

Lesson ①

Starter
Explain that you will hold up a multiplication fact for the 2, 5 or 10 times-table. Ask the children to say the answer. Repeat this, this time asking a division fact that is derived from the multiplication, for example for 5 × 2 you might ask: What is 10 divided by 2? Keep the pace sharp.

Main teaching activities
Whole class: Explain that in today's lesson the children will be considering how to present and use lists. Use the OHT of CD page 'Fishy business menu' and ask: *Can you spot the mistake?* (Lobster and chips prices have been switched.) Encourage the children to look carefully at the list. What can they tell about this fish and chip shop just from reading the menu? Explain that people tend to try and show their information so the public will be tempted to buy items or use services; these forms of presentation are not always for information only. Ask: *Which item is most/least expensive? How much would two bags of chips cost? Which item do you think is bought most often and why?* (Deducing information) *How else could the prices have been listed and organised?* Discuss ways of presenting information so that it will encourage others to read it.

Group work: Provide the children with activity sheet 'Fishy business!' Ask them to decide what they would like to buy from the sheet, and to write their own menu and calculate the total cost. They should make two different menus.

Differentiation
Less able: Decide whether to use the version with smaller prices to aid calculation.
More able: Decide whether to use the more challenging prices version.

Plenary and assessment
Discuss the menus that the children have made. They are likely to have chosen their favourite food, so make a class survey of what has been selected. This can be done on the board making a list of the foodstuff, and writing how many have chosen it next to each food. Ask questions such as:
- *Which is the most popular item?*
- *Which is least popular?*
- *Which is more/less popular than…? How can you tell?*

Discuss the way in which the activity sheet 'Fishy business!' presented its menu. Ask: Was it easy to read? How could you change it to make it easier to read? Children may suggest re-ordering items so that, for example, drinks are together. Invite a child to write their suggestions onto the board. Ask if the others agree. There is likely to be disagreement about the ordering, so try to come to a consensus by voting.

Lesson ②

Starter
Repeat the Starter from Lesson 1.

Main teaching activities
Whole class: Explain that today the children will learn how to make a simple Carroll diagram. On the board draw a two-region Carroll diagram and write the title above it:
Ask: *What numbers will go in the even box? What will go into the not even box?* Write in the suggested numbers: 20, 22, 24… 40 in the 'even' box and 21, 23… 39 in the 'not even' box.

	Not even	Even
Numbers 20 to 40		

Repeat this for another simple Carroll diagram for sorting, for example: 'All numbers with a 9 as a digit from 1 to 30', so that 9, 19, 29 are in the '9 digit'

box and 'not 9 digit' box contains the other numbers. Explain that 'not' will be in the heading for the second box in a Carroll diagram.

Group work: Ask the children to work in pairs. They will need two sets of 0 to 9 digit cards from CD page 'Numeral cards 0 to 20'. Ask them to take turns to take two cards and to make a TU number which they think will fit into the Carroll diagram. They sort their numbers onto a two-region Carroll diagram which they can draw for themselves on squared paper, with the title 'Multiples of 2, 5 and 10'. Then they head one region 'even' and the other 'not even'.

Multiples of 2, 5 and 10

Not even	Even

Ask the children to keep a list of numbers which will not fit. Remind them that they can choose the ordering of their two digits.

Differentiation

Less able: Work with this group. The activity can be undertaken as a group task, and the recording completed on a large sheet of paper, with children taking turns to decide where to write their number.
More able: Challenge the children to choose three cards each time and to make three-digit numbers.

Plenary and assessment

Invite the children to discuss what they have done and to give examples of numbers that would not fit. Ask: *Why would these numbers not fit on your chart?* Encourage them to use vocabulary such as multiple: *These numbers are not a multiple of 2, 5 or 10.* More able children may be able to explain why: multiples of 2 have an even units digit; multiples of 5 have a 5 or 0 units digit, and multiples of 10 have a 0 units digit.

 **Lesson** ③

Starter

Explain that you will say a number, and that you would like the children to say back to you the number that is 1 more or less than the number that you say. Begin by saying, for example: *What is 1 more/less than 23? 245?* Repeat this for 10 more/less then 100 more/less.

Main teaching activities

Whole class: Explain that today the children will learn how to make a simple frequency table. On the board, write a list of favourite pets which the children suggest, such as cats, dogs, etc. Now ask the children to vote for their favourite. Explain that they can have just one vote each. Complete how many votes each pet receives.

Now ask questions about the frequency table data, such as: *Which is the most/least popular pet? How can you tell? Which had fewer than/more than… votes? How would the table change if you all had two votes? Who might find it useful to know which are children's favourite pets?*

Group work: Ask the children to work in mixed-ability groups of six to eight. Explain that each group will have the task of making a frequency table for data for their group, working on large sheets of sugar paper. Suggestions for data collection include:

● the number of brothers and sisters in each family in the group
● the number of letters in first names in family members
● favourite sports
● favourite TV shows.

Each group should prepare a short presentation of their findings for the others to see, and to ask and answer questions on the data.

Differentiation

With mixed-ability groups, ensure that the less able children are encouraged by the others to take an active part. The more able children may try to take over the activity and this should be

discouraged. When working as a mixed-ability group, this is the opportunity for children to develop their social skills as well as their mathematical understanding.

Plenary and assessment

Invite each group to explain what they had to find out, how they went about it, and how they recorded their data. Encourage the children in the audience to ask questions about the data. You may need to model this by asking, for example: *Which is the least/most popular? Which had more than/less than…? What if all the children had had two votes. How would the table change then do you think? Who would find it useful to know about this data?*

Lesson 4

Starter

Explain that you will say multiples of 100. The children respond by writing the complement to 1000 on their whiteboards then, when you say 'Show me', they hold up their boards for you to check. Keep the pace sharp.

Main teaching activities

Whole class: On the board draw a two-region Carroll diagram, write in the title 'Shapes' and the region headings of 'squares' and 'not squares'. Ask a child to pick up a shape from the box of 2-D shapes and ask: *Where will this shape fit?* Fix the shape to the diagram using Blu-Tak. Repeat this for other shapes. Discuss how all the squares are together, and the other shapes, which are not squares, are together.
Paired work: Provide the children with sets of mixed shapes. Ask them to decide how to sort these onto a Carroll diagram. They should draw four different diagrams, for example, 'triangles' and 'not triangles', 'has 4 sides' 'does not have 4 sides', and so on. Suggest that they begin by considering the properties of the shapes in their box and how these could be sorted.

Differentiation

Less able: Decide whether to limit the range of shapes for these children to, for example circles, triangles, rectangles and pentagons.
More able: Challenge the children to draw six different Carroll diagrams.

Plenary & assessment

Invite pairs from each ability group to show one of their Carroll diagrams. Ask questions of all of the children, such as: *How can you tell that this shape fits here? What other properties does this shape have?* Praise those children who used properties other than just the names of the shapes, such as 'has right angles'; 'has more than 4 sides', and so on.

Lesson 5

Repeat the Starter from Lesson 4. This time you say the multiple of 100, such as 300, and the children respond by saying the complement to make 1000, eg 700. Keep the pace sharp. For the Main teaching activities, ask the children to refer back to the data that they collected in a frequency table yesterday. Remind them of how to make a two-region Carroll diagram. Ask them to say whether they think that their data can be placed in a two-region Carroll diagram and what the title and headings would be, such as 'Family members' and 'brothers' and 'not brothers'. Repeat this for each of the surveys completed yesterday. Now ask the children to work together in their groups again, with sugar paper, and make a two-region Carroll diagram for their data. If time permits, ask the groups to complete another frequency table and Carroll diagram for 'Children who are 8 years old' so that they will need to think about headings of '8 years old' and 'not 8 years old'. During the Plenary, invite each group to show their work and discuss the suitability of their titles and headings. Ask: *Did all your data fit? How could you alter this to make it fit?*

Name	Date

Fishy business!

These are the items that the takeaway shop sells.

Decide which items you would like to buy to make a meal.

Write them into your menu.

Calculate how much your meal would cost.

Pot of curry	50p		Chips	£1
Cod	£2.00		Chicken	£2.50
Sausage	£1.00		Cola	£1.00
Mushy peas	80p		Salmon	£2.50
Beef burger	£1.50		Milkshake	£1.00

my menu

This will cost

Now make a different menu from the list.

Work out how much it will cost.

My menu

This will cost

EVERY DAY: Practise and develop oral and mental skills (eg counting, mental strategies, rapid recall of +, –, × and ÷ facts)			

- Describe and extend number sequences: **count on/back in 10s or 100s starting from any two and three digit number.**
- **Know by heart all addition and subtraction facts for each number up to 20.**
- **Know by heart** all pairs of multiples of 100 with a total of 1000 (eg 300 + 2001).
- **Count on or back in 10s or 100s starting from any two- and three-digit number.**
- Count on or back in twos starting from any two-digit number, and recognise odd and even numbers to at least 100.
- **Know by heart multiplication facts of the 2, 5 and 10 times-tables, and derive quickly corresponding division facts.**
- Compare two given three-digit numbers, say which is more or less, and give a number which lies between them.
- Identify near doubles, using doubles already known, eg 80 + 81).

Units	Days	Topics	Objectives
1	3	Place value and ordering	• Read and begin to write the vocabulary of comparing and ordering numbers, including ordinal numbers to 100. Compare two given three-digit numbers, say which is more or less, and give a number which lies between them.
		Estimating and rounding	• Read and begin to write the vocabulary of approximation. Give a sensible estimate of up to about 100 objects. • Round any two-digit number to nearest 10 and any three-digit number to the nearest 100.
		Measures	• Read scales to the nearest division (labelled or unlabelled).
2–3	10	Mental calculation strategies (+ and -)	• Use knowledge that addition can be done in any order to do mental calculations more efficiently. For example: add three or four small numbers by putting the largest number first; add three or four small numbers by finding pairs totalling 9, 10 or 11; partition into '5 and a bit' when adding 6, 7, 8 or 9 (eg 47 + 8 = 45 + 2 + 5 + 3 = 50 + 5) = 55).
		Understanding addition and subtraction	• Extend understanding that more than two numbers can be added; add three or four single-digit numbers mentally, or three or four two-digit numbers with the help of apparatus or pencil and paper.
		Problems involving 'real life', money and measures	• Solve word problems involving numbers in 'real life', money and measures, using one or more steps, including finding totals and giving change, and working out which coins to pay.
		Making decisions	• **Choose and use appropriate operations (including multiplication and division) to solve word problems,** and appropriate ways of calculating: mental, mental with jottings, pencil and paper. • Check with an equivalent calculation.
4–6	13	Shape and space	• Make and describe shapes and patterns. • Relate solid shapes to pictures of them. • Read and begin to write the vocabulary of direction. • Make and use right-angled turns including turns between the four compass points.
		Reasoning about numbers or shapes	• Solve mathematical problems or puzzles, recognise simple patterns and relationships, generalise and predict. Suggest extension 'What if…?' • **Explain methods and reasoning** orally and, where appropriate, in writing.
		Measures	• Read the time to 5 minutes on an analogue and a 12-hour digital clock, and use the notation 9:40. • Read and begin to write the vocabulary related to mass. • Measure and compare using standard units (kg, g). • Know the relationship between kilograms and grams. • Suggest suitable units and measuring equipment to estimate or measure mass. • Read scales to the nearest division (labelled or unlabelled).
		Making decisions	• Record estimates and measurements to the nearest whole or half unit (eg 'about 3.5kg') or in mixed units. • **Choose and use appropriate operations (including multiplication and division) to solve word problems,** and appropriate ways of calculating: mental, mental with jottings, pencil and paper.
7		Assess and review	

EVERY DAY: Practise and develop oral and mental skills (eg counting, mental strategies, rapid recall of + and – facts)

- **Know by heart multiplication facts in 2, 5 and 10 times-tables,** and derive quickly corresponding division facts.
- Begin to know the 3 times-table.
- Derive quickly doubles of multiples of 5 to 50.
- Identify near doubles, using doubles already known.
- **Count on or back in 10s or 100s starting from any two- and three-digit number.**
- Derive quickly all pairs of multiples of multiples of 5 with a total of 100.
- **Know by heart all addition and subtraction facts for each number to 20.**
- Say or write a subtraction statement corresponding to a given addition statement, and vice versa.
- **Read and write whole numbers to at least 1000 in figures and in words.**
- Order a set of three-digit numbers.
- Know by heart all pairs of multiples of 100 with a total of 1000 (eg 300+700).

Units	Days	Topics	Objectives
8	5	Counting, properties of numbers and number sequences	• Describe and extend number sequences: count on in steps of 3 or 4 or 5 from any small number to at least 50, and then back again.
		Reasoning about numbers	• Investigate a general statement about familiar numbers by finding examples that satisfy it. **Explain methods and reasoning** orally and, where appropriate, in writing.
9–10	10	Understanding addition and subtraction	• Extend understanding that more than two numbers can be added; add three or four single-digit numbers mentally, or three or four two-digit numbers with the help of apparatus or pencil and paper.
		Mental calculation strategies (+ and –)	• Use knowledge that addition can be done in any order to do mental calculations more efficiently. For example: partition into tens and units, then recombine (eg 34 + 53 = 30 + 50 + 4 + 3).
		Understanding multiplication and division	• **Understand division** as grouping (repeated subtraction) or sharing. • Read and begin to write the related vocabulary. • **Recognise that division is the inverse of multiplication**, and that halving is the inverse of doubling.
		Mental calculation strategies (× and ÷)	• Use doubling or halving, starting from known facts (eg 8 × 4 is double 4 × 4). • Say or write a division statement corresponding to a given multiplication statement.
		Problems involving 'real life', money and measures	• Solve word problems involving numbers in 'real life', money and measures, using one or more steps, including giving change, and working out which coins to pay. Explain how the problem was solved.
		Checking results of calculations	• Check subtraction with addition, halving with doubling and division with multiplication.
11	5	Fractions	• Begin to recognise simple equivalent fractions, eg five tenths and one half, five fifths and one whole.
12	5	Handling data	• **Solve a given problem by organising and interpreting numerical data in simple lists, tables, and graphs,** for example simple frequency tables; bar charts – intervals labelled in ones then twos; Venn diagrams (one criterion).
13		Assess and review	

Comparing and ordering numbers

Children compare and order numbers, find which is more or less, and place numbers between them. They estimate and approximate, rounding to the nearest 10 or 100. They read dial scales for weight and round the weights to the nearest 100g.

LEARNING OBJECTIVES

		Topics	Starter	Main teaching activity
Lesson	1	Place value and ordering	● Describe and extend number sequences: **count on/back in tens or hundreds, starting from any two- or three-digit number.**	● Read and begin to write the vocabulary of comparing and ordering numbers, including ordinal numbers to at least 100. Compare two given three-digit numbers, say which is more or less, and give a number which lies between them.
Lesson	2	Estimating and rounding	As for Lesson 1.	● Read and begin to write the vocabulary of approximation. Give a sensible estimate of up to about 100 objects. ● Round any two-digit number to the nearest 10 and any three-digit number to the nearest 100.
Lesson	3	Measures	As for Lesson 1.	● Read scales to the nearest division (labelled or unlabelled).

Lessons overview

Preparation
Thread 12 beads on each of the laces to make: an abab pattern; an aabbaabb pattern; an aaabbbaaabb pattern. Make OHTs of CD pages 'Chickens' and 'Hundred square'.

Learning objectives
Starter
● Describe and extend number sequences: **count on/back in tens or hundreds, starting from any two- or three-digit number**.
Main teaching activity
● Read and begin to write the vocabulary of comparing and ordering numbers, including ordinal numbers to at least 100. Compare two given three-digit numbers, say which is more or 'less, and give a number which lies between them.
● Read and begin to write the vocabulary of approximation. Give a sensible estimate of up to about 100 objects.
● Round any two-digit number to the nearest 10 and any three-digit number to the nearest 100.
● Read scales to the nearest division (labelled or unlabelled).

Vocabulary
first, second, third... tenth... twentieth... twenty-second... last, order, halfway between, round (up or down), nearest, how many...? about the same as, just over, just under, about the same as, measure, size, compare, measuring scale, division, guess, estimate, nearly, roughly, about, close to

You will need:
Photocopiable pages
'Rounding' (page 93) and 'Reading scales' (page 94), one for each child.

CD pages
'Hundred square', 'Numeral cards 0 to 20' for each child (Autumn term); 'chickens' (Spring term), 'Rounding' and 'Reading scales' less able and more able versions (Spring term, Unit 1) (see General resources).

Equipment
Two colours of beads, three laces; an OHP, NNS animation for mass; dial scale.

Lesson

Starter

Explain that you would like the children to count on in tens from a number that you say, until you say *Back*, when they count back to the starting number. Begin with two-digit numbers, such as 25, 89 or 47, then use three-digit starting numbers, such as 123, 361 and 456. Keep the pace sharp. Repeat for counting in hundreds.

Main teaching activities

Whole class: Explain that today the class will be comparing and ordering numbers. On the board write 56 and 65. Ask: *Which is more: 56 or 65? How can you tell?* Discuss the place value of the 5, then the 6, in each of these numbers and what it represents. Ask: *What number could go between 56 and 65?* Invite a child to write the numbers that are suggested. Repeat for other examples.

Now show the children the abab bead pattern and ask questions such as: *What colour is the first/third/twelfth bead? What colour would the 18th bead be? How did you work that out?* Repeat this for the other laces. Discuss how, when ordering numbers or things, we can use ordinal vocabulary, such as *twelfth*, *twenty-first*.

Paired work: Provide each pair with three sets of 0 to 9 numeral cards from CD page 'Numeral cards 0 to 20'. Taking turns, one child takes three cards and makes a three-digit number (eg 123). The second child uses the same cards to make another three-digit number (eg 321). They write their two numbers, in order, and write five numbers, in order, which will fit between their numbers. They must make sure that they have chosen numbers/cards to allow them to write five more numbers, and so this may mean that they will need to rearrange the digits in one of their numbers to do this.

Differentiation

Less able: Decide whether to ask the children to take two cards to make TU numbers only.
More able: Challenge the children to make all the numbers possible with three cards. Ask them to order their numbers, then to insert five more numbers between the lowest and highest numbers.

Plenary & assessment

Invite children from each group to give their two or three starting digits to the other children. Ask: *Which numbers can you make? Which is lowest? Highest?* Ask what might fit between these numbers. Invite the more able children to show what they have done. They can write their ordered numbers on the board. Challenge all the children to think of more numbers which might fit between the lowest and highest, and where these numbers would go in the ordered list.

Lesson

Starter

Repeat the Starter from Lesson 1. This time, however, begin by counting back from and to given numbers, then count on to the start number.

Main teaching activities

Whole class: Put the OHT of CD page 'Chickens' onto the OHP for five seconds. Invite the children to estimate how many chickens they can see. Ask: *What made you decide upon your number?* Note down the range of the answers on the board. Show the OHT again, but this time allow ten seconds – just enough time so that some children start to use a counting strategy, but not quite enough complete it. Discuss counting strategies used and any changes to estimates. Now show the OHT once more and invite the children to count how many chickens there are. Ask: *What counting strategy did you use?* Praise those who counted in tens and suggest to all of the children that they should always look for quicker ways of counting than counting in ones, such as counting in groups of twos, fives, tens…

Explain that when estimating, it is really useful to round numbers up or down to the nearest 10. Explain that numbers with 5 to 9 in their units round up to the next 10, and unit digits of 0 to 4 round down to the nearest 10. Draw a number line marked in tens from 0 to 100 on the board. Explain that you will say a number and ask the children to decide how it will round: up or down. Say, for example, *18, 29, 11, 14, 75*… and ask the children to point with their finger up or down as they say the number to which it rounds. Write each number onto the number line on the board and then point to the decade number to which it rounds as the children say this number. Repeat this for different TU numbers, this time using an OHT of CD page 'Hundred square'. Ask a child to point to the nearest 10 for the different two-digit numbers.

Explain that three-digit numbers can be rounded to the nearest 100 in the same way: 50 to 99 rounds up; 00 to 49 rounds down. Invite the children to say which way these numbers round: 124, 287, 650 and 449.

Individual work: Provide activity sheet 'Rounding', and ask the children to round the distances to the nearest 10km, then calculate the difference between the actual and the rounded distance.

Differentiation
Less able: Decide whether to use the version of the sheet for the less able children, which asks them to plot numbers and where they round to onto a hundred square.
More able: Decide whether to use the more able version of the sheet, which asks them to suggest possible original quantities for some rounded measures. This involves rounding to the nearest 100.

Plenary & assessment
Say some two-digit numbers for the children to round up or down to the nearest 10, such as 44, 65 and 99. Then repeat this for three-digit numbers, rounding to the nearest 100. However, instead of saying the answer, the class can jump up to show round up or crouch down for round down. Ask individuals to explain how they know whether to round up or down.

Use an empty number line to show just how far it is from 160cm to 200cm. Then discuss the range of three-digit numbers that round up to 200 (150 to 199) and down to 100 (101 to 149).

Lesson ③

Starter
Using the Starters for Lessons 1 and 2, ask children to count on, count back, in tens and hundreds.

Main teaching activity
Whole class: Explain that today is about being able to weigh accurately and read from different types of scales. Use the NNS animation to show the children how to read a kitchen scales accurately. Ask: *What happens when the weights are increased? What happens if you take some weight away?* Show the class how to adjust the reading arrow to zero on a dial scale. Use the NNS animation to show adding 50g and 50g. Ask: *In what other ways could you make 100g?*
Individual work: Provide activity 'Reading scales' for the children to complete. They are asked to draw in the reading arrow onto the dial scales for given weights, then to round the readings on more scales to the nearest 100g.

Differentiation
Less able: There is a version of the sheet which uses 10g intervals and rounding to the nearest 10g.
More able: There is a version of the sheet with more challenging readings and roundings.

Plenary & assessment
Review the core version of 'Reading scales' together. Ask: *Where will the reading arrow point for… weight? How would you round this weight to the nearest 100g?*

| Name | Date |

Rounding

Round the distances to the nearest 10km.

Write these into the chart.

Now write in the difference between the distance and the rounded distance.

	Distance	Rounded distance	Difference between distance and rounded distance
Ashford to Tenterden	8 km	10km	2km
Ashford to Canterbury	19km		
Ashford to London	53km		
Ashford to Brighton	46km		
Ashford to Hastings	27km		

Name	Date

Reading scales

Write in the missing arrows to show the weight.

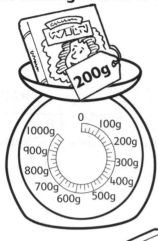

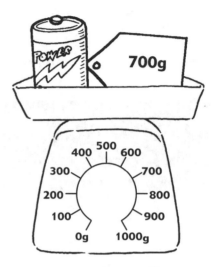

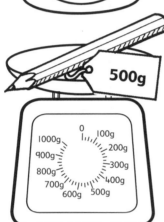

Now read these scales and write the weights to the nearest 100g.

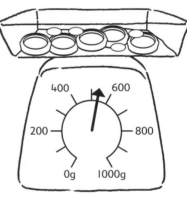

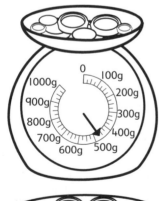

Spring term
Unit 2
Mental calculation strategies

Children extend their understanding of addition calculation strategies by working with larger numbers. They recognise that adding numbers in different orders still produces the same answer and use a calculator to check answers by adding in a different order. They put the larger number first; find pairs to make 9, 10 or 11, and partition into '5 and a bit'.

LEARNING OBJECTIVES

	Topics	Starter	Main teaching activity
Lesson 1	Mental calculation strategies (+ and –)	● **Know by heart: all addition and subtraction facts for each number to 20.**	● Use knowledge that addition can be done in any order to do mental calculations more efficiently. For example: add three or four small numbers by putting the largest number first.
Lesson 2	Mental calculation strategies (+ and –)	As for Lesson 1.	● Use knowledge that addition can be done in any order to do mental calculations more efficiently. For example: add three or four small numbers by finding pairs totalling 9, 10 or 11.
Lesson 3	Mental calculation strategies (+ and –)	As for Lesson 2.	● Use knowledge that addition can be done in any order to do mental calculations more efficiently. For example: partition into '5 and a bit' when adding 6, 7, 8 or 9 (eg 47 + 8 = 45 + 2 + 5 + 3 = 50 + 5). = 55).
Lesson 4	Mental calculation strategies (+ and –)	● **Count on or back in tens or hundreds, starting from any two- or three-digit number.**	● Extend understanding that more than two numbers can be added; add three or four single-digit numbers mentally, or three or four two-digit numbers with the help of apparatus or pencil and paper.
Lesson 5	Mental calculation stategies (+ and –).	As for Lesson 4.	As for Lesson 4.

Lessons overview

Learning objectives
Starter
● **Know by heart: all addition and subtraction facts for each number to 20.**
Main teaching activity
● Use knowledge that addition can be done in any order to do mental calculations more efficiently. For example:
– add three or four small numbers by putting the largest number first and/or finding pairs totalling 9, 10 or 11
– partition into '5 and a bit' when adding 6, 7, 8 or 9 (eg 47 + 8 = 45 + 2 + 5 + 3 = 50 + 5).

Vocabulary
add, addition, more, plus, make, sum, altogether, is the same as, equals, sign, tens boundary

You will need:
Photocopiable pages
'Counting on' (page 99), on for each child.

CD pages
'Counting on' less able and more able versions (see Spring term, Unit 2) (see General resources).

Lesson ①

Starter

Explain that you will say a number, between 0 and 20, and challenge the children to say the number that adds to your number to make 20. So, if you say *Five*, the children say *15,* and so on. Begin slowly, giving the children about ten seconds thinking time. As they become more confident, increase the pace.

Main teaching activities

Whole class: Explain that in today's lesson, children will be asked to put the larger number first and count on. Write on the board 7 + 56. Invite the children to count on from the larger number. Say together: *56 and 57, 58, 59, 60, 61, 62, 63.* Agree that 7 + 56 is 63. Some children may point out that they can add 4 to 56 to take them to 60, then another 3 because 4 + 3 = 7. If children are unsure, model this using an empty number line. Provide further examples such as: 7 + 136, 8 + 237, each time counting on in ones from the larger number. Now write up 30 + 44. Invite suggestions for how this can be calculated. Suggest that counting on in tens from 44 would be useful and say together: *44 and 54, 64, 74. So 30 + 44 = 74.* Repeat the counting in tens procedure for other examples.
Individual work: Provide activity sheet 'Counting on' and invite the children to complete the addition sentences using the counting on in ones or tens strategy.

Differentiation

Less able: There is a version of 'Counting on' with simpler numbers.
More able: Decide whether to use the sheet which involves adding three numbers.

Plenary & assessment

Write on the board 40 + 57 and ask: *How would you work this out?* Invite a child to demonstrate adding by counting on in tens. Repeat for 9 + 133 for counting on in ones. Provide further examples.

Lesson ②

Starter

Explain that you will keep a steady beat by clapping quietly. Ask the children to say the number that adds to make 1000 to the number that you say. Begin with 100, then 200, and so on up to 1000. Repeat this, this time clapping a little faster but still keeping a steady beat.

Main teaching activities

Whole class: Explain that today the children will be adding by finding pairs that total 9, 10 or 11. Write on the board 15 + 6 + 2 + 8 and ask: *Which numbers shall we pair? Why did you choose those?* A solution would be: (15 + 5 + 1) + (2 + 8) = 20 + 1 + 10 = 31. Repeat this for other examples, such as 16 + 7 + 5 + 3, where one way of calculating would be: (16 + 5) + (7 + 3) = 10 + 6 + 5 + 10 = 31. In this example children can make 11 by adding 6 and 5. Now provide an example where the children can add to make a 9, such as 13 + 8 + 6 + 5 = (10 + 3 + 6) + (8 + 5) = 19 + 13 = 10 + 10 + 9 + 3 = 32.
Individual work: Write up some addition sentences, such as: 14 + 7 + 8 + 1; 19 + 2 + 7 + 3… Also include some with missing numbers such as 15 + □ + 5 = 33 for the children to complete.

Differentiation

Less able: Decide whether to work with this group and discuss with the children how they would calculate each question.
More able: Challenge the children, when they have completed the work from the board, to write three addition sentences of their own and swap these with a partner. Ask the children to explain during the Plenary & assessment how they calculated.

Plenary & assessment

Review the number sentences on the board. Invite children from each ability group to explain how they calculated. There is likely to be more than one way of doing this for some questions, so ask, for example: *Who tried a different way? Tell us what you did. Was this easier/harder to do than Marc's way?* Invite the more able children to write up their own sentences and invite all the children to suggest how these could be calculated.

Lesson

Starter

Repeat the Starter from Lesson 2, but this time use a faster, steady pace. Repeat, increasing the pace so that the children will need to answer almost immediately. This will give you the opportunity to identify who has rapid recall of these facts.

Main teaching activities

Whole class: Explain that in today's lesson the children will be partitioning into '5 and a bit' when adding. On the board write 19 + 8 and ask: *How can we work this out?* Children may reply: (10 + 5 + 4) add (5 + 3). Write up, for example: 10 + 5 + 4 + 5 + 3 = 10 + 5 + 5 + 4 + 3 = 20 + 7 = 27. Explain that breaking down the numbers 6, 7, 8 and 9 into '5 and a bit' is a very useful strategy. Provide more examples, such as 27 + 36 and 28 + 29, and invite individual children to demonstrate the method of partitioning and recombining, writing this on the board.

Paired work: Write these numbers on the board: 26, 37, 48, 29. Ask the children to work in their pairs and to take turns to choose two of the numbers. They both write addition sentences, partition into '5 and a bit' and recombine. They compare what they have done, then combine two more of these numbers until they have completed all six possible addition combinations.

Differentiation

Less able: Decide whether to simplify the TU numbers, using, for example, 16, 17, 18 and 19.
More able: Decide whether to challenge the children to total three of these numbers each time.

Plenary & assessment

Invite pairs to explain how they worked out their answers. Ask: *How would you partition 48/57/69/96 into '5 and a bit'?* Remind the children that this week they have considered putting the larger number first; looking for pairs that make 9, 10 or 11, and today partitioning into '5 and a bit'. Explain that next week the children will be using these strategies to solve problems.

Lessons   overview

Learning objectives
Starter
● **Count on or back in 10s or 100s starting from any two- and three-digit numbers.**
Main teaching activity
● Extend understanding that more than two numbers can be added; add three or four single-digit numbers mentally, or three or four two-digit numbers with the help of apparatus or pencil and paper.

Vocabulary
add, addition, more, plus, make, sum, altogether, is the same as, equals, sign, tens boundary

You will need:
Photocopiable pages
'Inspector Add-it' (page 100), one for each child.

CD pages
'Inspector Add-it' less able and more able versions (Spring term, Unit 2) (see General resources).

Equipment
Calculators; OHP calculator; OHP; large Post-It Notes; calculators.

Lesson

Starter

Ask the children to work as two groups. They take turns to count in tens from a number that you say, each group saying the alternative number. So, for example, starting on 158 they would say 168, 178, 188, 198… until you say *Back*. Then repeat this, counting back to the starting number. Repeat this for other numbers, such as 199, 174 and 182. Check that the children cross the hundreds barrier appropriately.

Main teaching activities

Whole class: Explain to the class that they will be adding small numbers, using the strategies that they have learned so far in this unit. Ask them to add the following numbers, making jottings as they choose (some children will need to be reminded to use an empty number line if they need to): 10 + 15 + 10 + 11 = □. Take suggestions from the children how they could do this, such as 10 + 10 + 10 + 5 + 10 + 1 = 20 + 20 + 6 = 46. Using an OHP and OHP calculator, show the children that they still obtain the same answer by inputting the numbers in a different order.

Now ask the children to try the next example, adding mentally: 15 + 7 + 15 + 3. Invite a child to explain how they worked this out. They may have doubled 15, added 7 and 3, to make 40. Invite other suggestions. Discuss whether any ways of adding were more efficient and why this is so. Provide calculators and invite the children to use the calculators to check their answer, by inputting the numbers in a different order. Repeat this for other examples, still working mentally.

Individual work: Ask the children to complete activity sheet 'Inspector Add-it'. Core and more able children can check their answers using a calculator.

Differentiation

Less able: This version of the activity page focuses on smaller totals.
More able: This version of the activity page focuses on crossing the tens boundary when adding.

Plenary & assessment

Ask a child to show how they would try 10 + 17 + 13 = □. Acknowledge that personal preference is allowed so spotting that 17 + 13 = 30 and then adding the 10 is fine. Write the numbers in the sum on large Post-It Notes and move their order. Invite the children to work out the answer each time you move the Notes. Now write up 10 + □ + 10 = 35. Ask: *What do you think the missing number is? What number must be in the units of this number? Why do you think that?* Ask for examples of what the number *couldn't* be if the children are struggling to explain.

Now ask the children to work in pairs. Prompt them to find three numbers which when totalled make 40. Challenge the more able by asking them to find four numbers which total to make 60; and decide whether to limit the range for the less able to three numbers to total 20.

Lesson

Repeat the Starter for Lesson 1, this time counting hundreds, forwards and backwards. Then review the work done in Lesson 4. Use more examples, including checking with a calculator, such as 15 + 14 + 9, 8 + 9 + 6… Now ask the children to work in pairs. Prompt them to find three numbers which when totalled make 40. Challenge the more able by asking them to find four numbers which total to make 60; and decide whether to limit the range for the less able to three numbers to total 20. During the Plenary & assessment, review what the children have done and ask: *Which strategies did you use to find the totals?*

Name	Date

Counting on

Add the numbers.

Count on in ones from the larger number.

Write your answer.

1. 9 + 45 = ☐   **2.** 8 + 165 = ☐

3. 7 + 85 = ☐   **4.** 6 + 137 = ☐

5. 9 + 124 = ☐   **6.** 5 + 178 = ☐

Count on in tens from the larger number.

Write your answer.

7. 30 + 46 = ☐   **8.** 40 + 56 = ☐

9. 20 + 48 = ☐   **10.** 30 + 67 = ☐

Now try these.

Decide whether to count on in ones or in tens.

Write your answer in the strategy box that you used.

Add	Count on in ones	Count on in tens
7 + 168		
30 + 49		
40 + 58		
9 + 154		

Name	Date

Inspector Add-it

Decide how to add these numbers.

You can make jottings below to help you.

Which is the best order to add these in?

1. 10 + 13 + 10 + 14 = _____ ☐

2. 10 + 17 + 10 + 12 = _____ ☐

3. 17 + 10 + 10 + 13 = _____ ☐

4. 13 + 10 + 14 + 10 = _____ ☐

5. 8 plus 4 plus 9 = _____ ☐

6. What is the sum of 14, 15 and 6?= _____ ☐

7. How many altogether are 12, 15 and 7? = _____ ☐

8. What is the total of 16, 12 and 8?= _____ ☐

Check your answers with a calculator.

Put the numbers in a different order to check again.

Word problems

Children use the mental calculation strategies for addition that they learned in Unit 2 to help them to solve problems. They check answers using an equivalent calculation.

LEARNING OBJECTIVES

		Topics	Starter	Main teaching activity
Lesson	1	Problems involving 'real life', money and measures	● Count on or back in twos starting from any two-digit number, and recognise odd and even numbers to at least 100.	● Solve word problems involving numbers in 'real life', money and measures, using one or more steps, including finding totals and giving change, and working out which coins to pay.
Lesson	2	Problems involving 'real life', money and measures.	As for Lesson 1.	As for Lesson 1.
Lesson	3	Making decisions	● **Know by heart: multiplication facts for the 2, 5 and 10 times-tables.** ● Derive quickly: division facts corresponding to the 2, 5 and 10 times-tables.	● **Choose and use appropriate operations (including multiplication and division) to solve word problems,** and appropriate ways of calculating: mental, mental with jottings, pencil and paper.
Lesson	4	Making decisions.	As for Lesson 3.	As for Lesson 3.
Lesson	5	Making decisions Checking results of calculations	As for Lesson 3.	● **Choose and use appropriate operations (including multiplication and division) to solve word problems,** and appropriate ways of calculating: mental, mental with jottings, pencil and paper. ● Check with an equivalent calculation.

Lessons   overview

Preparation
Prepare an OHT of CD pages 'Word problem frame' and 'Word problems'.

Learning objectives
Starter
● Count on or back in twos starting from any two-digit number, and recognise odd and even numbers to at least 100.
Main teaching activity
● Solve word problems involving numbers in 'real life', money and measures, using one or more steps, including finding totals and giving change, and working out which coins to pay.

Vocabulary
pattern, puzzle, calculate, calculation, mental calculation, method, jotting, answer, right, correct, wrong, what could we try next? how did you work it out? sign, operation, symbol, equation

You will need:
CD pages
'Word problem frame' for each child, 'Word problems' for the teacher's/LSA's reference (see General resources).

Equipment
OHP.

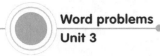
Lesson ①

Starter

Firstly, practise with the children walking forwards and then backwards four steps. You could do this to music. The children count one on the first step then count two and clap on the second step, count three on the third step and then clap and count four on the fourth step. Moving backwards, they say five, clap six, say seven, clap eight. Ask whether they are clapping on odd or even numbers. Continue the pattern up to 40.

Change the starting number to 15. What happens? Invite the children to suggest two-digit numbers to start on, discussing the odd and even patterns each time.

Main teaching activities

Whole class: Explain to the class that they will be using the mental calculation strategies that they practised in Unit 2 to solve problems. Solve the following problem with the class using an OHT of CD page 'Word problem frame'. Say: *There are 17 books on the top shelf, eight books on the middle shelf and 13 books on the bottom shelf. How many books are there altogether?* Invite the children to say what sort of calculation they will need to do and write their suggestions on the board, such as 17 + 8 + 13. Ask: *How shall we work this out?* Children may suggest adding 17 and 13 because they can 'make a ten'. Write on the OHT 17 + 13 + 8 in the first column; 10 + 10 + 10 + 8 in the second column; and the answer 38 in the third column.

Repeat for another example, which this time is a two-step problem: *There are 15 apples, 22 pears and 28 bananas. If I eat three of each of the fruit, how many pieces of fruit are left?* (56)

Paired work: Put CD page 'Word problems' on the OHP and ask the children to work in pairs to complete these, using a copy of CD page 'Word problems frame'. Ask them to read each question carefully, discuss with their partner how to solve it, and fill in the table for each problem.

Differentiation

Less able: Decide whether to work with these children as a group. Discuss for each question how it can be calculated and say the calculation through together, counting on in ones as appropriate.
More able: Decide whether to limit the children to working mentally, rather than mentally with jottings.

Plenary & assessment

Review each question, and how the children solved it. Discuss the strategies that they used. Where different strategies were used, invite the children to compare them and discuss which is more efficient and why that is.

Lesson ②

Starter

Use the Starter from Lesson 1, but this time concentrate on counting backwards.

Main teaching activities

Whole class: Write on the board: 12 + 6 + 8 + 9 and ask: *What could the word problem be?* Give the children a few minutes to decide on their word problem, then take suggestions and together solve the addition sentence. Discuss the strategies that the children used, and their efficiency.
Paired work: Ask the children to work in pairs and to write some addition sentences choosing three numbers from a given list each time: 13, 14, 15, 17, 18, 19, 4, 5, 6, 7, 8, 9, 10 and 11. Write the list on the board. Now ask the children to write, using CD page 'Word problem frame', a word problem

in the first column as well as the calculation, and complete the rest of the row. Challenge them to write five problems in all.

Differentiation
Less able: Decide whether to simplify the numbers to 1 to 9 .
More able: You can challenge more able by including 26, 27, 28… Suggest to them that all of their problems must be two-step ones.

Plenary & assessment
Invite children from each ability group to give examples of their number sentences and, using the OHT of 'Word problems frame' to write their calculations, strategies and answers. Ask the more able children to demonstrate some of their two-step problems.

At the end of the lesson, ask: *Which strategies do you feel confident in using now?* You may like to ask the children to write this down, and to write down which strategies they feel they need to practise more.

Lessons overview

Learning objectives
Starter
- **Know by heart: multiplication facts for the 2, 5 and 10 times-tables.**
- Derive quickly: division facts corresponding to the 2, 5 and 10 times-tables.

Main teaching activity
- **Choose and use appropriate operations (including multiplication and division) to solve word problems**, and appropriate ways of calculating: mental, mental with jottings, pencil and paper.
- Check with an equivalent calculation.

Vocabulary
pattern, puzzle, calculate, calculation, mental calculation, method, jotting, answer, right, correct, wrong, what could we try next? how did you work it out? sign, operation, symbol, equation

You will need:
Photocopiable pages
'Sparky – Queen of the chickens part 2' (page 106) and 'Checking activity sheet' (page 107), one for each child.

CD pages
'Multiplication facts for 2, 5 and 10 times-tables' (Autumn term); 'Sparky – Queen of the chickens part 1'; 'Sparky – Queen of the chickens part 2' more able and less able versions (Spring term, Unit 3) (see General resources).

Equipment
Individual whiteboards and pens; balance; interlocking cubes; calculators.

Word problems
Unit 3

Lesson ③

Starter

Use the cards from CD page 'Multiplication facts for 2, 5 and 10 times-tables'. Ask the children to respond quickly to the multiplication facts. They write the answer each time onto their whiteboard and, when you say Show me, they hold this up for you to see. Keep the pace sharp. This activity will give you the opportunity to check which children have rapid recall and which need further practise.

Main teaching activities

Whole class: Explain that today's lesson is all about using the appropriate calculation to solve problems. Invite the children to respond by writing a symbol: +, −, × or ÷ on their whiteboards during the following story. Pause each time you want them to do this, as there is a calculation to do. Now read the story below.

Poultry Productions Presents… the story of Sparky Queen of the chickens!
Sparky had been playing lead guitar with the 'screaming bantums' for two decades.
How many years is this? (20) Pause for × or + sign and the calculation.
She had played to many chickens in many coups.
Looking back it must have been at least three concerts a week.
How many concerts is that every month, she wondered. (12) Pause for × or + and the calculation.
There were only four of them left in the band. That's half what we started with, she remembered. (8)
Pause for ÷ and the calculation.

Read the story again. This time ask, for each pause. *How can you tell which calculation is needed? What clues are there in the story?* Discuss the vocabulary that is used and what it tells about the calculation needed.

Group work: Ask the children to use their version of Sparky – Queen of the chickens and to solve the problems, deciding which calculation to use each time.

Differentiation

Less able: This group has smaller numbers to use the the differentiated CD page 'Sparky – Queen of the chickens part 2'.
More able: More complex numbers are used on the differentiated activity sheet.

Plenary & assessment

Read through the core activity sheet 'Sparky – Queen of the chickens part 2' together and ask for answers. Invite children to explain which strategies they used for working out their answers. Repeat this for the less able and more able sheets. For each question ask: *Which calculation do you think you should use? What tells you that in the sentence?*

Lesson ④

Repeat the Starter from Lesson 3. This time, ask a division fact for the multiplication on the card that you choose. Invite the children to think about coins. On the board, list all the coins there are. Then say: *Sammy gave two silver coins to pay for a 16p toy. Which coins do you think he chose? How much change did he get?* Invite the children to suggest different solutions for this and write the calculation strategies on the board.

Set a similar problem for the children to tackle in pairs: *You have a 50p piece. You buy a toy and receive two silver coins as change. Which coins could these be? How much did the toy cost?* Remind the children that there are several answers to this, and challenge them to find as many as they can. Review the children's answers during the Plenary & assessment, and ask questions such as: *Which calculation/strategy did you use to work that out?*

Lesson 5

Starter

Use the Starters from Lessons 4 and 5, providing a mix of multiplication and division questions.

Main teaching activities

Whole class: Introduce the idea of an equation as calculations that balance. It is useful to show this actually using a balance and some cubes of equal weight: two cubes + three cubes = four cubes + one cube. Extend this idea to 2 + 3 = 6 − 1. Now try these as a class, again reasoning what the symbol could be: 5 ☐ 5 = 4 + 6; 11 + 9 = 12 ☐ 8.

Discuss how the children could check this calculation using an equivalent calculation, for example 30 + 56 = 86 using 56 + 10 + 10 + 10 or 30 + 50 + 6 = 80 + 6 = 86. Repeat for another example, such as 9 + 7 + 11. Remind the children of the mental strategies that they practised in the previous unit, as they will find all of these useful to help them to complete this task.

Group work: Ask the children to work individually using 'Checking' activity sheet. Prompt them to check their calculations using a calculator when they have completed the sheet.

Differentiation

Less able: Decide whether to work together as a group to complete the activity sheet. Encourage the children to use the vocabulary of addition and subtraction to explain how they wish to carry out the calculation.

More able: Challenge the children to write two check calculations for each question.

Plenary & assessment

Collect some examples from the children that show they have used a different calculation to check the answer. Write these up on the whiteboard, asking the whole group for an explanation of how the child who did the example would have been thinking and which calculation strategies they have used. Conclude by asking the children what they think they have learned, when they would find this useful, and which strategies they feel confident with and which they need to practise further.

Name	Date

Sparky – Queen of the chickens part 2

Read the story.

Write the answers in the boxes.

Sparky and her 3 band players were not happy.

They were laying 5 double-yolker eggs each, every week.

How many eggs did they lay in 4 weeks? ☐

_____

_____

The farmer was pleased.

He charged double price for double yolkers. Normally eggs cost 20p each.

How much would he get for 5 double yolkers? ☐

_____

_____

Sparky found out the farmer was putting special double-yolker feed in their trays.

The feed cost him 30p each day.

So how many eggs did he have to sell in a week to earn more than the feed cost

him? ☐

_____

_____

The farmer sold 6 double-yolker eggs on Monday,

4 on Tuesday and 5 on Wednesday.

How much money did he take? ☐

_____

_____

Remember the feed cost him 30p each day.

How much did he have left after paying for the feed? ☐

_____

_____

Name   Date

Checking activity sheet

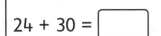

Write your answer in the box.

Write your check calculation in the checking box.

When you have finished, use a calculator to check your calculations.

24 + 30 = ☐

jottings

checking box:

---

11 + 8 + 19 = ☐

jottings

checking box:

---

14 + 8 + 7 = ☐

jottings

checking box:

---

19 + 6 + 7 = ☐

jottings

checking box:

---

40 + 54 = ☐

jottings

checking box:

---

30 + 65 = ☐

jottings

checking box:

---

13 + 17 + 8 = ☐

jottings

checking box:

---

21 + 10 + 9 = ☐

jottings

checking box:

Shape and space

Children make sketches of 3-D models and compare views of models from one aspect to work out what has been used to make these. They use compass directions to describe position and movement. They solve problems about shapes and explain their methods and reasoning.

LEARNING OBJECTIVES

	Topics	Starter	Main teaching activity
Lesson 1	Shape and space	● Compare two given three-digit numbers, say which is more or less, and give a number which lies between them.	● Make and describe shapes and patterns. Relate solid shapes to pictures of them.
Lesson 2	Shape and space.	As for Lesson 1.	As for Lesson 1.
Lesson 3	Shape and space	● Identify near doubles, using doubles already known (eg 80 + 81).	● Read and begin to write the vocabulary related to direction. ● Make and describe right-angled turns, including turns between the four compass points.
Lesson 4	Reasoning about numbers or shapes	As for Lesson 3.	● Solve mathematical problems or puzzles, recognise simple patterns and relationships, generalise and predict. Suggest extensions by asking 'What if…?' ● **Explain methods and reasoning** orally and, where appropriate, in writing.
Lesson 5	Shape and space Reasoning about numbers or shapes	As for Lesson 3.	As for Lesson 4.

Lessons ① ② overview

Preparation
Photocopy three sets of digits 0 to 9 each to A3 from CD page 'Numeral cards 0 to 20'. Copy CD page 'Pictures of 3-D shapes' onto acetate. Prepare eight 3-D 4-cube models (all different) from interlocking cubes and seal each one inside an opaque carrier bag. Keep aside two of the models to use in during the lesson. Make a shape with five interlocking cubes, ensuring that at least one cube will be hidden from view when the shape is placed onto the OHP.

Learning objectives
Starter
● Compare two given three-digit numbers, say which is more or less, and give a number which lies between them.
Main teaching activity
● Make and describe shapes and patterns. Relate solid shapes to pictures of them.

Vocabulary
hollow, solid, corner, face, side, edge, end, make, build, draw, surface, match, size

You will need:
CD pages
'Numeral cards 0 to 20' (Autumn term); 'Pictures of 3-D shapes' for each child (see General resources).

Equipment
Three sets of A3 numeral cards 0 to 9; 3-D shapes such as cube, cuboid, triangular prism, hemisphere, sphere, cone, pyramid; OHP; interlocking cubes; some examples of Kandinsky's artwork which use mathematical shapes.

Lesson ①

Starter

Shuffle the three sets of 0 to 9 numeral cards and ask a child to select three cards. He or she orders the cards to make a three-digit number. Hold the cards up so that all can see. Repeat this to make another, different, three-digit number. Write each of these numbers on the board along an empty number line, so that the lower number is to the left, and the higher to the right at the end of the line. Invite the children to suggest numbers that will fit between and to take turns to write them on the board in their approximate place along the line. Repeat for other pairs of three-digit numbers.

Main teaching activities

Whole class: Explain that in this lesson children will be exploring the properties of 3-D shapes. Introduce the vocabulary of 'corner', 'face', 'edge', 'end' and 'hollow' by showing shapes that exemplify the words. Invite the children to offer examples for the word 'solid' (often used in daily speech to mean good). Write the vocabulary on the board.

Hand out the carrier bags and ask the children to describe the shape they can feel using some of today's vocabulary. Now ask them to sketch what they felt. Share afterwards the conventions for drawing 3-D shapes by using dotted lines for edges you can't see. Ask the children to open the bags and check the shape that they drew with the model. Prompt them with questions such as: *How many faces are touching in each shape?* (Mostly three, but not always.) *Look down on the shape. How does it look now? Look at the shape from the front... side... What does it look like?*

Put one of the spare 4-cube models that was not placed into a carrier bag on the OHT. Ask the children to sketch what they see and to predict where any cubes that might be hidden are placed. Turn the shape to show a different view and repeat. Finally show the children all of the shape and encourage them to check their drawing. Repeat for the second spare shape.

Group work: The children now work in pairs. One child makes a shape with four interlocking cubes; their partner asks for the view to be sketched from the top, front and side and then using the sketches makes the shape. They check to see if it is correct, then swap over roles.

Differentiation

Less able: You may wish to work with the children as a group, with you describing your hidden shape while the children sketch. Encourage them to use the vocabulary of shape in order to describe what they draw and what they see when you show them the hidden shape.

More able: Challenge the children to complete all eight possible shapes made with four cubes.

Plenary & assessment

Place a 5-cube shape that you have made onto the OHP. Challenge the children to describe what they see. Tell them that there are five cubes and that one of them is hidden. Ask: *Where do you think the hidden cube might be?* Provide the children with five cubes each and invite them to make the model as they think it is. Now change the orientation, showing a different view of the model on the OHP. Ask: *What shape can you see now? How do you need to change your model?* Repeat this for a different view. Discuss with the children that when looking at shapes from the front, back or side, we do not see all of the shape.

Lesson ②

Starter

Repeat the Starter from Lesson 1. This time ask the children to make all the three-digit numbers that they can with the three cards, order these on the number line, then fit another three-digit number between each pair of numbers on the number line.

Main teaching activities

Whole class: Explain that today the focus is on recognising images of 3-D shapes. If possible, look at some of Kandinsky's work and invite the children to describe what they see in the pictures.

Place the acetate of CD page 'Pictures of 3-D shapes' onto the OHP. Ask the children to describe the shapes that they see and where they are placed. Invite a child to use the shapes in the box to make the model that they can see. Remove the OHT and ask the children to sketch the model. Replace the OHT and invite the children to check that their drawing is similar to that on the OHT. If not, ask for differences and explanations of why there are differences. These may be to do with the size of the shape models used.

Group work: Encourage the children to work in groups of four with a set of 3-D shapes. They take turns to make a model then they all sketch what is made. If they do this from different angles, that is side, front, back and top, then they can compare what they have drawn and discuss whether or not they could make the complete model from their sketches. Ask the children to preserve the last model and sketches for the Plenary & assessment.

Differentiation

Less able: Decide whether to limit the range of shapes offered in order to simplify the models made.
More able: Challenge the children to make more complex structures, particularly with 'hidden' shapes, then to compare sketches to see in which orientation the 'hidden' shape will show.

Plenary & assessment

Ask children from each group to put their models on view, and collect all of the sketches for these models. Give each group another group's sketches. Now invite the children to go from model to model, as a group, comparing the sketches that they have with the models. Challenge them to find the appropriate model for their sketch. Ask questions such as: *How did you recognise the model? What clues were there in the sketches? Is there anything else that could have been sketched to help?*

Lessons overview

Preparation
Mark the four points of the compass clearly on the floor.

Learning objectives
Starter
- Identify near doubles, using doubles already known (eg 80 + 81).

Main teaching activity
- Read and begin to write the vocabulary related to direction.
- Make and describe right-angled turns, including turns between the four compass points.

Vocabulary
underneath, above, below, top, bottom, side, on, in, in front, behind, beside, next to, clockwise, anticlockwise, North, South, East, West

You will need:
Equipment
Whiteboards and pens; Roamer; ten beanbags.

Lesson

Starter

Remind the class that 19 and 21 are near doubles. Ask the children for other examples of near doubles. Tell them to divide their whiteboards into two with a vertical line. Ask for a double and near double, such as 34/35, where 34 is double 17 and 35 is, for example, 17 + 18. Share the responses and test out the 'doubleness' of the left-hand number by halving. What is the hardest example they can show you?

Main teaching activities

Whole class: Give out five beanbags, one to each of five children. The first child moves around the room and places their beanbag saying 'My beanbag is underneath the chair'. The next child has to remember this and then repeat this by touching the first child's bag and moving to place their own beanbag in their choice of place. Continue until all five bags are out. Ask the children what positional vocabulary has been used from today's list. Extend to ten beanbags.

Now point to the four compass points on the floor and ask the children to explain what these mean. Write 'North', 'South', 'East' and 'West' on the board, spread well out, to show the four points of the compass. Repeat the beanbag activity, this time asking the children to place their beanbags using compass directions, such as the first child steps North, 1 step (drop bag); second child repeats and adds turn clockwise through a right angle, 1 step (drop bag), and so on. Each time the children decide in which direction the child is when the beanbag is dropped. Sketch the route on the board, marking the route and referring to the compass direction each time.

Group work: Using the vocabulary of compass points, direction and movement, the children work in teams of three or four to script a short route to drop beanbags. Each child tries out their script before making a drawing of the route.

Differentiation

Less able: You act as a scribe for this group.
More able: Challenge the children to program Roamer to follow their route.

Plenary & assessment

Ask one group to walk their route. Then display two of the drawn routes. Can the children reason which is the correct drawing? Encourage the children to direct a child along a beanbag route. Ask: *Which way should s/he turn next? How can you tell that? In which direction is s/he facing now?* If the more able children have programmed Roamer, invite them to show what they have done and to explain how they programmed Roamer.

Lessons   overview

Preparation
Make an OHT of CD page '2-D shapes and patterns'. Collect and display the repeated patterns.

Learning objectives
Starter
- Identify near doubles, using doubles already known (eg 80 + 81).

Main teaching activity
- Solve mathematical problems or puzzles, recognise simple patterns and relationships, generalise and predict. Suggest extensions by asking 'What if…?'
- **Explain methods and reasoning** orally and, where appropriate, in writing.

Vocabulary
right angle, left, right, up, down, horizontal, vertical, diagonal, forwards, backwards

You will need:
CD pages
'2-D shapes and patterns' for each child (see General resources).

Equipment
Samples of wallpaper border patterns; Aztec repeated patterns; squared paper; OHP; shape tiles such as square, rectangle, circle, triangle… Roamer.

Lesson

Starter
Ask for a pair of teen numbers near doubles. Now ask: *How would you total these?* Children may have different suggestions. For example, for 18 and 19 they might say Double 20, subtract 1 and then 2. Double 18 add 1. Double 10, then add 9, then 8… Repeat this for other pairs of near doubles.

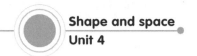

Main teaching activities

Whole class: Use the wallpaper borders and Aztec art to see how patterning is used in real life. Ask: *Are there any examples in the class of repeated patterns?* On the OHP, show a rectangle cut from CD page '2-D shapes and patterns'. Place another beside it to make a larger rectangle.

Ask: *In what other ways could we place two rectangles together?* Invite the children to make suggestions. For each shape, ask: *How many sides/vertices does it have? Does it have a special mathematical name?* Now invite the children to think about how to place the strips together to make an octagon.

Discuss which of the shapes made with two rectangles are symmetrical and where the line of symmetry is.

Now use the shape tiles from '2-D shapes and patterns' to make a repeating ABAB pattern on the OHP. Ask: *What is the pattern? What will the next piece in the pattern be? What will the tenth/twentieth/twenty-ninth piece be? How can you tell?*

Group work: Explain that there are three tasks to be completed during this and the next lesson:
1. Using shapes cut from '2-D shapes and patterns', ask the children to make a symmetrical shape by fitting together two of the shapes. Challenge them to find as many different ways as they can of doing this, and to record their work by sketching what they make.
2. Using Roamer, the children programme the robot to draw shapes with right-angled corners. Suggest that they draw shapes with three, four, five… up to eight sides, and name each shape.
3. Use shape tiles to make repeating patterns such as AABBCCAABBCC… Challenge the children to make their patterns more complex by placing some pieces in a line horizontally, and some above so that there is both horizontal and vertical movement in the pattern.

Differentiation

Less able: The tasks can be simplified if necessary. For example:
● Limit the children to finding three different symmetrical combinations of two shapes.
● Ask the children to draw different shapes with just four sides, but each shape to have at least one right angle.
● Suggest that the children make patterns with pieces 'moving' horizontally only.
More able: Challenge the children by asking them to make patterns that are also symmetrical.

Plenary & assessment

Choose two children to give verbal descriptions of their patterns. Ask the children to close their eyes and visualise the pattern, and to sketch their idea. Opening their eyes, they compare their drawing to the real pattern. Note: they will need to hear the description more than once. Ask: *How could you make the description easier to follow?* Agree a common approach such as 'First draw a horizontal line for one square. Next…'

Lesson ⑤

Repeat the Starter from Lesson 4. This time explain that you will say near doubles of numbers to 20. Ask the children to find the total quickly. Say, for example, 17 + 16; 15 + 16… Keep the pace sharp. Stop every so often to ask: How did you work that out? Who used a different way? During the Main teaching activity, review with everyone how to programme Roamer to turn through a right angle. Invite children who worked with Roamer in the previous lesson to demonstrate the shapes that they made and how they programmed Roamer. Ask the children to continue to work on the activities from Lesson 4. During the Plenary & assessment, review the symmetrical shapes that were made. Ask: *Where is the line of symmetry? How many lines of symmetry does this shape have?*

Time and weight

Children review reading the time to five minutes on analogue and digital clocks, and learn how to use am and pm. They estimate, weigh and record masses in kilograms and grams. They use decimal notation to record masses such as 1.5kg.

LEARNING OBJECTIVES

		Topics	Starter	Main teaching activity
Lesson	1	Measures	**Read and write whole numbers to at least 1000** in figures and words.	● Read the time to 5 minutes on an analogue and a 12-hour digital clock, and use the notation 9:40.
Lesson	2	Measures	As for Lesson 1.	● Read and begin to write the vocabulary related to mass. ● Measure and compare using standard units (kg, g). ● Know the relationship between kilograms and grams. ● Suggest suitable units and measuring equipment to estimate or measure mass.
Lesson	3	Measures	As for Lesson 1.	● As for Lesson 2.
Lesson	4	Measures	● Identify near doubles, using doubles already known (eg 80 + 81).	● As for Lesson 2.
Lesson	5	Measures	As for Lesson 4.	● As for Lesson 2.

Lesson overview

Preparation
Photocopy three sets of digits 0 to 9 each to A3 from CD page 'Numeral cards 0 to 20'.

Learning objectives
Starter
● **Read and write whole numbers to at least 1000** in figures and words.
Main teaching activity
● Read the time to 5 minutes on an analogue and a 12-hour digital clocks and use the notation 9:40.

Vocabulary
morning, afternoon, evening, night, midnight, am, pm, bedtime, dinnertime, playtime, yesterday, today, tomorrow

You will need:
Photocopiable pages
'Beat the clock' (page 118) and 'Passing time' (page 119), one for each child.

CD pages
'Numeral cards 0 to 20' (Autumn term) (see General resources).

Equipment
Whiteboards and pens; analogue teaching clock; 12-hour digital clock; three sets of A3 numeral cards 0 to 9.

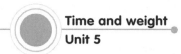

Time and weight
Unit 5

Lesson

Starter

Shuffle the three sets of numeral cards. Take three cards and ask a child to make a three-digit number from the numerals and write it on the board as numerals. Invite the children to write this number in words on their white boards and to hold these up for you to see when you say Show me. Invite another child to make another three-digit number from the original cards and repeat until all six possible numbers have been made, written on the board by you in numerals and by the children as words. (For example, for 1, 2, 3: 123; 132; 213; 231; 312; 321). Repeat for another set of three digits.

Main teaching activities

Whole class: The main emphasis for this lesson is knowing the parts that make up a full day and how we tend to mark these times collectively in most parts of Britain. You may wish to pursue cross-curricular links with cultural expectations, for example, use of prayer punctuating the day for Muslims. Gather assessment information by asking questions such as:

- *How many hours does the average person sleep every night?* (8 hours)
- *What time do you go to bed/get up each day?*
- *What kinds of things tend to happen before lunch?* (Going to school, breakfast, walking the dog…)
- *What kinds of things happen after lunch?* (People relax after eating…)

Relate each of these events to time, before inviting a child to set the hands on the analogue clock to show that time, whilst another child writes the time in digital format on the board. Explain about am (*ante meridian* or before noon) and pm (*post meridian* or after noon). Write 'am' and 'pm' on the board and say: *am begins at 12 o'clock midnight; pm begins at 12 o'clock noon.* Suggest events during the day and ask for an approximate time for these and whether these will be am or pm events, such as: *At what time do we have morning/afternoon break? At what time do you go home from school?* Record these times as digital time on the board. Discuss how we write, for example 3:40, but say *twenty to four.* Repeat this for other 'past the hour times', showing each one on an analogue clock, saying it as a 'past the hour' time, and recording it digitally.

Group work: This is in two distinct parts today. Provide activity sheet 'Beat the clock'. The children have ten minutes to see how many of the digital times they can write on the analogue clock face, vice versa. Then provide activity sheet 'Passing time' and ask the children to work in pairs to discuss the times and what they did yesterday.

Differentiation

Less able: Decide whether to concentrate on telling the time in five-minute intervals. The activity sheet 'Beat the clock' can be completed as a group activity, using teaching analogue and digital clocks for setting the hands or the digits for each question. Encourage the children to say the time for each question.

More able: If these children finish more quickly, challenge them to write what they do on a typical Saturday, with the times written as am or pm.

Plenary & assessment

Discuss what the children have done since they woke up today. Ask:

- *What were you doing at 8.30am?*
- *What did you do next?*
- *Do you think you will be doing the same thing at 8.30am tomorrow?*

On the board write 'am' 'pm', 'yesterday', 'today' and 'tomorrow' and ask the children to suggest sentences which use this vocabulary. Practise reading the times from a large clock face for the following times: 2.20, 4.35, 5.55, 10.15. Assess whether most of the children are able to use past and to the hour accurately.

Lesson   ⑤ overview

Preparation
Photocopy three sets of digits 0 to 9 each to A3 from CD page 'Numeral cards 0 to 20'. Make an OHT from CD page 'Dial'. For Lesson 5, place a dial scale onto each table and a pack of potatoes.

Learning objectives
Starter
- **Read and write whole numbers to at least 1000** in figures and words.
- **Identify near doubles, using doubles already known (eg 80 + 81).**

Main teaching activity
- Read and begun to write the vocabulary related to mass.
- Measure and compare using standard units (kg, g).
- Know the relationship between kilograms and grams.
- Suggest suitable units and measuring equipment to estimate or measure mass.
- Read scales to the nearest division (labelled or unlabelled).
- Record estimates and measurements to the nearest whole or half unit (eg 'about 3.5kg') or in mixed units.

Vocabulary
weigh, weighs, balances, heavy/light, heavier/lighter, heaviest/lightest, kilogram, half kilogram, gram, balances, scales, weight, too much, too little, enough, not enough, about the same as, just over, just under, approximately

You will need:
Photocopiable pages
'Two-egg cake' (page 120), for each child.

CD pages
'Numeral cards 0 to 20' (Autumn term); 'Dial' for each child (see General resources).

Equipment
OHT; tray, strong carrier bag and food items such as cans, packs of teabags, so that there is a total weight of about 1.5kg; various types of weighing instruments including pan balances and weights, dial scales, and digital scales; strong paper bag; strong bags containing, for example, potatoes, which weigh amounts such as 500g, 1kg, 1.5kg… up to 4kg; A4 numeral cards 0 to 9; whiteboards and pens.

Lesson

Starter
Repeat the Starter from Lesson 1, using different sets of three digits.

Main teaching activities
Whole class: Show the OHT made from CD page 'Dial'. Explain it is the dial on some scales. Mark zero at one end and 500g at the other. Draw the needle in different positions and ask the children to read the mass shown. Ask questions such as:
- *What is each division worth? How did you work that out?*
- *Can you think of an item that might have a mass near 100g?*
- *Can you think of an item that would force me off the end of my 0–500g scale?*

Change the range of the dial to 500 to 1000g, and repeat the activity and questions. Check that the children understand that 1 kilogram weighs the same as 1000 grams. Write this on the board, and the shortened forms of kg and g.

You may like to address the issue of 'mass' and 'weight' by explaining that scales measure mass. Mass remains constant, but weight is a force and can change according to the force of gravity. Our mass is the same on Earth and on the Moon, for example, but our weight is less on the Moon because there is one-sixth as much gravity there.

Now ask the children to look at the mass measuring equipment that you have put out. Ask them to check that the dial scales are correctly set and that the pans are in equilibrium, and to alter them if not. Remind the children of how to do this, if necessary.

Group work: This work continues during the next two lessons. Choose from this circus of activities.
1. Provide activity sheet 'Two-egg cake'. Ask the children to work in pairs to complete this sheet.
2. The children can work in groups of three or four for this activity. Provide the items and shopping bag on the tray. Ask the children to pack the bag so that it weighs about 1kg. Encourage them to

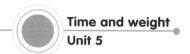
estimate first, then to check by balancing. Suggest that they find different ways of doing this and decide how to record their work on paper.

3. The children can work in groups of three or four for this activity. Ask them to pack a paper bag with classroom items that weigh about 300g. The children can collect their own items, and should estimate first before checking by weighing. Suggest that they find different ways of doing this and decide how to record their work on paper.

Differentiation

The children can work in mixed-ability groups for these tasks. As they work, ensure that the less able children are taking an active role and contributing to the work. Challenge the more able children to work out the difference between the net weights of the packs in activity 2, compared with their gross weight, and to explain why these are different to the other children during the plenary.

Plenary & assessment

Here are three Plenaries, one for each of the activities. Decide which to use on each of the successive days.

1. Discuss with the children that this really is a recipe that has been used for a long time. Ask: *Why do you think people used this recipe?* (It was probably handed down, from parent to child, and is very easy to remember. Perhaps, too, with little or no education, this was an easy way of remembering what would work.) Ask the children who have completed this activity to explain how they worked out the new weights for the ingredients. Discuss how much is needed for six, then 12 people each to have cake. Finally, ask: *How much would we need of each ingredient if only three people wanted cake?*

2. Ask for suggestions of how to fill the bag. *How close to 1kg did you get? How many different ways did you find to do this? How did you record your work?* Discuss the merits of the ways of recording. Some children may have drawn pictures; others may have shown totals of weights. Ask which way gives most information (probably showing weights so that items could be substituted to find a new way of making 1kg.) Invite the more able children to explain about the differences between the net weight on the packs and their actual weight, and to explain why there is a difference (the packaging as the net weight refers to the contents of the pack).

3. Ask the children to explain how they found their totals. Discuss how close to their target of 300g they were, again, inviting children to discuss how they recorded their work and how effective this was.

Lesson ③

For the Starter explain that you will write some three-digit numbers on the board in words. As you write each one, ask a child to write the number using digits. Repeat this, this time beginning with writing the number in digits and asking a child to write it in words. During the whole-class session, invite the children to suggest things that they would expect to weigh in grams, and things that they would expect to weigh in kilograms, listing the items on the board. Choose from the circus of activities for Lesson 2 for group work. During the Plenary & assessment, ask questions about how much children would expect items to weigh, such as: *Would you expect an apple to weigh about 100g or 1kg?* Choose one of the activities from the circus and use the Plenary for it from Lesson 2.

Lesson  ④

For the Starter, explain that you will say a number between 1 and 19. Ask the children to respond by saying its double. Keep the pace of this sharp. During the whole-class work, ask the children to suggest items in the classroom which they think weigh about 500g, then, using a balance, to check their estimates. Invite the children to complete the activity from Lesson 2's circus which they still have to complete. During the Plenary & assessment, choose the Plenary from Lesson 2 which is still to be covered. Discuss how important it is to check an estimate by measuring in order to improve the ability to estimate with reasonable accuracy.

Lesson ⑤

Starter
Repeat the Starter for Lesson 4. This time explain that you will say a number to be halved. Say even numbers between 2 and 40.

Main teaching activities
Whole class: Use bags of potatoes or similar to estimate with the children weights of more than 1kg. Let the children feel a 1kg bag of sugar to get a good idea first. Show them how to express 1 1/2kg as 1.5kg. Write on the board: 1kg 500g =1 1/2kg = 1.5kg. Repeat with other examples involving 500g, such as 2500g, 5500g…

Group work: Ask the children to work in groups of four. They begin at their own table, pass the bag of potatoes around the group to estimate its weight, then check by weighing. They record the weight in grams, in kilograms and grams, and as a decimal fraction of a kilogram. For example, for 2500g they write 2500g, 2kg 500g, 2.5kg. On your signal, the groups move to a different table and repeat this, until every group has estimated, weighed and written their results for each bag of potatoes.

Differentiation
Less able: If the children need help with the recording of decimal fractions, move around the room with this group, offering support with estimating, weighing and recording.
More able: Challenge the children to work out the total of the weight of all of the potatoes.

Plenary & assessment
On the board draw this spidergram.

Ask the children: *How many different ways can I write 1.5kg?* (In words, as 'g', as a fraction, etc.) Write all their ideas onto the diagram, discussing the ease/complexity of each one. Ask the children to decide which one they prefer and which they have seen used most frequently. Now review the estimates, weights and ways in which the potato weights were recorded. Invite a child to record each bag of potatoes' weight on the board as a decimal fraction of a kilogram. Now challenge the children to put these in weight order, beginning with the lightest. If the more able children have totalled the weights of the potatoes, review this as a group. Ask: *If all the potatoes were in a sack, do you think you could lift them? Would this be sensible?* (Probably not, because of their weight.)

| Name | Date |

Beat the clock

Write the time on the digital clock face.

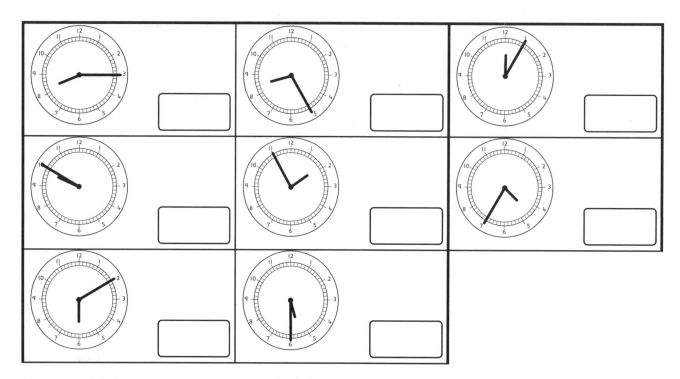

Now draw in the hands to show the times on the digital clocks.

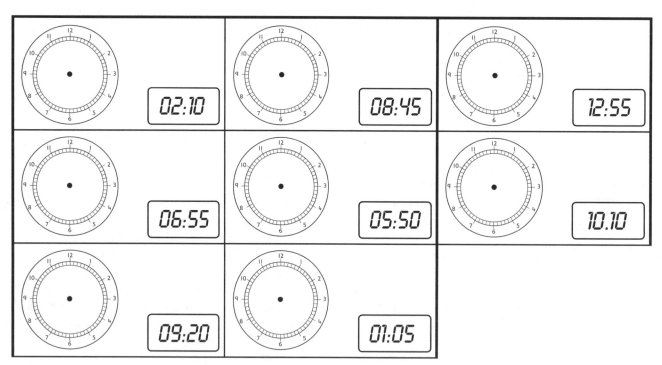

Name	Date

Passing time

Write what you were doing at these times yesterday.

Morning

7am   I was _____

8am   I was _____

9.30am   I was _____

10.45am   I was _____

12 o'clock midday   I was _____

Afternoon

1.30pm   I was _____

4pm   I was _____

Evening

6pm   I was _____

Night

9pm   I was _____

My favourite part of the day yesterday was

_____

Name	Date

Two-egg cake

This is a list of ingredients for making a cake.

Read it carefully.

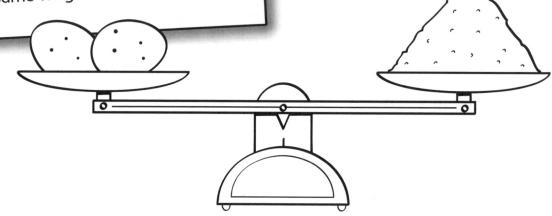

Two standard eggs.
The same weight of flour as the eggs weigh still in their shells.
The same weight of sugar as flour.
The same weight of margarine as flour.

Write the answers to these questions.

1. If each egg weighs 50g how much do both eggs weigh?

2. How much will the flour and the sugar weigh together?

3. Approximately how much will all the ingredients weigh in total?

The recipe makes a cake large enough for six people to enjoy.

Write the recipe again so that there will be enough for 12 people to eat some cake.

standard eggs.

grams of flour.

grams of sugar.

grams of margarine.

The recipe really works if you add about 15ml of milk to the mixture.

You might like to try to make the cake!

Making decisions

Children decide which operation to choose for particular problems and explain why. They solve problems, make jottings where appropriate, and check with an equivalent calculation.

LEARNING OBJECTIVES

	Topics	Starter	Main teaching activity
Lesson 1	Making decisions	● Say or write a subtraction statement corresponding to a given addition statement, and vice versa.	● **Choose and use appropriate operations (including multiplication and division) to solve word problems,** and appropriate ways of calculating: mental, mental with jottings, pencil and paper.
Lesson 2	Making decisions	As for Lesson 1.	As for Lesson 1.
Lesson 3	Making decisions	As for Lesson 1.	As for Lesson 1.

Lessons   overview

Preparation
Make an A3 enlargement of activity sheet 'Guess my rule'.

Learning objectives
Starter
● Say or write a subtraction statement corresponding to a given addition statement, and vice versa.
Main teaching activity
● **Choose and use appropriate operations (including multiplication and division) to solve word problems**, and appropriate ways of calculating: mental, mental with jottings, pencil and paper.

Vocabulary
start with, arrange, choose, record, work out, check, answer, question, solve.

You will need:
Photocopiable pages
'Guess my rule' (page 123) and 'Bugs alive' (page 124), for each child.

CD pages
'Guess my rule' and 'Bugs alive' less able and more able versions (see Spring term, Unit 6).

Equipment
Stopwatches.

Lesson

For the Starter, some subtraction sentences on the board, e.g. 47 – 25 = 22, and ask the children to think of three related sentences: two for addition and another for subtraction. Now ask them to decide which operation was used for the following problems.
- *I start with the number 10 but end up with 15.*
- *I start with 25 and end up with 17.*
- *I start with 54 and end up with 27.*

Discuss each question in turn, invite the children to explain why it is addition or subtraction. Give each child a copy of the differentiated activity sheet 'Guess my rule' and ask them to work out the rule for the function machines. For Plenary & assessment, use an A3 enlargement of 'Guess my rule', invite all the children to help explain what the rule is for each function machine. Ask questions such as: How did you work out whether to add, subtract, multiply or divide? Encourage the children to explain this in their own words. Give praise to those who use mathematical vocabulary appropriately.

Making decisions
Unit 6

Lesson ②

Starter

Repeat the Starter for Lesson 1. This time, write up, for example, 45 + 36 =, or 95 – 67 = and ask the children to complete the number sentence, before deriving the other three sentences.

Main teaching activities

Whole class: Explain that the problems to be solved in this lesson centre around a class on a science trip who are collecting minibeasts. Pose this problem. *Dana has 15 slugs. Andy has 23 slugs. How many more slugs does Andy have?* On the board, write this grid formation and solve it.

Problem	Calculation	Final answer	Checking calculation
15 slugs, 23 slugs how many more?	23 – 15	8 slugs more	15 + 8 = 23

Explain to the children that by carrying out a checking calculation they will be able to check their answer. Repeat for another problem, such as: *Seema has collected 24 woodlice. Mark has only half as many woodlice as Seema. How many woodlice does Mark have?*

Individual work: Ask the children to complete the activity sheet 'Bugs alive'.

Differentiation

Less able: Decide whether to use the activity sheet with simpler calculations. Discuss with the children the range of calculation strategies that they could use to solve these problems.
More able: There is a version available which extends the number range for these children.

Plenary & assessment

Choose some of the problems from each of the differentiated CD pages used, and review these together. Ask: *What calculation strategy did you choose? Who did this in a different way?*

Lesson ③

Starter

Write four two-digit numbers on the board, such as 26, 78, 39 and 45. Ask the children to choose pairs of these numbers and, with their partner, to add their choice and write an addition sentence. Now ask them to write another addition sentence using the numbers in their addition sentence and the corresponding subtraction sentences. After five minutes, invite pairs to say their addition and subtraction sentences.

Main teaching activities

Whole class: Explain to the children that today they will invent their own number stories to reflect number sentences. On the board write: 145 + 155 = ☐. Ask: *How can you calculate this equation?* Invite suggestions, such as 100 + 100 + 45 + 55 = 200 + 90 + 10 = 300. Now ask: *What could the number story be for this equation?* Repeat this for other examples, including subtraction.
Group work: In pairs, the children make stories to accompany equations. Ask the children to complete the number sentences which you write on the board, then write a number story for each one. Write, for example: 124 + 165 = ☐; 92 – ☐ = 50; ☐ × 5 = 60; 36 ÷ ☐ = 9.

Differentiation

Less able: Decide whether to work as a group.
More able: Challenge the children to invent more number sentences and stories; one each for addition, subtraction, multiplication and division.

Plenary & assessment

Review the answers to the number sentences on the board, then ask: *How did you work that out? Who used a different method?* Invite suggestions for the number stories. For each story, ask: *How can you tell what sort of strategy would be needed to work this out?*

Name		Date

Guess my rule

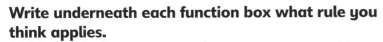

Look at the numbers in the first column.

Decide how they have been changed into the numbers in the second column.

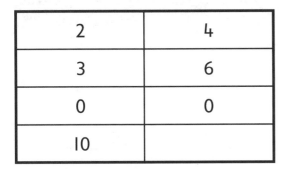

Write underneath each function box what rule you think applies.

Write in the missing numbers.

2	4
3	6
0	0
10	

My rule is _____

44	35
	59
36	27
22	13

My rule is _____

25	21
52	48
	6
100	96

My rule is _____

27	32
41	46
75	80
58	63

My rule is _____

24	8
30	10
15	5
	9

My rule is _____

36	
42	21
68	34
44	22

My rule is _____

| Name | Date |

Bugs alive

Read the following brain teasers and use the boxes to write your thinking.

Write a check calculation to prove to yourself that your answer is correct.

The story so far...

Class 3 have gone on a science trip. They have to collect lots of bugs to study.

Brain teaser	Your jottings	Final answer	Check calculation
Collette collected 5 more spiders than Adam. She had 26 in total. How many did Adam have?			
Carole counted 13 worms. Tony saw 8 more than Carole. How many did Tony see?			
Peter chased Nora with a jar of 23 flies but 6 escaped. How many did he have left?			
Ronnie, Simon and Carl each had a jar with 16 ladybirds. How many ladybirds altogether?			
Waseem caught 27 ants. He separated them equally into 3 jars. How many in each jar?			
Sarah had twice as many slugs as Iain. Iain collected 6. How many did Sarah have?			

Sequences, reasoning about numbers, and explaining methods

Children complete number chains which contain sequences which count in threes, fours and fives. They find missing numbers in incomplete sequences. They describe the rules for making sequences, and make their own sequences. The 3 times-table is introduced, then the children investigate number statements, decide whether they are true by finding examples to satisfy these, explain why the statements are true, and explain their methods.

LEARNING OBJECTIVES

	Topics	Starter	Main teaching activity
Lesson 1	Counting, properties of numbers and number sequences	● **Know by heart multiplication facts for the 2, 5 and 10 times-tables.** ● Derive quickly: division facts corresponding to the 2, 5 and 10 times-tables.	● Describe and extend number sequences: count on in steps of 3, 4 or 5 from any small number to at least 50, then back again.
Lesson 2	Counting, properties of numbers and number sequences	As for Lesson 1.	As for Lesson 1.
Lesson 3	Reasoning about numbers	● Begin to know the 3 times-table.	● Investigate a general statement about familiar numbers or shapes by finding examples that satisfy it. ● **Explain methods and reasoning** orally and, where appropriate, in writing.
Lesson 4	Reasoning about numbers	As for Lesson 3.	As for Lesson 3.
Lesson 5	Reasoning about numbers	As for Lesson 3.	As for Lesson 3.

Lessons overview

Preparation
Make an A3 enlargement of 'Hundred square' and 'Spot the pattern'.

Learning objectives
Starter
● **Know by heart multiplication facts for the 2, 5 and 10 times-tables.**
● Derive quickly: division facts corresponding to the 2, 5 and 10 times-tables.
Main teaching activity
● Describe and extend number sequences: count on in steps of 3, 4 or 5 from any small number to at least 50, then back again.

Vocabulary
bigger, larger, smaller, pattern, between, missing numbers, sequence

You will need:
Photocopiable pages
'Spot the pattern' (page 130) and 'Patterns' (page 131) for each child.

CD pages
'Hundred square', 'Multiplication facts for 2, 5 and 10 times-tables' for each child (Autumn term); 'Spot the pattern' and 'Patterns' less able and more able versions (Spring term, Unit 8) (see General resources).

Equipment
Counters in sets of the same colour; Blu-tack; sheets of paper.

Lesson ①

Starter

Explain to the children that you will show them a multiplication card for the 2, 5 or 10 times-tables from CD page 'Multiplication facts for 2, 5 and 10 times-tables'. Ask them to say quietly the answer to the question on the card when you hold up your hand. Give the children a few seconds of thinking time, so that most have time to recall the table fact. You may prefer to sort the cards and to deal with, for example, the 2 times-table first. Give very little time for recalling the facts as the children should all know these well by now.

Main teaching activities

Whole class: Show the children the A3 CD page 'Hundred square'. Using one colour of counters, ask the children to say the pattern of two starting on 2, and cover each number said with a counter, sticking it with Blu-Tack. Repeat this for counting in fives, starting at 5, using a different colour counter, then in tens, starting at 10. Now ask:

- Does the pattern of twos cover odd or even numbers? Can you explain why this is?
- What do you notice about the pattern of fives? What are the digit numbers?
- Which numbers are in both the pattern of fives and tens? What about in the pattern of twos and tens? And twos, fives and tens?

Now use paper to mask parts of the hundred square so that only the squares 1, 2, 3, 4, 5 to 25 are visible. Ask the children to count in threes, starting from 2, and again cover the numbers said with a counter. Ask: *What do you notice about this pattern?* (It forms diagonal lines.) *What would the next number in the sequence be?* (26) *And the next?* (29) *Would 41 be in the sequence?* (Yes) *How do you know?*

Remove the counters and ask the children to think out the pattern of counting in threes, this time starting on 1. Ask: *What would the pattern be?* Repeat this, moving the masking sheets so that the number squares 1 to 36 are visible. Ask the children to count in steps of 4, from 1, then 2, then in steps of 5, and so on.

Paired work: Provide copies of activity page 'Spot the pattern' to each child. Ask the children to work in pairs to complete the sequences. Encourage them to discuss the sequences. They may find it helpful to say each one aloud so that they hear the numbers making the pattern. Children may find a copy of the hundred square helpful.

Differentiation

Less able: Decide whether to use the differentiated activity sheet for this group, which uses lower TU numbers.

More able: There is a version of the sheet which takes the sequences beyond 100.

Plenary & assessment

Use an A3 version of 'Spot the pattern' and have the hundred square handy. Invite individual children to give missing numbers. Ask a child to point to each number in the sequence on the hundred square for the others to check the pattern. You may wish to use the Blu-Tacked counters again to cover the numbers to help the less able children to keep the pattern in their heads. Ask questions such as: *Does this sequence make a pattern on the hundred square?* (For example, straight line, diagonal, every other number…) *What would the next number in the sequence be? And the number before the first in the sequence?* (Where the pattern begins, for example, with a teen number.)

Lesson

Starter

Repeat the Starter from Lesson 1, but this time decrease the thinking time before you hold up your hand for the answer in order to encourage rapid recall of these multiplication facts. Include division facts.

Main teaching activities

Whole class: Explain to the children that you would like them to play *Guess my rule* using adding and subtracting 3, 4 or 5 to random numbers from 1 to 50. Say, for example: *16, 19, 22. What is the rule?* (Add three each time.) *What would the next number be? And the next? What would the number before 16 be?* Ask the children to explain how they decided what your rule was. Encourage the children to explain: 'It can't be adding 1 because…'.

Write up the numbers 26, 41, 31, 46 randomly on the board. Invite a child to order the numbers: 26, 31, 41, 46, then say: *There is a missing number. Where should it go? What number is it?* (36) *What number do you think comes next in this sequence?* (51) *Why do you think that?* Repeat this for another set of four numbers such as 24, 27, 30 and 36 written randomly on the board.

Group work: The children complete missing number 'chains' on activity sheet 'Patterns' and write the rule for each chain.

Differentiation

Less able: The children will find it helpful to have a hundred square handy to plot the number sequences.
More able: There is a version of the activity sheet available which includes numbers beyond 100.

Plenary & assessment

Write up this sequence onto the board: 15, 19, □ , 27, 31, □ , □ . Ask questions such as: *What are the missing numbers? How did you work that out? What is the rule for the pattern? Are the numbers in the sequence getting larger or smaller?* Repeat this for another sequence, such as 3, 8, 13, 18…

Lessons   overview

Preparation
Enlarge 'Work it out' to A3.

Learning objectives
Starter
● Begin to know the 3 times-table.
Main teaching activity
● Investigate a general statement about familiar numbers or shapes by finding examples that satisfy it.
● **Explain methods and reasoning** orally and, where appropriate, in writing

Vocabulary
pattern, puzzle, calculate, calculation, mental calculation, method, jotting, answer, right, correct, wrong, what could we try next? how did you work it out? number sentence, sign, operation, symbol, equation

You will need:
CD pages
'Work it out', core, less able and more able versions (Spring term, Unit 8) (see General resources).

Equipment
Whiteboards and pens; interlocking cubes.

Lesson ③

Starter

Ask the children to count aloud with you, starting from zero. Whenever they reach a number in the pattern of threes (3, 6, 9…), ask them to clap their hands gently at the same time as they say the number. Continue to 36, then repeat from zero. When the children have done this several times, repeat again, this time counting backwards. Finally, say the sequence of threes: 3, 6, 9 to 36.

Main teaching activities

Whole class: Explain that in this lesson the children will be considering statements about how numbers work, and finding examples to fit those statements. Say, for example: *Any odd number is one more than an even number.* Write the statement onto the board. Ask for examples that satisfy this statement, such as $37 = 36 + 1$ and $45 = 44 + 1$. Write the examples on the board. Challenge the more able children to explain why this statement is always true. They might say, for example: 'The counting numbers always go odd, even, odd, even. So any even number is always followed by an odd number, which is one more'. Repeat this for another statement, such as: *Any even number is one more than an odd number.*

Paired work: Ask the children to work in pairs to find examples which match the following statements:

- *Any odd number can be written as the sum of an odd and even number.*
- *A multiple of 5 is always half a multiple of 10.*
- *The multiplication table for 10 is always even.*

Remind the children that you will expect them to be able to explain why the statements are true.

Differentiation

Less able: Decide whether to work as a group to find examples to match the statements. Encourage the children to explain why the statements are true, using mathematical vocabulary. You may need to say their explanations in mathematical language if the children find this difficult.

More able: Encourage the children to write explanations for each of the statements, using mathematical vocabulary.

Plenary & assessment

Review each of the statements in turn. Ask for examples, which the children can write on the board. Say: *Is this example correct? Who can explain why this statement is true?* Now say: *Is it true that the sum of two even numbers is odd. Why not? Explain.*

Lesson ④

Starter

Say together the 3 times-table. Write the number sentences on the board, in order: $0 \times 3 = 0$; $1 \times 3 = 3$… Using the vocabulary of multiplication, invite the children to say the answers to questions such as: *What is 3 times 3? What is … multiplied by 3? Can you work out what 12 divided by 3… 4 is?*

Main teaching activities

Whole class: Explain that you would like the children to continue to think about general statements about numbers. Write on the board: *The difference between two even numbers is even.* Ask: *Is this true? Talk to your partner and write down four number sentences to show that this is true.* Invite the children to take turns to write their number sentences on the board, such as $8 - 4 = 4$;

96 – 10 = 86… Invite the children to think about why this statement is true. They may find it helpful to model a simple number sentence, such as 6 – 4 = 2 using cubes.

Now repeat this for the difference between odd and even numbers. Write up: *The difference between an odd and an even number is…* Ask the children to work with their partner to decide how to complete the statement, then to find four examples to satisfy the statement. Again, invite the children to explain why the difference between an odd and an even number is always odd.

Paired work: Ask the children to consider the following statements, which should be written onto the board:

● *The difference between two odd numbers is always even.*
● *If you multiply numbers either way round the answer is the same.*

Ask the children to decide whether the statements are true and to find six examples to satisfy each statement. Remind them that you may ask how they worked out their six examples so that they are ready to explain.

Differentiation

Less able: Decide whether to work as a group to find examples to match the statements. Encourage the children to explain why the statements are true, using mathematical vocabulary. You may need to say their explanations in mathematical language if the children find this difficult.
More able: Challenge the children to explain why these statements are true. They may find it helpful to have cubes to model their explanations.

Plenary & assessment

Begin with the statement 'The difference between two odd numbers is always even.' Invite the children to take turns to write up on the board examples which show that the statement is true. Ask: *How did you work out this number sentence?* Encourage the children to explain this, using mathematical vocabulary. Ask the more able children to explain why the statement is true. They may say that the difference between any two odd numbers, such as 5 and 7, is even, because they are two away from each other. This would be a good start to the discussion. Repeat for the second statement.

Lesson ⑤

For the Starter, invite the children to say the answer to multiplication questions for the 3 times-table, such as: What is… multiplied by 3? At this stage give plenty of thinking time, so that the majority of children can find the answer. For the Main activity, ask the children to consider number sentences such as 24 + 18, 40 – 19, 15 × 2 and 48 ÷ 2, and to explain how they worked out the answer. Provide differentiated CD page 'Work it out' and ask the children to write the answer, as well as a brief explanation of how they worked this out. Encourage them to explain to their partner their explanation. Review the core version of the sheet during the Plenary & assessment, and ask the children to explain their working out, using mathematical language.

Name   Date

Spot the pattern

Write the missing numbers in these number patterns.

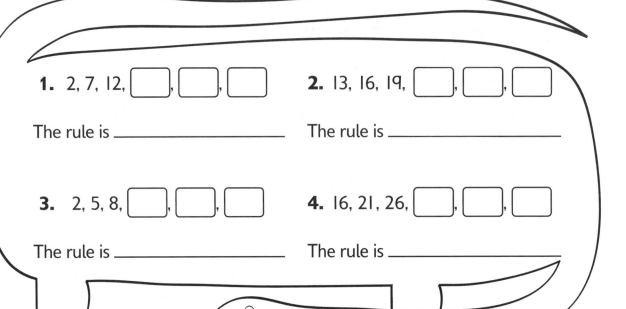

1. 2, 7, 12, ☐, ☐, ☐

The rule is _____

2. 13, 16, 19, ☐, ☐, ☐

The rule is _____

3. 2, 5, 8, ☐, ☐, ☐

The rule is _____

4. 16, 21, 26, ☐, ☐, ☐

The rule is _____

Write the rule for each of these patterns.

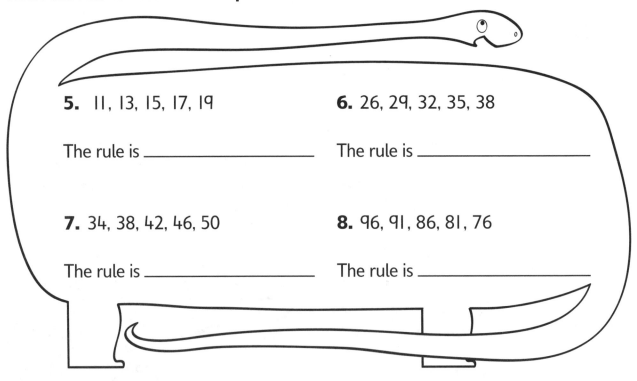

5. 11, 13, 15, 17, 19

The rule is _____

6. 26, 29, 32, 35, 38

The rule is _____

7. 34, 38, 42, 46, 50

The rule is _____

8. 96, 91, 86, 81, 76

The rule is _____

Now write your own sequence.

It must include the numbers 8 and 17 in it.

Write the rule.

| Name | Date |

Patterns

Fill in the missing numbers.

Write the rule for the chain.

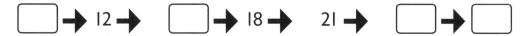

The rule is _____

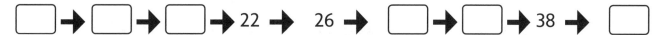

The rule is _____

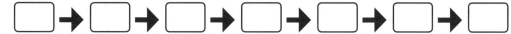

The rule is _____

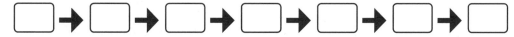

The rule is _____

Write your own pattern.

Write the rule for your pattern.

The rule is _____

The rule is _____

The rule is _____

The rule is _____

Addition and division

Children add several one- and two-digit numbers, using mental strategies such as reordering and partitioning into tens and units. They use paper and pencil strategies such as the empty number line. Division is revisited, reinforcing understanding that this can be seen as by grouping or by sharing. They begin to understand that division is the inverse of multiplication.

LEARNING OBJECTIVES

	Topics	Starter	Main teaching activity
Lesson 1	Understanding addition and subtraction Mental calculation strategies (+ and –)	● Derive quickly: doubles of multiples of 5 to 100.	● Extend understanding that more than two numbers can be added; add three or four single-digit numbers mentally, or three or four two-digit numbers with the help of apparatus or pencil and paper. ● Use knowledge that addition can be done in any order to do mental calculations more efficiently.
Lesson 2	Understanding addition and subtraction Mental calculation strategies (+ and –)	As for Lesson 1.	● Extend understanding that more than two numbers can be added; add three or four single-digit numbers mentally, or three or four two-digit numbers with the help of apparatus or pencil and paper. ● Use knowledge that addition can be done in any order to do mental calculations more efficiently. For example: partition into tens and units, then recombine (e.g. 34 + 53 = 30 + 50 + 4 + 3).
Lesson 3	Understanding addition and subtraction Mental calculation strategies (+ and –)	As for Lesson 1.	As for Lesson 2.
Lesson 4	Understanding multiplication and division	● Identify near doubles, using doubles already known (eg 80 + 81).	● **Understand division** as grouping (repeated subtraction) or sharing. Read and begin to write the related vocabulary. ● **Recognise that division is the inverse of multiplication**, and that halving is the inverse of doubling.
Lesson 5	As for Lesson 4.	As for Lesson 4.	As for Lesson 4.

Lessons   overview

Preparation
Make an A3 photocopy of 'Hundred square'.

Learning objectives
Starter
● Derive quickly: doubles of multiples of 5 to 100 (eg 75 × 2, 90 × 2).

Main teaching activity
● Extend understanding that more than two numbers can be added; add three or four single-digit numbers mentally, or three or four two-digit numbers with the help of apparatus or pencil and paper.
● Use knowledge that addition can be done in any order to do mental calculations more efficiently. For example: partition into tens and units, then recombine (e.g. 34 + 53 = 30 + 50 + 4 + 3).

Vocabulary
missing number/s, number facts, number pairs, number bonds, start from, talk about, explain how you got your answer, tell me, describe

You will need:

Photocopiable sheets
'Hop it' (page 137) for each child.

CD pages
'Hundred square' for each child (Autumn term); 'Splitting tens and units' core, less able and more able versions (see General resources).

Equipment
Counting stick.

Lesson ①

Starter

Practise counting in fives, starting from zero, using a counting stick. Point to different positions on the stick asking both whole-class and individual questions such as: How many fives in 50? Ask the children to only think of multiples of five when responding to your questions. Then invite them to close their eyes and think of a multiple less than 25, and double it. *What possible answers are there?* List the answers and ask the children to spot which possible answers are missing.

Main teaching activities

Whole class: Explain to the children that in this lesson they will be adding three or four numbers together. Provide each child with a copy of CD page 'Hundred square', which they can use as an aid for addition, and remind them that they can also use an empty number line if they find this helpful. Write the addition 15 + 35 + 45 = on the board. Ask the children to calculate the answer. Ask: *How did you work this out?* Invite different methods, such as beginning with the larger number or adding the tens first. Repeat for another addition such as 31 + 26 + 37.

Now ask the children to find different ways to make a total of 200. Write 130 + □ + △ = 200 on the board and ask for suggestions for solutions. Invite individual children to write their solution on the board, and to explain how they found the answer. For example, some may have worked out that 70 needs to be added to 130 to make a total of 200, then made a partition of 70, such as 40 + 30; 25 + 45… You may want to hint that using numbers that have a 0 or 5 as their unit will make it easier to calculate such a number sentence! Repeat for another example, such as 160 + □ + △ = 300.

Individual work: Ask the children to complete the 'Hop it' activity sheet. They are asked to find six different solutions to the addition sentence 150 + □ + △ = 500.

Differentiation

Less able: Decide whether to work with this group to find different solutions. Use an empty number line to demonstrate each possible solution.

More able: Challenge the children to find more solutions, say ten, in total. They can write their additional solutions on the back of their sheet.

Plenary & assessment

Ask for volunteers to draw one of their solutions for 'Hop it' activity sheet on an empty number line on the board. Move their box and triangle numbers around, asking the class what difference it makes to the total (none). However, they may express a preference to which order they would like to add the numbers. For example, for 150 + 100 + 250 discuss in which order children would prefer to add, and why.

Addition and division
Unit 9

Lesson ②

Starter
Explain that you would like the children to halve some numbers. Ask them to halve 100, 90, 80, 70, 60, 50, 40, 30, 20 and 10. Ask: *Which numbers did you find easier to halve? How did you halve 90?* For example, did they consider $80 \div 2$ and $10 \div 2$ and recombining them?

Main teaching activity

Whole class: Explain that today you would like the children to consider for addition in which order they would add a series of numbers, and to add by partitioning into tens and units. Write on the board: $26 + 43 =$ and ask the class to think about how they would calculate the answer. Now write up $26 + 43 = (20 + 6) + (40 + 3) = (20 + 40) + (6 + 3) = 60 + 9 = 69$.

Then write up $43 + 26 = (40 + 3) + (20 + 6) = (40 + 20) + (3 + 6) = 60 + 9 = 69$ and ask: *Does it make any difference in which order we add? No. Which way round do you think was easier? Why do you think that?* Children may vary in their views, so be accepting of this. Repeat for $17 + 52$, $25 + 61$ and $34 + 25$.

Individual work: Provide copies of CD page 'Splitting tens and units' and ask the children to complete them, working individually.

Differentiation

Less able: There is a differentiated version of the CD page for this group. Decide whether to provide apparatus such as an A3 hundred square or number line as a calculation aid.

More able: There is a more challenging version of the CD page for this group, where children will probably find it useful to think about the order of the two-digit numbers to be added.

Plenary & assessment

Write on the board the numbers 24, 67 and 82. Ask the children to partition each of these. Now ask: *How would you add 24 and 67?* Invite suggestions and ask a child to record the suggestions on the board. Discuss whether it is easier to calculate $24 + 67$ or $67 + 24$ and why they think this. Now challenge the more able. Invite them to calculate $67 + 82$. Discuss the size of the answer before beginning, saying: *Will the answer be more or less than 100? How do you know?* Record a suggestion for calculating on the board, such as:

$67 + 82 = 82 + 67$
$= (80 + 60) + (2 + 7)$
$= 140 + 9 = 149$.

Repeat for adding 24 and 82.

Lesson ③

Repeat the Starter for Lesson 2, increasing the pace for recall of facts and for deriving halves. For the Main teaching activity write on the board $15 + 26 + 37$ and ask the children to suggest how to calculate this. Repeat for another set of three two-digit numbers, such as $32 + 14 + 26$. Now write on the board the numbers 18, 54, 63, 107 and 87, and ask the children to work in pairs. They choose three numbers each time, write an addition sentence and decide how to calculate the answer. Challenge them to write ten different addition sentences. Decide whether to simplify the numbers for the less able by using two-digit numbers between 11 and 30. For the more able include another HTU number and challenge them to write 15 addition sentences. During the Plenary & assessment, invite children from each ability group to write one of their number sentences on the board, and show how they calculated. Discuss with the children different ways of working each one out, which they considered an easier method, and why.

Lessons   overview

Preparation
Make an A3 enlargement of CD page 'Number line 0 to 30'.

Learning objectives

Starter
● Identify near doubles, using doubles already known eg 80 + 81).

Main teaching activity
● **Understand division** as grouping (repeated subtraction) or sharing. Read and begin to write the related vocabulary.
● **Recognise that division is the inverse of multiplication**, and that halving is the inverse of doubling.

Vocabulary
one each, two each, three each…, group in pairs, threes… tens, equal groups of, divided by, divided into, left over, remainder

You will need:

CD pages
'Number lines 0 to 30' for each child (see General resources).

Lesson

Starter
Explain that you are going to ask the children to add two numbers. Ask them to decide if the numbers will make a double or near double. Say, for example, *What is 35 + 35? How did you work that out? So what is 35 + 36? 34? 37? How did you work that out?* Repeat for other near doubles such as 16 + 18 and 50 + 60…

Main teaching activity
Whole class: Explain to the children that for this and the next lesson they will be learning about division. Say: *I have 35 sweets. How many can I give to each of five children? How did you work this out?* Discuss how the sweets could be shared out equally, giving one to each child until all have gone, so that each child receives seven sweets. Also remind the children that if they remember that $7 \times 5 = 35$, then they can work out that $35 \div 5 = 7$. Write the word 'sharing' on the board. Now say: *If I have 27 apples, how many bags can I fill with three apples in each?* Discuss how the children worked out the answer. Say: *We could keep subtracting three; 27, 24, 21… How many times can we do this? Yes, nine.* Illustrate this on the board using an A3 copy of CD page 'Number line 0 to 30'. Mark in the hops back from 0 to 27 and ask the children to count the number of hops. Remind the class that they can also use what they know about the 3 times-table: $9 \times 3 = 27$, so $27 \div 3 = 9$. Write 'grouping' on the board. Repeat for another example, such as: *If I have 30 oranges, how many bags can I fill with five oranges in each?*

Paired work: Provide each pair with copies of CD page 'Number lines 0 to 30'. Ask them to find the solutions to the problems that you write on the board. Write, for example:

● *Find $21 \div 3$ by counting how many hops of 3 are needed to reach 21.*
● *Find $25 \div 5$ by counting hops.*
● *Find $30 \div 10$ by counting hops.*
● *Find $24 \div 2$ by counting hops.*
● *Find $20 \div 5$ by counting hops.*
● *Find $15 \div 3$ by counting hops.*

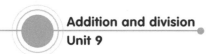
Ask the children to write the division sentence, using ÷, and the corresponding multiplication sentence by each number line.

Differentiation

Less able: Decide whether to simplify the task by providing examples from the 2 times-table.
More able: Challenge the children to use their recall of multiplication facts to derive the answers.

Plenary & assessment

Review the answers to the division questions. Invite children to demonstrate the hops on an A3 number line. Now ask: *What would 3 divided by 1 be?* If the children are unsure, demonstrate by making hops of 1 from 0 to 3 along a number line. Repeat for another example, such as 6 ÷ 1. Now ask: *What is 14 divided by 2?* Invite a child to mark the jumps along a number line. Now ask: *Is this the same as 2 divided by 14? Why not?*

Lesson ⑤

Starter

Repeat the Starter for Lesson 4, choosing different numbers to find doubles and near doubles. Again, invite the children to explain how they calculated.

Main teaching activities

Whole class: Ask the children to double numbers that you say, such as double 15, 18, 7… Write these as multiplication sentences on the board: 15 × 2 =… with their answers. Now ask: *What is half of 30? So 30 divided by 2 is15.* Write alongside the multiplication sentences the relevant division sentences, such as 30 ÷ 2 = 15.

Now write up 5 × 3 and ask the children to work out the answer. Write up 15 ÷ 3 and ask for the answer. Discuss how, if you know a multiplication fact, you can work out a division. Write: 5 × 3 = 15; 3 × 5 = 15; 15 ÷ 3 = 5; 15 ÷ 5 = 3. Repeat this for another fact, such as 7 × 3.
Paired work: Ask the children to work in pairs. They take turns to write a multiplication fact for which they know the answer. They write two multiplication facts and two division facts, such as 8 × 3 = 24; 3 × 8 = 24; 24 ÷ 3 = 8; 24 ÷ 8 = 3. Ask the children to complete ten different sets of facts.

Differentiation

Less able: Decide whether to limit the children to facts from the 2, 5 and 10 times tables.
More able: Challenge the children to use their knowledge of multiples of 2 to derive multiplication and division facts for 4.

Plenary & assessment

Invite children to give examples of their multiplication and division facts. Discuss how each fact can be seen to be part of a family of multiplication and division facts, and how useful this is; children can find division facts from multiplication facts that they know. Ask questions such as: *What is double 30? So what is half of 60? What is 4 multiplied by 5? So what is 40 divided by 10?* Check from their responses that children understand the inverse nature of multiplication and division, and of doubling and halving.

Name	Date

Hop it

Write in the missing numbers.

Find six different solutions.

 +  + =

 +  +  =

 +  +  =

 +  +  =

 +  +

 +

Multiplication and division and solving word problems

Children use doubling and halving, extending this to finding multiples of four and quarters. They begin to learn their 4 times-table. They understand that multiplication is the inverse of division. They solve problems using doubling and halving strategies and check answers using the inverse operation.

LEARNING OBJECTIVES

	Topics	Starter	Main teaching activity
Lesson 1	Mental calculation strategies (× and ÷)	**Count on or back in tens or hundreds starting from any two- or three-digit number.**	● Use doubling or halving, starting from known facts (eg 8 × 4 is double 4 × 4). ● Say or write a division statement corresponding to a given multiplication statement.
Lesson 2	As for Lesson 1.	As for Lesson 1.	As for Lesson 1.
Lesson 3	As for Lesson 1.	As for Lesson 1.	As for Lesson 1.
Lesson 4	Problems involving 'real life', money and measures Checking results of calculations	● Derive quickly: doubles of multiples of 5 to 100 (eg 75 × 2, 90 × 2).	● Solve word problems involving numbers in 'real life', money and measures, using one or more steps, including giving change, and working out which coins to pay. Explain how the problem was solved. ● Check subtraction with addition, halving with doubling and division with multiplication.
Lesson 5	As for Lesson 4.	As for Lesson 4.	As for Lesson 4.

Lessons overview

Preparation
Photocopy activity sheet 'Halving and halving again' to A3.

Learning objectives
Starter
● **Count on or back in tens or hundreds starting from any two- or three-digit number**.
Main teaching activity
● Using doubling or halving, starting from known facts (eg 8 × 4 is double 4 × 4).
● Say or write a division statement corresponding to a given multiplication statement.

Vocabulary
half, halve, multiple of, product, divided by, remainder

You will need:
Photocopiable pages
'Multiplying by 2 and 4' (page 143) and 'Halving and halving again' (page 144) for each child.

CD pages
'Halving and halving again' less able and more able versions (Spring term, Unit 10) (see General resources).

Equipment
NNS interactive programs *Counter* and *Function machine*; drum or tambourine; counting stick.

Lesson ①

Starter

Ask the children to count with you in tens, forwards and back, from a given two-digit number. Say, for example: *Count on in tens from 56. When I say 'back', count back in tens to the start number.* Ask the children to count back when they have counted at least to 156 in tens. Repeat this for other starting numbers, such as 89 and 27. Then repeat, this time starting with a three-digit number, with the children counting back until you say 'forward', with the children stopping at the start number. Use starting numbers such as 147, 152 and 129. To keep a good, even pace to the count, decide whether to use a tambourine or drum so that the children can hear the counting rhythm.

Decide whether to use the *Counter* program to demonstrate counting in tens from the numbers listed above.

Main teaching activities

Whole class: The children should be able to apply doubling and halving strategies to help them calculate quickly by the end of this lesson. Begin by using a counting stick. Label one end of the stick 0 and the other end 20, and ask the children to count along the stick in twos with you. Now point to any position on the stick, such as 8, and ask: *What number goes here? Two multiplied by what makes eight?* Repeat this for other positions on the stick. Now wipe the numbers from the stick and re-label it 0 to 40, so you can count in fours as the children count along with you. Now point to any position on the stick and ask the class to say what number is at that position. Challenge the children to say the 4 times-table fact for, for example, 12 ($3 \times 4 = 12$).

On the board write up the 2 times-table facts. Now write up the beginning of the 4 times-table facts, 0×4 and 1×4, then 2×4, so that the 'doubles' appear next to each other in a list. Ask the children to supply the answers.

Ask the children to explain what they see – that is, that if the 2 times-table facts are doubled, then the result is the 4 times-table facts.

Cover the table facts on the board so that the children can no longer see them, and ask questions such as: *What is double 4? 5? 8? 10? How did you work that out? What is the product of 6 and 4?* Repeat, this time asking for halves, such as: *What is half of 20? 40? 36? How did you work that out?* Write up the halves as a division sentence, such as $20 \div 2 = 10$. Invite the children to give examples of doubling and halving that they have noticed in real life, such as 'buy one get one free', 'two for the price of one', 'half-price sale', '50% off'.

Now ask: *What is double 16?* Write on the board $16 \times 2 = 32$. Ask: *What is half of 32?* and write up $32 \div 2 = 16$. Discuss how multiplication and division facts are linked, and that if you can recall a multiplication fact then you can find the linked division facts. Repeat for other examples, such as 18×2 and $36 \div 2$.

x	2	4	1
1			
2			
4			

Draw this grid on the board.
Point to a square and ask for suggestions as to what should be written in it. Check that the children understand that they multiply the row and column numbers together for the chosen square. For each answer ask: *How did you work that out?* Children may have remembered facts, and used doubles.
Individual work: Provide each child with a copy of activity sheet 'Multiplying by 2 and 4'. Ask them to complete the tables chart, then challenge them to work out the doubles for the numbers entering the function machine.

Differentiation

Less able: Decide whether to provide number lines or hundred squares as an aid for this group to calculate their 4 times-tables facts. You may prefer to work as a group to find the answers for the function machine challenge.

More able: Challenge these children to work quickly to complete the table facts. Decide whether to provide more numbers for doubling, such as 26, 27, 29 and 30.

Plenary & assessment

Ask the children to say together the 4 times-table facts as a chant. To begin with, the children can read the answers from their sheet. Now ask them to cover their sheet and to say these number facts again, this time without a prompt. Remind them that they can use doubling to help them. Ask questions such as: *What is 8 × 4? So what is half of 32? How do you know this?* Repeat for other facts from the 4 times-table.

Lesson ②

Starter

Repeat the Starter from Lesson 1, but this time count forwards and back in hundreds from 456, 527, 999 and 1001. If the children are confident, you can work round a circle with each child having their own turn or each pair having their own turn.

Main teaching activities

Whole class: Explain to the children that today they will be finding new doubles and halves. Write on the board: $1 \times 25 =$ and agree that the answer is 25 and write it on the board. Now write up 2×25 and ask: *What is the answer? How did you work it out?* Some children may 'know' the answer; others may have doubled 20 and added double 5. Repeat for the double 4×25. Again discuss strategies, then work out 8×25, 16×25 and so on. Ask: *What do you notice about the answers for $4 \times 25, 8 \times 25, 16 \times 25$?* (100, 200, 400… are all 'hundreds')

Now write on the board 8×5 and ask the children to supply an answer. Ask: *What other multiplication sentence could we write which uses the same numbers?* Write up $5 \times 8 = 40$. Now ask: *What division sentences could we write which use the same numbers?* Agree that you could write $40 \div 5 = 8$ and $40 \div 8 = 5$. Repeat for another example, such as 6×4.

Paired work: Write ten sets of three numbers which form a multiplication sentence, such as 3, 5 and 15, on the board. Ask the children to work in pairs and to take turns to write two multiplication sentences and two division sentences for each set of three numbers.

Differentiation

Less able: Decide whether to limit the children to specific table facts which you would like to reinforce, such as those for the 2, 5 and 10 times-tables.
More able: Decide whether to provide a challenge by including facts which the children could derive by using doubles, such as 6, 7, 21, 42… 8, 6, 48…

Plenary & assessment

Explain that you will write up another set of three numbers, such as 2, 25 and 50. Ask: *What multiplication sentence could you write? Think of another. Now, can you think of two different division sentences which use all three numbers each time?* Write up the sentences on the board. Repeat for another example, such as 16, 25 and 400. If the more able children completed the challenge that was set, invite them to write up one of their multiplication sentences, and to explain how they worked out the answer by using doubling. Challenge all of the children to give another multiplication and two division sentences which use these numbers.

Lesson ③

Starter

Combine the Starters for Lesson 1 and 2, so that the children count forwards and back in tens and hundreds.

Main teaching activity

Whole class: Explain to the children that they will be learning how to find a quarter by finding a half and halving that. Write up the number 20 on the board and ask: *What is half of 20? Yes, ten. So what is half of ten? Yes, five. So a quarter of 20 is five.* Remind children of the 4 times-tables facts that they have begun to learn, and ask: *What is 5 multiplied by 4? What is 20 divided by 4?* Explain that in finding a quarter of a number, the children will be doing the same as dividing it by 4. Repeat this for another fact, such as finding a quarter of 32 by halving and halving again. Extend this to include finding a quarter of 100, 600 and 800.

Paired work: Provide copies of the activity sheet 'Halving and halving again' and ask the children to complete these in pairs. The sheet has a double function machine, so you may wish to work through the first example together to ensure that the children understand how this works. Encourage them to discuss, quietly, how they will work out each answer.

Differentiation

Less able: There is a version of the activity sheet available which uses 4 times-table facts, and multiples of ten.

More able: There is a more challenging version of the sheet, where children will need to derive halves from what they know.

Plenary & assessment

Review 'Halving and halving again' using the A3 version. Ask individual children to explain how they worked out their answers. Remind the class that finding a half then a half of that is the same as finding a quarter.

Lessons   overview

Learning objectives

Starter
- Derive quickly: doubles of multiples of 5 to 100 (eg 75 × 2, 90 × 2).

Main teaching activity
- Solve word problems involving numbers in 'real life', money and measures, using one or more steps, including giving change, and working out which coins to pay. Explain how the problem was solved.
- Check subtraction with addition, halving with doubling and division with multiplication.

Vocabulary

calculate, calculation, mental calculation, method, jotting, answer, right, correct, wrong, what could we try next? how did you work it out? number sentence, sign, operation, symbol, equation

You will need:

Photocopiable pages
'Easter egg parade' (page 145) for each child.

CD pages
'Easter egg parade' less able and more able versions (Spring term, Unit 10) (see General resources).

Lesson

Starter

Explain that you will say a number and that you want the children to say its double. Choose numbers that are multiples of 5, from 5 to 50, such as 15, 10, 25, 40, 35… Give sufficient thinking time for the majority of the children to derive the answer.

Main teaching activity

Whole class: Explain that this and the next lessons are about solving problems. Tell the class that you will read a story about a disastrous dinner party. Ask the children to jot down their answers, using mental or pencil and paper methods as necessary, each time you pause. Here is the story:

There are six visitors coming to tea. How many pieces of cutlery will you need if they and you each have a knife, spoon and fork? (7 × 3 = 21)

You only have five table settings-worth of cutlery, so you decide to have a Chinese meal instead for which you will need seven pairs of chopsticks. How many chopsticks will be on the table? (14)

Sadly, the dog decides to chew two chopsticks, so how many do you have left? (12)

You think to yourself, 'I wish we'd eaten out!'

You find some plastic picnic spoons. You discover that you have twice as many spoons as there will be people at the party – but don't forget yourself! So how many spoons are there? (14)

Review the children's answers to each part of the story and ask individuals to explain how they worked out the answer.

Individual work: Provide copies of the activity sheet 'Easter egg parade'. Ask the children to work individually to calculate their answers.

Differentiation

Less able: There is a version of the activity sheet available for this group which uses halving and doubling.

More able: There is a version of the sheet available for this group which included finding quarters.

Plenary & assessment

Explain that you are going to tell another story. Ask the children to keep a note of their answers, and make jotting as necessary. Say:

I decided to take my friends on a picnic. There were four of us altogether. Each of us would eat four sandwiches. How many sandwiches would I need to make? (16)

We all like cakes. I made six chocolate cakes and four times that number of strawberry cakes. How many cakes did I make altogether? (6 + (6 × 4) = 30).

Another friend gave me two more cakes. How many cakes are there now? (32)

But only a quarter of the cakes were eaten. How many were eaten? (8)

Review the children's answers, and encourage them to explain how they worked each one out. Ask them to check each answer, for example by doubling or halving, as appropriate.

Lesson

Repeat the Starter from Lesson 4, this time increasing the pace to encourage rapid recall. For the Main teaching activity, ask word problems such as: *I have 60 apples. I put a quarter of the apples into a bowl. How many apples are in the bowl?* Discuss how the children worked out the answer, such as halving and halving again. Discuss also how the answer can be checked by doubling and doubling again. Repeat this for another example, such as: *There are 48 chickens to go to market. Only a quarter of them will fit into each crate. How many chickens is that?* On the board write some number sentences such as 80 ÷ 4, 100 ÷ 4, 25 × 4, 400 × 4… Challenge the children to work in pairs to invent their own word problem for each number sentence, find the answer, then check it by halving for doubling, or doubling for halving. You may wish to offer the less able children simpler number sentences, and add in some more complex ones for the more able, such as 160 ÷ 4… During the Plenary & assessment, invite the children to read out their number sentences, say their answers and explain how they checked. Ask questions such as: *How did you work that out? Did anyone try a different method? Which do you think was the more effective method? Why do you think that?*

Name		Date	

Multiplying by 2 and 4

Write in the missing numbers

Use halving and doubling to help.

	1 times-table	2 times-table	4 times-table
1	1		
2			
3		6	
4			
5			
6			24
7			
8	8	16	
9	9		
10	10	20	40

Challenge

Double these numbers.

19

21

22

23

25

Name	Date

Halving and halving again

Work with a partner.

Find a half of the number and write it into the function machine.

Now find a half of that number. Write that into the next machine.

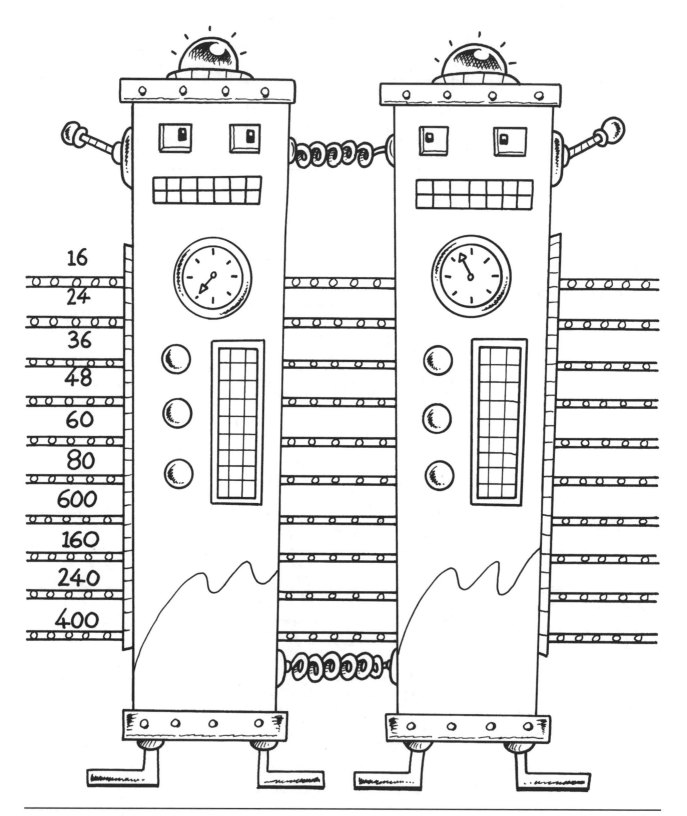

16
24
36
48
60
80
600
160
240
400

Name	Date

Easter egg parade

Read each piece of information carefully.

Write the answers to the questions.

1. There are 3 dozen chocolate eggs in a box. Half of the eggs have stripy wrapping paper. How many eggs is that?

2. If half of the eggs cost £8 how much did the whole box cost?

3. Each egg weighs 30 grams. How many eggs would it take to make a total of 210 grams?

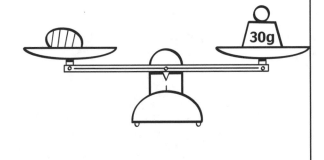

4. It takes 25cm of ribbon to tie a bow around each egg. How much ribbon would you need for 8 eggs?

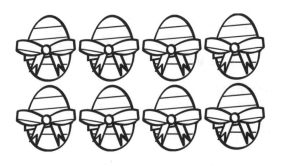

Children learn about simple equivalent fractions. They recognise equivalences through using apparatus to model fractions, and sketch their results. They recognise what must be added to a fraction to make a total of 1.

LEARNING OBJECTIVES

	Topics	Starter	Main teaching activity
Lesson 1	Fractions	● Derive quickly: all pairs of multiples of multiples of 5 with a total of 100 (eg 35 + 65).	● Begin to recognise simple equivalent fractions: for example five tenths and one half, five fifths and one whole.
Lesson 2	Fractions	As for Lesson 1.	As for Lesson 1.
Lesson 3	Fractions	● Begin to know the 3 times-table.	As for Lesson 1.
Lesson 4	Fractions	● **Know by heart: all addition and subtraction facts for each number to 20.**	As for Lesson 1.
Lesson 5	Fractions	● **Know by heart all addition and subtraction facts for each number to 20.** ● Say or write a subtraction statement corresponding to a given addition statement, and vice versa.	As for Lesson 1.

Lessons overview

Preparation
Copy 'Smiley hundred square 1' onto acetate.

Learning objectives
Starter
● Derive quickly: all pairs of multiples of multiples of 5 with a total of 100, eg 35 + 65).
● Begin to know the 3 times-table.
● **Know by heart all addition and subtraction facts for each number to 20.**
● Say or write a subtraction statement corresponding to a given addition statement, and vice versa.
Main teaching activity
● Begin to recognise simple equivalent fractions: for example five tenths and one half, five fifths and one whole.

Vocabulary
part, fraction, one whole, one half, two halves, one quarter, two… three… four quarters, one third, two thirds, one tenth

You will need:
Photocopiable pages
'Equivalent fractions' (page 151) and 'Fractions' (page 152) for each child.

CD pages
'Smiley hundred square' (Autumn term); 'Equivalent fractions' and 'Fractions' less able and more able versions (Spring term, Unit 11) (see General resources).

Equipment
OHP; two A4 sheets of coloured transparency paper; whiteboards and pens; interlocking cubes in various colours; a selection of the following as available, in various colours: Learning links, Compare Bears, beads, Polydron, counters; OHT calculator; squared paper; container.

Lesson ①

Starter

Display the OHT of CD page 'Smiley hundred square 1'. Use the coloured transparency sheets to cover up 65 of the squares, leaving 35 uncovered (leave uncovered three rows/columns of ten squares, and one row/column of five squares). Explain to the children that you want them to calculate in their head how many you cover with the coloured transparency each time – in this case, 65. Repeat by quickly covering different numbers of squares, each time asking the class to write on their whiteboards how many are covered, e.g. 25, 30, 95, 70, 10… Ask: *What do all the numbers have in common?* (They are multiples of 5.)

Repeat, but this time ask the children to notice how many are covered and to write on their whiteboard how many they would need to add to that number to get 100, e.g. if 25 are covered, 75 should be written on the whiteboard. Cover, for example, 30, 50, 85, 35, 15. You are aiming for these to be rapid recall facts so the answers should be given within five seconds.

Main teaching activities

Whole class: Explain that today and for the next four sessions the children will be learning about fractions. Draw a number line on the board, label one end 0 and the other 10 and ask a child to place 5 on the line. Now ask: *Where would 6 go? And where would 5 1/2 fit?* Repeat this, for, for example, 7 1/2, 1 1/2, 6 1/2… Now explain to the class that they will be considering fractions that are worth the same but are written differently (equivalent fractions). On the board, draw a rectangle which is divided into four sections.

Now ask a child to colour in one of the sections, and another to choose another section to colour. Ask: *How many sections are there altogether? How many are coloured? So what fraction is coloured? Yes, two quarters or one half.* Write the fractions 2/4 and 1/2 next to the drawing on the board. Repeat this, colouring in different combinations of two of the four sections of the rectangle so that the children understand that even if this is done in a different way, still 2/4 or 1/2 has been coloured. Ask: *What fraction is not coloured? Say this fraction in two ways.* (1/2 and 2/4).

Now show two interlocking cubes of different colours joined together. Ask: *What fraction is red? Blue?* (1/2) Repeat this for four (1/2, 2/4), then eight (1/2, 4/8), then ten (1/2, 5/10) cubes. Point out that when they have more than two cubes, but still an even number, they have a choice about how they join the two colours together. This results in different patterns but the overall result is the same – one half is red and one half is blue.

Paired work: Explain that you would like the children to work in pairs. Their challenge is to work with one resource to make patterns that show the equivalent fractions for 1/2. Provide each child with a copy of activity sheet 'Equivalent fractions'. Suggest that they compare their work with their partner in order to consider different ways in which they can make the fraction patterns. Provide some equipment in two colours for the children to use to help them to make their patterns.

Differentiation

Less able: There is a version of the activity sheet which uses the equivalents 1/2, 2/4 and 4/8.
More able: There is a version of the sheet which challenges the children to find further equivalent fractions for 1/2 and to find fractions that are not 1/2.

Plenary & assessment

Invite the children to spend a couple of minutes comparing their results with others who completed the same version of the activity sheet. Now write the following sentence starters for the children to complete in pairs.

- *It is true to say that one half…*
- *This fraction* (show one of more able children's work) *cannot be worth the same as one half because…*
- *To work out one half of something…*
- (For the more able) *An equivalent fraction…*

Invite the more able children to explain what is meant by 'equivalent'.

Lesson 2

Starter

Repeat the Starter from Lesson 1, but develop a pattern for the children to fill in the missing numbers using the CD page 'Smiley hundred square 1' to help, as they did yesterday.

$5 + \square = 100, 10 + \square = 100, 15 + \square = 100, 20 + \square = 100, 25 + \square = 100$. Continue until you reach $95 + \square = 100$.

Ask the children about the pattern. How can they quickly work out the pair $25 + 75 = 100$? Remind them that once they know this they also know that $75 + 25 = 100$.

Main teaching activities

Whole class: On the board, draw a rectangle divided into ten equal sections. Ask: *How many tenths can you see? Yes, ten. So how many fifths are there?* Point to two sections at a time and count the fifths. Agree that 5/5 is the same as 10/10, and that both of these are the same as one whole. Now colour in two sections and ask: *What fraction have I coloured? What other fraction could this be?* (1/5 or 2/10) Repeat for colouring in another two sections (2/5 or 4/10), then colour in one more section and ask: *What fraction is coloured?* Agree that this is 5/10 or 1/2, but that it is not a fraction of fifths because each fifth needs to have two sections coloured in.

Group work: Write some fractions related to tenths on the board, such as 4/10, 2/5, 8/10, 1/5… Ask the children to work in pairs to model the fractions using the apparatus from Lesson 1's paired work. Ask them to sketch their fractions onto squared paper, to decide which fractions have equivalents and to write these in both forms.

Differentiation

Less able: Decide whether to work as a group to carry out this task. Encourage the children to use the vocabulary of fractions as they explain what they have made with the apparatus.

More able: Challenge the children by asking them to find an equivalent fraction for each one that you write on the board. Remind them, if necessary, that, for example, 6/20 is equivalent to 3/10.

Plenary & assessment

Invite children to show their sketches for 4/10. Discuss how the sketches all show the same number of sections coloured in but that the patterns are not the same. Say: *Tell me another fraction that is worth the same.* (2/5) Encourage the more able children to suggest other equivalent fractions, such as 8/20. Repeat for the other fractions.

Lesson 3

Starter

Use an OHT calculator to repeatedly add in threes (3++=) up to 30. Ask the children if they can spot any patterns, such as alternate odd/even in the units. Continue adding in threes up to 90, each time writing the result on the board so the children can begin to see the 3, 6, 9, 2, 5, 8, 1, 4, 7 and 0 repeating in the units. Encourage the class to predict each time what will come next, using the pattern that they have already spotted.

Main teaching activities

Whole class: Invite a child to count out 12 interlocking cubes and agree that 12 cubes make a whole stick of cubes. Ask: *How many would half of these be?* Write on the board 1/2 + 1/2 = 1. Demonstrate this by breaking the stick into two halves, then combining to make a whole again. Repeat for 1/4, asking the children to say how many that would be. Now ask: *So how many is 1/4?* Agree that 3 + 9 = 12 (number of cubes) so that 1/4 + 3/4 = 1. Repeat this for ten cubes, using tenths, such as 5/10 + 5/10 = 1; 6/10 + 4/10 = 1, and so on.

Individual work: Ask the children to use one of the resources from Lesson 1, and some squared paper. Suggest they use their resource to show 10/10 and to sketch this. Then ask them to make and sketch each combination of tenths to make a whole and to order these: 1/10 + 9/10; 2/10 + 8/10, and so on.

Differentiation

Less able: Decide whether to carry out the task as a group. Help the children to use the vocabulary of fractions appropriately.

More able: When they have completed the task, ask the children to look at each fraction sentence they have written and to decide which ones could be written using fifths or halves, and to include these too.

Plenary & assessment

Ask the children to take turns to show one of their sketches. If the less able need further help, model each one using two colours of interlocking cubes. Write the fraction sentences on the board, then challenge the more able to identify which ones could be written in simpler form using halves or fifths. Ask questions such as: *How many tenths would I need to add to three tenths to make a whole? How many tenths/fifths/halves/quarters make one whole?*

Lesson 4

Starter

Explain that you will say a number between 0 and 20, and that you would like the children to put up their hands to say an addition fact with that number as the answer. For example, say 17 and the class might suggest 8 + 9 or 10 + 7. Repeat, choosing a different number. Now explain that you would like the class to think of a subtraction sentence that has the number that you say as the answer, such as for 9 they might say 20 – 11 or 17 – 8.

Main teaching activities

Whole class: Count out ten randomly coloured cubes from the container. Agree that each cube is worth one tenth of the whole group. Ask the children what fraction is red/green/yellow. Repeat for another set of ten randomly drawn cubes. Write the fractions for the colours on the board, and total them to show 1, such as 3/10 + 2/10 + 5/10 = 1. Ask the children to describe the order of fractions of each colour from smallest to largest. These can be mapped onto a number line, marked from 0 to 1, in tenths, on the board.

Group work: Ask the children to work in pairs, again using the resources from Lesson 1 but this time in three colours and using squared paper. They take, randomly, eight items and make a pattern. They draw this, then write the fractions for the colours as a fraction sentence, such as 3/8 + 4/8 + 1/8 = 1. Challenge the children to spot any equivalent fractions and to write these, too.

Differentiation

Less able: The activity can be simplified by providing just two colours of resource.
More able: When the children have completed sufficient patterns for eight items, suggest that they try it with 12 items.

Plenary & assessment

Ask the children to show some of their fraction sketches and to write up their fraction sentences. Ask: *How many eighths make a whole? What other fraction is the same as 2/8?* (1/4) *4/8?* (1/2) *6/8?* (3/4) *What is 2/8 add 6/8?* Write this as a fraction sentence on the board: 2/8 + 6/8 =. Now ask: *What other fractions are worth the same as 2/8 and 6/8? So 1/4 + 3/4 is worth the same as 2/8 + 6/8.* Using the challenge set to the more able children, review with them the fractions that they found and write these on the board with their equivalents, such as 6/12, 1/2, 3/6, and so on.

Lesson ⑤

Starter

Explain that you will write an addition statement on the board, which uses numbers from 0 to 20. Ask the children to work in pairs to write three more statements (one addition, and two subtraction) which belong to this family, such as 14 + 3 = 17, 3 + 14 = 17, 17 − 3 = 14 and 17 − 14 = 3. The children can write these on their whiteboards, one between two, and hold these up when you say Show me. Do not write the whole addition statement, just, for example, 14 + 3, so that they must total before finding the remaining statements. Repeat, this time for a subtraction statement, such as 18 − 11. Repeat, keeping a good pace to encourage rapid recall.

Main teaching activities

Whole class: Write 1 on the board and ask the children to suggest as many equivalent fractions as they can think of. Write these on the board, such as 2/2, 3/3, 4/4… Now say: *Tell me two fractions that will total 1.* Write the suggestions on the board, such as 1/4 + 3/4. Challenge the more able children to give more examples, such as 15/20 + 5/20.

Now explain that you are going to ask some word problems about fractions. Say, for example: *There are ten apples in the box. If 3/10 are sold, how many apples are left?* Ask the children to explain how they worked out the answer. Repeat for another word problem, such as: *4/5 of the pattern is red and the rest is white. What fraction is white?* (1/5) *If the pattern has ten sections altogether, how many sections are white?* (2)

Individual work: Provide the children with copies of activity sheet 'Fractions'. Ask them to complete the sheet, which covers equivalent fractions, and fractions totalling 1.

Differentiation

Less able: There is a version available which covers just halves, quarters and eighths.
More able: There is a version of the sheet available which includes twelfths and twentieths.

Plenary & assessment

Explain that you will write a fraction on the board and that you want the children to say an equivalent fraction. Write, for example, 1/4, 2/8, 4/10 and 6/8. Now ask the children to suggest what they can add to each of these fractions to make a total of 1. Some of the more able children may suggest using an equivalent fraction, such as 5/10 + 1/2. Praise them if they suggest this. Finish by asking the children to say what they have learned about fractions during these five sessions. Ask them to discuss with a partner where they feel confident with fractions and where they need further help. Take feedback about their levels of confidence by asking partners to describe how the other child is feeling.

Name	Date

Equivalent fractions

Ask your teacher for some equipment in two different colours.

Use your equipment to show the following fractions.

$$\frac{1}{2} \qquad \frac{2}{4} \qquad \frac{4}{8} \qquad \frac{5}{10}$$

Now sketch your results in the correct box.

$\frac{1}{2}$	$\frac{2}{4}$
$\frac{4}{8}$	$\frac{5}{10}$

Write a sentence about your drawings using 'the same as'.

_____

_____

_____

Name	Date

Fractions

Write the fraction for the shaded part.

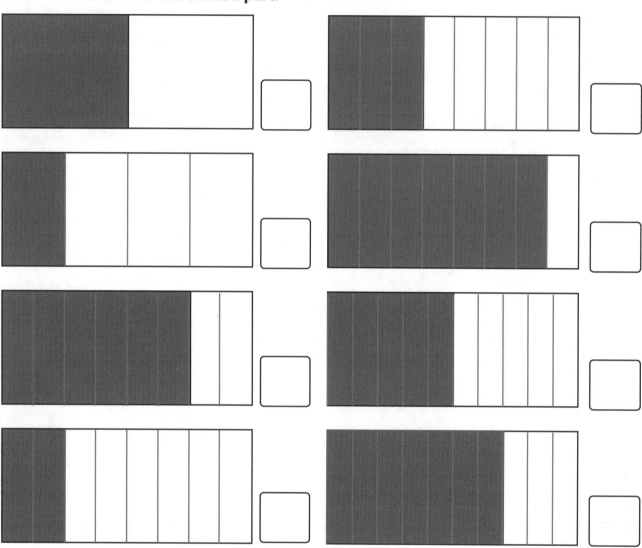

Write in the fraction to make 1 whole.

$\frac{1}{2}$ + ☐ = 1

$\frac{3}{4}$ + ☐ = 1

$\frac{3}{8}$ + ☐ = 1

$\frac{7}{10}$ + ☐ = 1

Spring term
Unit 12
Handling data

Children use simple frequency tables and one-criterion Venn diagrams to solve problems.

LEARNING OBJECTIVES

	Topics	Starter	Main teaching activity
Lesson 1	Handling data Fractions	● **Read and write whole numbers to at least 1000** in figures and in words.	● **Solve a given problem by organising and interpreting numerical data in simple lists, tables and graphs,** for example: Venn diagrams (one criterion).
Lesson 2	Handling data	As for Lesson 1.	● **Solve a given problem by organising and interpreting numerical data in simple lists, tables and graphs,** for example: simple frequency tables.
Lesson 3	Handling data	● **Order whole numbers to at least 1000** and position them on a number line.	● **Solve a given problem by organising and interpreting numerical data in simple lists, tables and graphs,** for example: simple frequency tables; bar charts – intervals labelled in ones then twos; Venn diagrams (one criterion).
Lesson 4	Handling data	As for Lesson 3.	As for Lesson 3.
Lesson 5	Handling data	● **Know by heart:** all pairs of multiples of 100 with a total of 1000 (e.g. 300 + 700).	As for Lesson 3.

Lessons overview

Preparation
Make A3 photocopies of CD pages 'Data handling vocabulary', 'Pencils' and 'Favourite fruit'.

Learning objectives
Starter
● **Read and write whole numbers to at least 1000** in figures and in words.
● **Order whole numbers to at least 1000** and position them on a number line.
● **Know by heart**: all pairs of multiples of 100 with a total of 1000 (eg 300 + 700).
Main teaching activity
● **Solve a given problem by organising and interpreting numerical data in simple lists, tables and graphs,** for example: simple frequency tables; bar charts – intervals labelled in ones then twos; Venn diagrams (one criterion).

Vocabulary
table, chart, Venn diagram, axis, diagram, least popular, group, set, interpret, count, tally

You will need:
Photocopiable pages
'Footwear fun' (page 158) and 'Sports activities' (page 159) for each child.

CD pages
'Venn diagrams', 'Data handling vocabulary', 'Three-digit numbers' (Autumn term), 'Bar chart', 'Pencils', 'Favourite fruit' for each child (see General resources); 'Footwear fun' less able and more able versions (Spring term, Unit 12) (see General resources).

Equipment
Post-It Notes; tambourine.

Lesson ①

Starter

Explain that you will write a number on the board using figures. Ask the children to read the number aloud when you hold up your hand. The children will read the number as you write, so hold up your hand as soon as you have finished writing in order to check that they read quickly and accurately. Write numbers such as 123, 560, 807, 900, 999, 11147 and 10001. Repeat, this time writing similar, but different, numbers as words.

Main teaching activities

Whole class: Ask the children what they can remember about handling data and write specific data handling vocabulary that the children use on the board. There is a lot of new vocabulary this week, so display the A3 enlargement of CD page 'Data handling vocabulary' for the children to refer to during the week. Make a point of sharing the vocabulary and highlighting words as you use them.

Introduce the idea of Venn diagrams by sketching the following diagram.

Ask the boys quickly to sort the girls into the two groups of 'Have ponytails' and 'Do not have

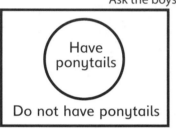

ponytails', and write this information in the diagram. Discuss which piece of sorted information goes where, and how this can be recorded by, for example, drawing a stick picture for each girl, or by putting their initials into the appropriate place on the diagram.

Collect data from the class for the following and make a Venn diagram for each result. Note: It is quicker to give each child a Post-It Note upon which they write their initials. Then, when a question is asked, they place their Post-It Note in the correct place on the diagram.

- *Who has/does not have any red on their clothes?*
- *Who ate/did not eat toast this morning?*
- *Who walked/did not walk to school today?*
- *Who likes/dislikes swimming?*

Now choose one of the Venn diagrams and ask: *How many children like/dislike swimming? How can you tell? How many girls like swimming? Is that easy to find out? Why/Why not?*

Ask the children to sit in a circle and remove one shoe. The children place their shoe in front of them so everyone can see it. Invite the class to guess your criterion/rule for choosing your group of shoes. As you select shoes place them in the centre of the circle, encouraging the children to look closely at them but also to look at the ones you don't pick. Here are some suggestions for criteria.

- *The shoes all have laces/buckles/Velcro.*
- *The shoes all have a bit of red/blue/white.*
- *The shoes all belong to girls/boys.*
- *The group are all types of trainers.*
- *The shoes are made from patent/suede/other.*
- *The shoes are all turned on their side/upside down.*

Once you have given the children plenty of ideas for sorting the shoes, ask for a volunteer to make a group with their own sorting criteria. (Individuals may need some whispered encouragement for the first few tries!)

Group work: Ask the children to work in groups of about four. Give each child a copy of CD page 'Venn diagrams'. Encourage them to fill the labels in according to their own sort criteria and to write the initials of the children to whom the shoe belongs. Ask them to discuss how they could sort their shoes into the two sets of 'Have…' and 'Do not have…' Challenge the children to find four different ways of sorting their shoes.

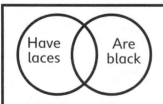

Differentiation

Less able: Give the children a starting criterion such as 'Have laces' and 'Do not have laces'. Now challenge the children to think of three more ways of sorting their shoes.

More able: When the children have finished the task of sorting by one criterion, challenge them to sort by two, such as 'Have laces' and 'Are black'. Show them how to make a two-region Venn diagram. Discuss what goes into the intersection of the Venn diagram, and what will go outside the two circles.

Plenary & assessment
Discuss the interesting ideas for criterion that children have come up with. Invite each group to show, by copying their Venn diagram on the board, one of their ways of sorting. Invite the rest of the class to ask questions about the sorting, such as: *How many had…? Was this everyone in your group? Can you tell whether the person was male or female? How? Why not?*

If the more able children have undertaken the two–region challenge, decide whether to discuss their work now during the Plenary, or whether to find another time just for this group. This decision will depend upon the confidence of the other children in the class with making and using Venn diagrams.

Lesson ②

Starter
Repeat the Starter for Lesson 1, but this time ask the children to write down the numbers that you say, firstly as figures, then as words. Include numbers such as 608, 990, 1051 and 1003 so that the children think about the position of the zero digit and its place value.

Main teaching activity
Whole class: Ask the children how many different types of footwear they can think of and make a list, such as: Wellingtons, slippers, tap dancing shoes, riding boots, ballroom dancing shoes, ice skates, walking boots, 'best shoes', trainers, flip flops, sandals. Ask questions such as:

- *Which footwear is easy to walk in?*
- *Which footwear is most suitable for wearing in the rain?*
- *Which footwear do you prefer?*

Make a table of their votes surrounding each question (25 children thought walking boots were easiest to walk in; 30 children thought trainers; 3 children thought riding boots; 2 children disagreed that riding boots were comfortable to walk in).

Referring to the answers, show the class how to represent their information in a sentence like this: 'Most of the class think that walking boots and trainers are the easiest footwear to walk in. Three people thought that riding boots were also comfortable to walk in. Two people disagreed and thought that riding shoes were not very comfortable for walking in.'

Ask the class if they can work out how many children are in the class simply by reading the information (they can't!). Whilst no precise answer can be given, they can deduce that it is around 30 as we have written 'most' of the children in our sentences. Encourage the children to think about what the information DOES NOT tell them as well as what it does tell them.

Individual work: Provide copies of activity sheet 'Footwear fun'. Ask the children to read the information in the table carefully, and then to complete the sentences about the families.

Differentiation
Less able: There is a version of the activity sheet which contains information and sentences to be completed about just one family.
More able: The version of the sheet for these children contains data in tables, then space for the children to write their own sentences about the families and their footwear.

Plenary & assessment
Ask the children to explain their deductions from the activity sheet 'Footwear fun'. Of course, there is no conclusive proof for their interpretations, just likelihoods. Ask questions such as: *How did you*

decide that? Who thinks something different? Why do you think that? You may like, at the end of the lesson, to give the children the following information about the families, then ask: *What information could we not tell from the table?*

For information
The Davies family: 2 adults, 3 children aged 14, 19 and 21. The family like walking. They live on a farm in a wet part of the country, so need Wellingtons. They like to go hill walking. One person is a keen cyclist; this happens to be the father who has size 11 feet. The extra pair of Wellingtons are size 4. These are kept for a cousin who visits often. The children aren't allowed to wear trainers to school.

The Williams family: 2 adults, 3 children aged 6, 6 and 14. The family like to wear slippers on their new carpet. The twins have just starter to roller skate. The adults and teenager sometimes go walking. They are digging up their garden so they all have to wear Wellingtons often. However, Dad has a hole in his and has thrown them away.

Ask the more able children to share what they had decided they couldn't definitely tell from the chart, e.g. exactly how many people lived in the house; what style of trainer/shoe they would have; whether they preferred lace ups.

Lesson ③

Starter
Explain that you will give a three-digit number card (from CD page 'Three-digit numbers') to each of three children. Ask them to stand at the front of the class, out of number order. Invite another child to reorder the group holding the cards so that the numbers are in order, starting with the smallest number. Repeat this for other sets of three cards and different children.

Main teaching activities

Colour	Votes
Black	12
Brown	10
Blue	4
Green	1
Red	2

Favourite shoes

Whole class: Explain that today the children will be collecting data, putting it into a frequency table, then making a bar chart from the data in their table. Ask them to collect data for their group about their favourite pair of shoes at home. Say: *Find out the colour of these shoes.* Ask the children to collect this data, then explain that the data will be combined in order to make a frequency table for the whole class. On the board make a frequency table.

When the table is completed, ask questions about the data, such as: *How many children have blue shoes as their favourite? Which is more popular: green or blue? Which colour had fewer/more than six votes?*

Explain that this data can be put into a bar graph. Either using a computer graphing program, or drawing the graph onto the board, show the children how to compile a simple bar graph, where the vertical axis is labelled in ones.

Ask the children to compare the two ways of displaying the information. Ask the same questions as of the frequency table data, but ask the children to use the bar chart to answer.

Group work: Ask the children to work in mixed-ability groups of about four. Explain that you would like them to collect data about the types of shoes that

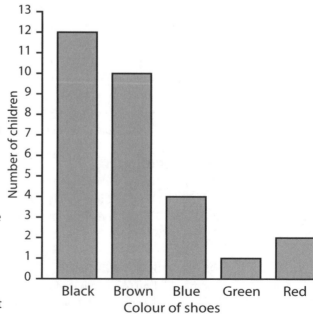

they have; both what they are wearing today and what they have at home. Suggest that each child can list up to five pairs of footwear. Explain that you would like them to construct a frequency table and a bar chart for the information that they collect. Provide CD page 'Bar chart' for the children to use to record their bar chart. Remind them to label the chart and its axes. Ask them to make their own frequency chart.

Differentiation
Less able: Check that the children are contributing to the work. Encourage them to use the vocabulary of handling data as they discuss what they are doing in their group.
More able: Encourage the children to ask questions of the other children in their group about the data that they collect.

Plenary & assessment
Choose one of the groups' frequency tables and bar charts and show it to the class. Ask questions about the data, for example: *How many more/fewer than… are there? How many shoes are there altogether? How did you work that out? So how many shoes in total do you think… has? Can you tell that from this data?* Repeat for other groups.

Lesson

Repeat the Starter from Lesson 3, this time asking for the three numbers in both ascending, then descending order. Display the data for CD page 'Pencils' and ask questions such as: *In which years were most/least pencils bought? Why do you think there were so few bought in 2002?* (This may have been an accumulation of spares.) *Do you think this is a lot of pencils for a school with 210 pupils? Why do you think that?* Now ask the children to work in mixed-ability pairs to create a bar chart to show how many pencils were bought each year. Then ask them to write some questions that they could ask the rest of the class from the data in their bar chart. You may wish some children to use computer software to design and complete their bar chart. During the Plenary & assessment, invite pairs of children to ask their questions of the others. Ask: *Is it possible to answer this? What else could we ask? What information does the bar chart not provide?*

Lesson

Say a number which is a multiple of 100 and invite the children to say the number that adds to this to make 1000. Give just a few seconds for thinking time, as the children should be able to work out the answers quickly based on number bonds for 10. Then ask the children to sort the numbers from 0 to 50 onto a one criterion Venn diagram labelled 'Multiples of 5'. *Where does the number 15 fit? Why? Where does 26 fit? Why?* Now ask the children questions about the bar chart on CD page 'Favourite fruit' such as: *How many fewer/more children like … than …? Which is the most/least popular fruit?* Now ask the class to sort onto a Venn diagram all the numbers between 1 and 50 and to label the Venn diagram circle 'Multiple of 3'. *What should the label be for the region outside the circle?* (Less able children can work with the number range to 1 to 20; more able children could make a Venn diagram for multiples of 6, from 1 to 100.) The second task is to make a bar chart for the information on activity sheet 'Sports activities'. For Plenary & assessment, ask questions about the completed Venn diagrams such as: *What numbers are inside the circle? What do we know about these numbers? What do we know about the numbers outside the circle?* Now ask the children to look at their completed bar charts and ask questions such as: *Which was the most/least popular sport? How many more liked swimming than gymnastics?* Now ask: *What information can you not tell from this bar chart?* Challenge the children to think of several things.

Name	Date

Footwear fun

Here is some information about two families and some of their footwear.
Complete the sentences after you have looked carefully at each table.

The Davies family

Type of footwear	How many pairs	Sizes of the pairs
Wellingtons	6	4, 5, 8, 9, 11, 11
Trainers	2	5, 8
Slippers	1	5
Walking boots	4	5, 8, 9, 11
Cycling shoes	1	11

The Williams family

Type of footwear	How many pairs	Sizes of the pairs
Wellingtons	4	11, 11, 6, 9
Trainers	5	11, 11, 6, 9, 10
Slippers	5	11, 11, 6, 9, 10
Walking boots	3	6, 9, 10
Roller skates	2	11, 11

1. I think there are [ ]

people in this family because

_____

2. I think this family like to

_____ because _____

_____

_____

3. In the family, there are

more _____ than _____

4. The least common shoes are

_____

5. The most popular footwear is

_____

6. I think there are [ ]

people in this family because

_____

7. I think this family like to _____

_____

because _____

_____

8. In the family, there are more

_____ than _____

9. The least common shoe is

_____

10. The most popular footwear is

_____

Name   Date

Sports activities

The children in Class 3 at Green Lane School were asked about their sports activities.

They made a frequency chart from the data that they collected.

Sport	Number of children who play
Football	12
Netball	10
Swimming	13
Tennis	8
Gymnastics	9

Fill in the bar chart.

Use the information in the frequency chart to help you.

Label the chart.

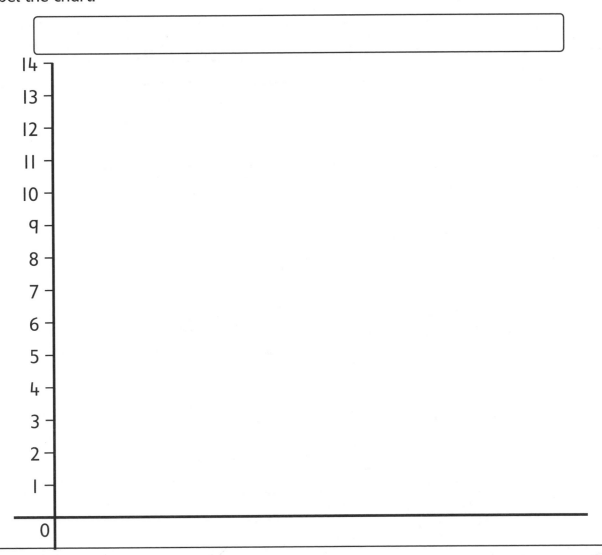

EVERY DAY: Practise and develop oral and mental skills (eg counting, mental strategies, rapid recall of +, −, × and ÷ facts)

- **Count on/back in tens or hundreds starting from any two and three digit number.**
- **Know by heart all addition and subtraction facts for each number up to at least 20.**
- Say the number that is 1, 10 or 100 more or less than any two- or three-digit number.
- Say or write a subtraction statement corresponding to a given addition statement, and vice versa.
- **Derive quickly doubles of multiples of 5 to 100** and all the corresponding halves (eg 36 ÷ 2, half of 130 .
- **Add and subtract mentally a 'near multiple of 10' to or from a two-digit number** by adding or subtracting 10, 20, 30… and adjusting.
- Derive quickly doubles of multiples of 50 to 500.
- **Know by heart multiplication facts for 2, 5 and 10 times tables, and derive quickly division facts corresponding to the 2, 5 and 10 times tables.**
- Order a set of three digit numbers.
- Derive quickly all pairs of multiples of 5 with a total of 100 (eg 35 + 65).
- **Know by heart** all pairs of multiples of 100 with a total of 1000 (eg 300 + 700).
- Count on in steps of 3 from any small number to at least 50, and back again.
- Begin to know the 3 times table.

Units	Days	Topics	Objectives
1	3	Counting, properties of numbers and number sequences	• Compare two given three-digit numbers, say which is more or less and give a number that lies between them. • **Order whole numbers to at least 1000**; and position them on a number line.
		Estimating and rounding	• Round any two-digit number to the nearest 10 and any three-digit number to the nearest 100.
		Measures	• Read scales to the nearest division (labelled or unlabelled).
2–3	10	Understanding + and –	• Extend understanding of the operations of addition and subtraction. Read and begin to write related vocabulary and continue to recognise that addition can be done in any order. • Use +,- and = signs.
		Mental calculation strategies (+ and -)	• Use knowledge that addition can be done in any order to do mental calculations more efficiently. • Add three or four small numbers by putting the largest number first and/or by finding pairs totalling 9, 10 or 11. • **Add and subtract mentally a 'near multiple of 10' to or from a two-digit number** by adding or subtracting 10, 20, 30…and adjusting. • Add three or four small numbers by putting the largest number first and/or by finding pairs totalling 9, 10 or 11. • Use patterns of similar calculations.
		Pencil and paper procedures (+ and –)	• Use informal pencil and paper methods to support, record or explain TU±TU, HTU±TU and HTU±HTU.
		Problems involving 'real life', money and measures	• Solve word problems involving numbers in 'real life', money and measures, using one or more steps, including finding totals and giving change, and working out which coins to pay.
		Making decisions	• **Explain methods and reasoning** orally and, where appropriate, in writing.
		Checking results of calculations	• Check with an equivalent calculation.
4–6	13	Measures	• Read and begin to write the vocabulary related to capacity. • Measure and compare using standard units (l, ml). • Suggest suitable units and measuring equipment to estimate or measure capacity. • Record estimates and measurements to the nearest whole or half unit or in mixed units. • Know the relationship between litres and millilitres. • Read scales to nearest division (labelled or unlabelled).
		Making decisions	• **Choose and use appropriate operations (including multiplication and division) to solve word problems,** and appropriate ways of calculating: mental, mental with jottings, pencil and paper.
		Shape and space	• **Identify and sketch lines of symmetry in simple shapes, and recognise shapes with no lines of symmetry.** • Sketch the reflection of a simple shape in a mirror line along one edge. • Read and begin to write the vocabulary related to position, direction and movement: for example, describe and find the position of a square on a grid of squares with the rows and columns labelled. • Recognise that a straight line is equivalent to two right angles. • Compare angles with a right angle.
		Reasoning about numbers or shapes	• Investigate general statements about shapes by finding examples that satisfy it. • **Explain methods and reasoning** orally and, where appropriate, in writing.
7		Assess and review	

EVERY DAY: Practise and develop oral and mental skills (eg counting, mental strategies, rapid recall of + and – facts)

- **Know by heart multiplication facts for the 2, 5 and 10 times-tables**, and derive quickly division facts corresponding to tge 2, 5 and 10 times-tables.
- Begin to know the 3 and 4 times-tables.
- Derive quickly doubles of multiples of 5 to 100 (eg 75 × 2, 90 x2) and all the corresponding halves (eg half of 130).
- Derive quickly doubles of multiples of 50 to 500 (eg 450 × 2) and all the corresponding halves (eg 900 ÷ 2).
- Begin to know the ×3 and ×4 tables.
- Say or write a division statement corresponding to a given multiplication statement.
- Know by heart pairs of multiples of 100 with a total of 1000 (eg 300 + 700).
- **Read and write whole numbers to at least 1000** in figures and words.
- Count on or back in tens or hundreds, starting from any two- or three-digit number.
- Round any two-digit number to the nearest 10 and any three-digit number to the nearest 100.
- **Add and subtract mentally a 'near multiple of 10' to or from a two-digit number** by adding or subtracting 10, 20, 30…and adjusting.
- **Order whole numbers to at least 1000**, and position them on a number line.
- **Know by heart all addition and subtraction facts for each number to 20.**
- Derive quickly all pairs of multiples of 5 with a total of 100 (eg 35 + 65).

Units	Days	Topics	Objectives
8	5	Counting, properties of numbers and number sequences	• Recognise two-digit and three-digit multiples of 2,5 and 10 and three-digit multiples of 50 and 100.
		Reasoning about numbers or shapes	• Solve mathematical problems or puzzles, recognise simple patterns and relationships, generalise and predict. Suggest extensions by asking 'What if..?' • **Explain methods and reasoning** orally and, where appropriate, in writing.
9–10	10	Understanding multiplication and division	• Begin to find remainders after simple division. • Round up or down after division, depending on the context.
		Problems involving 'real life, money and measures	• Solve word problems involving numbers in 'real life', money and measures, using one or more steps, including finding totals and giving change, and working out which coins to pay. • Explain how the problem was solved.
		Reasoning about numbers or shapes	• **Explain methods and reasoning** orally, and where appropriate, in writing.
		Mental calculation strategies × and ÷	• Use known number facts and place value to carry out mentally simple multiplications and divisions.
11	5	Fractions	• Compare familiar fractions: for example, know that on the number line one half lies between one quarter and three quarters. • Estimate a simple fraction.
12	5	Understanding addition and subtraction	• Extend understanding that more than two numbers can be added: add three or four two-digit numbers with the help of apparatus or pencil and paper.
		Pencil and paper procedures (+ and –)	• Use informal pencil and paper methods to support, record or explain HTU ± TU and HTU ± HTU. • Begin to use column addition and subtraction for HTU ± TU, HTU ± HTU.
		Problems involving measures	• Solve word problems involving numbers in 'real life', and measures.
		Pencil and paper procedures (+ and –)	• Begin to use column addition and subtraction for HTU ± TU, HTU ± HTU where one calculation cannot be done easily mentally.
		Reasoning about numbers and shapes	• Explain methods and reasoning orally, and where appropriate, in writing.
		Measures	• Use a calendar.
13	5	Organising and using data	• **Solve a given problem by organising and interpreting numerical data in simple lists, tables, and graphs**, for example: simple frequency tables; pictograms – symbol representing two units; bar charts – intervals labelled in ones then twos; Venn and Carroll diagrams (one criterion).
14		Assess and review	

Comparing, ordering and rounding numbers, and reading scales

Children compare pairs of three-digit numbers, note the values of their digits and find numbers that will fit between them. They order these numbers onto a number line. They revise rounding two-digit numbers to the nearest 10, and learn the convention for rounding three-digit numbers to the nearest 100. They read scales and, where appropriate, round these measurements to the nearest 10.

LEARNING OBJECTIVES

	Topics	Starter	Main teaching activity
Lesson 1	Place value and ordering	● **Count on/back in tens or hundreds starting from any two- or three-digit number.**	● Compare two given three-digit numbers, say which is more or less, and give a number that lies between them. ● **Order whole numbers to at least 1000**, and position them on a number line.
Lesson 2	Estimating and rounding	As for Lesson 1.	● Round any two-digit number to the nearest 10 and any three-digit number to the nearest 100.
Lesson 3	Place value and ordering Measures Estimating and rounding	● **Read and write whole numbers to at least 1000** in figures and words.	● Read scales to the nearest division (labelled or unlabelled). ● Round any two-digit number to the nearest 10.

Lessons   overview

Preparation
Sort out the 0 to 9 cards from CD page 'Numeral cards for 0 to 20'. Make three additional sets of enlarged 0 to 9 cards. Make an OHT of CD page 'Reading scales'.

Learning objectives
Starter
● **Count on/back in tens or hundreds starting from any two- or three-digit number.**
● **Read and write whole numbers to at least 1000** in figures and words.
Main teaching activity
● Compare two given three-digit numbers, say which is more or less, and give a number that lies between them.
● **Order whole numbers to at least 1000**, and position them on a number line.
● Round any two-digit number to the nearest 10 and any three-digit number to the nearest 100.
● Read scales to the nearest division (labelled or unlabelled).

Vocabulary
every other, round (up, down), nearest (round to the nearest ten)

You will need:
Photocopiable pages
'Ordering numbers' (page 166) and 'Detective Milly Litre' (page 167) for each child.

CD pages
'Numeral cards for 0 to 20' for the teacher's/LSA's and children's reference and 'Reading scales' (Autumn term) for each child; 'Ordering numbers' and 'Detective Milly Litre' less able and more able versions (Summer term, Unit 1) (see General resources).

Equipment
Beanbag; individual whiteboards and pens; Blu-Tack; OHT; metre stick marked in ten-centimetre increments.

Lesson

Starter

Ask the class stand in a circle to play a game, as follows. Give the beanbag to a child to hold and ask them to say a two-digit number. He or she then passes the beanbag to their left. The next person has to add 10 to the number, pass on the beanbag, and so on, until someone says *Inverse reverse*. This means the rule changes to subtract 10 and the direction of the beanbag also changes. Tell the children that they may each say 'Inverse reverse' only once during the game.

It may take a few tries before the children can pick up the speed! You may like to double up children if you have a large class by asking one child to stand behind a partner and to whisper the answer for the person in front to call out.

Main teaching activities

Whole class: Explain to the children that by the end of the lesson they should feel more confident in placing three-digit numbers in order quickly. Draw this simple grid on the board and ask the children to quickly draw it onto their whiteboards.

Hundreds	Tens	Units

Explain that you will show the children a number card with a single digit on it and they must decide where to write that number – that is, as a hundreds, tens or units digit. The aim of the game is to make the largest number they can, but once they have written the digit into a place it cannot be altered. Play the game two or three times, then ask questions such as: *Did you always make the largest number possible? What is the largest number we could make with these three digits? What is the smallest number that we could make?*

Now write two numbers on the board with a space between them, such as: 245 ☐ 368. Ask the children to give you as many facts as they can about the two numbers, such as: *Which is the larger number? Which is the smaller number? Think of some numbers that are larger than the smaller number.* Write the responses on the board, then repeat this for three-digit numbers that are smaller than the larger number. Again, write the children's responses on the board. Compare their answers, asking: *What is the hundreds digit? Is it a two or a three? Why is that important? What about the tens digit? Can that be any number? Why do you think that? What about the units digit – can that be any number in this example?* Discuss how the hundreds digit must be a 2 or a 3; and that the tens digit can be any number between 4 and 9 if the hundreds digit is a 2, or between 0 and 6 if the hundreds digit is a 3. Ask the children to explain what the units digit can or cannot be.

Now draw an empty number line and place the three digits on it: 245 ☐ 368. Repeat this for another example, such as 678 ☐ 804.

Paired work: Ask the children to complete activity sheet 'Ordering numbers'. This gives the children two numbers, and they must find a third, from a list given, which will fit between these two numbers. Point out that some answers will fit more than one question.

Differentiation

Less able: There is a version of the sheet which gives examples using just two-digit numbers.
More able: There is a version of the sheet that asks the children to write in two numbers, in order, to fit between each pair of numbers. There is no list of numbers so that the children must work these out for themselves.

Plenary & assessment

Ask a child to write a three-digit number on the board. Now invite another child to write a second three-digit number that is larger than the first number. Challenge the class to suggest numbers that will fit between so that the three numbers are in order. Ask: *How can you tell that that number will fit?* Repeat this for another pair of numbers. Challenge the more able children by including four-digit numbers.

Lesson ②

Starter

Repeat the Starter from Lesson 1, but extend the game so that the children now say 'Inverse reverse 100' and count forward and back in hundreds.

Main teaching activities

Whole class: Explain to the class the conventions of rounding numbers to the nearest ten: numbers ending in 1 to 4 round down; numbers ending in 5 to 9 round up. Then ask the children to round these distances to the nearest 10km: 24km (20km), 36km (40km), 12km (10km) and 55km (60km).

Now explain that numbers can be rounded to the nearest 100, and that this time it is the tens digit which is important for rounding. Tens digits which are 1 to 4 round down; tens digits which are 5 to 9 round up. Write on the board 160 and ask: *What number will this be if it is rounded to the nearest hundred? 200, because there are six tens so that it rounds up.* Repeat this for other numbers, such as 340, 890, 450…, each time checking that the children can explain the rounding. Now include numbers with a digit other than zero in the units and explain that for rounding to the nearest hundred the units digit is ignored. Give examples such as: 456, 137, 222, 361…

Group work: Ask the children to work in groups of four. They take turns to draw three single-digit cards from a pack of 0 to 9 cards. They make a three-digit number, then say what that number is rounded to the nearest 100. This can be recorded on paper if you wish. Challenge the children to work quickly.

Differentiation

Less able: Decide whether to limit this to making two-digit numbers, and rounding to the nearest 10.

More able: Challenge the children to make six different three-digit numbers with their cards, such as for the cards 5, 6, 3: 563, 536, 653, 635, 356 and 365. The children round each of these numbers to the nearest 100.

Plenary & assessment

Ask the children to think of a question that might give the answer 60, such as 'A tailor needed 55cm of cloth, so the tailor rounded the measurement up to 60cm so there would be plenty of material.' Share some of the responses from the children.

Ask each child to write a three-digit number on their whiteboard. They then pass their whiteboard along to another person who writes the nearest hundred number (rounded up or down as appropriate). The children then pass their whiteboards back to each other to check the answers.

Remind the class that you are interested to know when they next use the rounding up/down strategy.

Lesson ③

Starter

Use three sets of enlarged 0 to 9 cards. Choose three cards, and stick these to the board in a row, face down. Make sure that the rest of the cards are also face down so that the children cannot see their faces. Ask a child which card they would like to see – perhaps the units? Reveal the units number to the class. The children then have one minute to write down as many possibilities for the correct three-digit number as they can. Ask them to call out a few responses. Now reveal the tens digit. The children can eliminate all their wrong answers and try a few more guesses. Finally, reveal the hundreds digit. Did anyone get the correct number? Repeat this for another set of three digits.

Main teaching activities

Whole class: Explain to the children that in this lesson they will be considering scales used in measuring and how to read them. Show the children an OHT of 'Reading scales'. Draw in lines to represent measures, such as at the 24cm, 12cm, 19cm marks on the ruler. Invite the children to read the scale, then ask: *What would this measurement be rounded to the nearest ten centimetres?* Repeat this for the dial scale, this time marking, for example, 0.5kg and asking: *How many grams is this?*

Repeat for a position of about 800 grams. Now invite the children to read the scale on the water jug as you mark the position of the water, such as 200ml, 500ml and so on.

Individual work: Provide copies of activity sheet 'Detective Milly Litre' and ask the children to complete it, taking care to read the scales as accurately as they can.

Differentiation

Less able: There is a version of the sheet with jugs marked in 100ml increments to 1 litre.
More able: This sheet contains further work which asks the children to answer questions, comparing the amounts of liquid that have been drunk.

Plenary & assessment

Use a metre stick marked in ten-centimetre increments. Point to a position on the stick and ask a child to say how many centimetres that is. Repeat this several times, each time pointing to a decade marker. Now point in the centre of a decade, such as at the 75cm point, and ask the children to estimate this position. Repeat this for other points on the stick. Check that the children respond quickly and accurately. Now point near to, but not on, a decade marker, such as approximately 37cm, and ask: *What measurement do you think this is? What would it be rounded to the nearest ten centimetres?* Repeat this for other measurements, including both those that round up and those that round down.

Name	Date

Ordering numbers

Look at the pairs of numbers. Then read the list of numbers.

Choose a number from the list below to fit between each pair of numbers. Use each number only once.

899 375 555 502 146 101 700 292 624 209

1. 123 [　　] 156

2. 312 [　　] 398

3. 192 [　　] 392

4. 601 [　　] 715

5. 888 [　　] 999

6. 107 [　　] 654

7. 94 [　　] 888

8. 465 [　　] 503

9. 578 [　　] 776

10. 231 [　　] 642

Now write the numbers in order, so that the smallest number is first.

Name		Date	

Detective Milly Litre!

Each jug of juice had exactly 2 litres at the start of the day, but someone has been slurping secretly.

Help Milly decide how much is left and how much has been slurped from each jug!

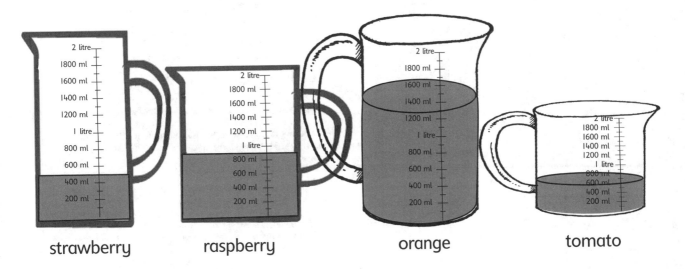

strawberry   raspberry   orange   tomato

	How much is left?	How much has been slurped?
strawberry		
raspberry		
orange		
tomato		

Addition and subtraction strategies

Children use, read and write the vocabulary of addition and subtraction, and write equations using + , – and = . They develop their mental strategies, including putting the largest number first, adding pairs to make a 9, 10 or 11, adding or subtracting using near multiples of 10, and using patterns of similar calculations.

LEARNING OBJECTIVES

	Topics	Starter	Main teaching activity
Lesson 1	Understanding addition and subtraction	● **Know by heart: all addition and subtraction facts for each number to 20.**	● Extend understanding of the operations of addition and subtraction, read and begin to write the related vocabulary, and continue to recognise that addition can be done in any order. ● Use the + , – and = signs.
Lesson 2	Understanding addition and subtraction	● Say the number that is 1, 10 or 100 more or less than any two- or three-digit number.	As for Lesson 1.
Lesson 3	Mental calculation strategies (+ and –)	As for Lesson 1.	● Use knowledge that addition can be done in any order to do mental calculations more efficiently. For example: – add three or four small numbers by putting the largest number first and/or by finding pairs totalling 9, 10 or 11. ● Use patterns of similar calculations.
Lesson 4	Mental calculation strategies (+ and –)	● Say or write a subtraction statement corresponding to a given addition statement, and vice versa.	● Use knowledge that addition can be done in any order to do mental calculations more efficiently. ● **Add and subtract mentally a 'near multiple of 10' to or from a two-digit number**… by adding or subtracting 10, 20, 30… and adjusting. ● Use patterns of similar calculations.
Lesson 5	Mental calculation strategies (+ and –)	As for Lesson 4.	● Use knowledge that addition can be done in any order to do mental calculations more efficiently. For example: – add three or four small numbers by putting the largest number first and/or by finding pairs totalling 9, 10 or 11. ● **Add and subtract mentally a 'near multiple of 10' to or from a two-digit number**… by adding or subtracting 10, 20, 30… and adjusting. ● Use patterns of similar calculations.

Lessons overview

Preparation
Make two sets of CD page 'Numeral cards 0 to 20'. Make sets of cards from CD page 'Add or subtract 10 or 100'.

Learning objectives
Starter
● **Know by heart: all addition and subtraction facts for each number to 20.**
● Say the number that is 1, 10 or 100 more or less than any two- or three-digit number.
Main teaching activity
● Extend understanding of the operations of addition and subtraction, read and begin to write the related vocabulary, and continue to recognise that addition can be done in any order.
● Use the + , – and = signs.

Vocabulary
more, add, sum, total altogether, equals, sign, take away, subtract, difference between, minus, + , –, =

You will need:
Photocopiable pages
'Missing numbers' (page 172) for each child.

CD pages
'Numeral cards 0 to 20' and 'Hundred square' (Autumn term) and 'Add or subtract 10 or 100' and 'Addition and subtraction vocabulary' for the teacher's/LSA's reference; 'Missing numbers' less able and more able versions (Summer term, Unit 2).

Equipment
Blu-Tack; seconds timer; individual whiteboards and pens; timer.

Lesson ①

Starter

Place two stacks of 0 to 20 cards face down on the table, and invite a child to take the top card from each stack, Blu-Tacking the cards to the board for everyone to see. Then ask the children to make an addition and subtraction number sentence using the two numbers, where the addition total does not exceed 20. For example, for 19 and 13 they might make 13 + 6 = 19 and 19 − 13 = 6. Set the timer to 'ting' at ten seconds, telling the children that as soon as the timer 'tings' they must hold up their whiteboards to show their number sentences. Share some of the responses and swiftly move on to the next two cards to be picked up.

82 add 19 = 101
83 plus 18 = 101
84 and 17 = 101
$\triangle$ + 16 = 101
86 + $\square$ = 101

Main teaching activities

Whole class: By the end of the lesson the majority of children should understand that $\triangle + \square = \bigcirc$ or $\bigcirc - \triangle = \square$. Review with the children the language of addition and subtraction, focusing on numbers that encourage the children to bridge the hundreds.

Discuss the children's strategies for calculating, and how they managed to cross the hundreds, such as: *82 add 10 is 92, add 8 is 100, add 1 is 101.*

Now draw an empty number line on the board and invite a child to demonstrate 82 + 19. Reinforce that whilst 82 + 19 = 101, 19 + 82 = 101 and 82 − 19 = 63, 19 − 82 *cannot* equal 63.

Now say: *I think of a number. I add 7. The answer is 15. What is my number?* (8)

15 added to a number is 65. What is the number? (50) Invite children to explain how they worked out the answers and to show this on an empty number line such as:

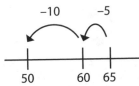

Paired work: Provide activity sheet 'Missing numbers' and ask the children to work in pairs to complete the questions. Encourage them to discuss their work with a partner and to compare methods for finding their solutions.

Differentiation

There are differentiated versions of the sheet available for the less and more able children.
Less able: Decide whether to provide a hundred square to assist the children in calculating.
More able: If the children are confident, challenge them to use mental methods as they work.

Plenary & assessment

Ask the children to substitute numbers so the statements are true.
$\triangle - \triangle = 0$ (both numbers must be the same)
$\square + \square = 102$ (51)
Ask for volunteers to model one of their answers using an empty number line (this can be done on the interactive whiteboard).

Move on to the following question: $\square - 12 = 101$. Again, invite children to model the answer using the empty number line.

Lesson ②

For the Starter, choose six volunteers and give each one an 'Add or subtract 10 or 100' card. Ask the six children to stand in a line in any order. The first child says any number greater than 100 and the other three children then say what their number would be if they applied the rule on their card. Now child two says a number, and so on. The class has to work out which child is adding or subtracting 1, 10 or 100. For the Main activity, review using an empty number line, using 36 − 15, then 176 − 43. Discuss whether there is just one way to a solution, or whether alternatives will work too. Write up $\triangle - \square = 15$ and, working in pairs again, ask the children to find as many solutions to this as they can in three minutes. Write some of these on the board and discuss how they worked them out. Repeat for other subtraction equations, such as $\triangle - \square = 18$ and $29 - \triangle - \square = 6$. During the Plenary & assessment, invite the children to give examples of their number sentences, making up number stories for some of the sentences using the vocabulary of subtraction.

Lessons ③ ④ ⑤

Preparation
Enlarge the core activity sheet 'Now I know!' to A3.

Learning objectives

Starter
- **Know by heart: all addition and subtraction facts for each number to 20.**
- Say or write a subtraction statement corresponding to a given addition statement, and vice versa.

Main teaching activity
- Use knowledge that addition can be done in any order to do mental calculations more efficiently. For example:
– add three or four small numbers by putting the largest number first and/or by finding pairs totalling 9, 10 or 11.
- **Add and subtract mentally a 'near multiple of 10' to or from a two-digit number**…
by adding or subtracting 10, 20, 30… and adjusting.
- Use patterns of similar calculations.

Vocabulary
more, add, sum, total altogether, equals, sign, take away, subtract, difference between, minus, +, −, =

You will need:

Photocopiable pages
'Now I know!' (page 173)
for each child.

CD pages
'Hundred square' for each
less able child (Autumn
term); 'Now I know!'
less able and more able
versions (Summer term,
Unit 2) (see General
resources).

Equipment
Timer.

Lesson ③

Starter
Repeat the Starter from Lesson 1, this time reducing the time allowed to about six seconds in order to keep the pace sharp.

Main teaching activities
Whole class: Explain that today the children will be totalling several small numbers. On the board write 17 + 4 + 3 + 6 and ask: *How can we work this out?* Discuss how the 17 and 3 can combine to make 20, and the 4 and 6 to make 10. Now ask the children to consider this example: 19 + 8 + 4 + 7. For example: (19 + 8) + (4 + 7) = (20 + 7) + (10 + 1) = 27 + 11 = 38. Repeat this for a further example, such as 15 + 6 + 8, where 15 + 6 makes 21 or 20 + 1. This relates to adding 11 by adding 10 and adjusting by 1. Now write on the board 14 + 8 + 5, where 14 + 5 = 19 or 20 − 1. This relates to adding 9 by adding 10 and adjusting by 1.

Individual work: Write these numbers on the board: 11, 12, 13, 14, 15, 16, 1, 2, 3, 4, 5, 6, 7, 8, 9 and 10. Ask the children to choose one of the two-digit numbers and three single-digit numbers, write an addition sentence and calculate the answer. Ask them to write six of these, making each one different.

Differentiation
Less able: Decide whether to ask the children to choose just two or three of the numbers for each addition sentence.
More able: Challenge the children to include one of these numbers each time: 21, 32, 43, 54 and 65.

Plenary & assessment
Choose some of the number sentences that the children have written and ask them to explain their calculation strategies. Ask questions such as: *How else could we work this out? Can you make a 10, 11, 9? How does that help you?*

Ask the more able children to write up some of their number sentences and to explain how they calculated their answers. Discuss how making a ten can also be used for making 20, 30, 40…

Lesson 4

Starter

Explain that you will write up a number sentence such as 45 + 36 = 81. Ask the children to write on their whiteboards another addition and two subtraction sentence which use the same numbers, such as 36 + 45 = 81; 81 – 36 = 45; 81 – 45 = 36. Repeat for other examples, such as 97 – 43 = 54.

Main teaching activities

Whole class: Write on the board: 36 + 30 = and ask for an answer. Invite children to explain how they worked this out, such as counting on three tens. Now write 36 + 29 and explain that we can use adding 9, 10, and 11 strategies for adding. Write up 36 + 29 = 36 + 30 – 1. Ask the children to calculate the answer. Repeat for another example, such as 45 + 39, or 45 + 40 – 1.

Now write up 64 + 21 and ask for suggestions for calculating this. Write up: 64 + 20 + 1 and discuss how this is a development from adding 11 by adding 10 and adjusting by 1. Now write up:

15 + 9 =
15 + 19 =
15 + 29 =

Ask the children to work out the answer to 15 + 9 (24) and then to deduce the answers to the other two addition sentences. Ask them to continue the pattern of number sentences and to write the answers. Discuss how patterns like this help us to find answers to questions quickly.

Individual work: On the board write: 17 + 11; 17 + 21; 17 + 31. Ask the children to write the answers to these, then to continue the pattern until the total is about 100. Then ask them to begin with 18 + 9 and to continue the pattern to find the answers for themselves. Finally, ask them to continue the subtraction pattern for 78 – 1, 78 – 11, 78 – 21 and so on to 78 – 71.

Differentiation

Less able: Provide a hundred square for the children to use to count on in tens, if necessary, to help them to find the answers.
More able: Ask the children to continue each pattern until the totals are about 200.

Plenary & assessment

Challenge the children to say the number sentence pattern as you write these on the board. Begin with 17 + 11… and continue to 17 + 81 = 98. Now ask the more able children to continue the pattern, prompting the other children to join in as they see this continue: 17 + 91 = 108; 17 + 101 = 118… Ask: *What do you notice?* Discuss how, as the tens number increases in 11, 21, 31… so does the total increase by 10 each time. Repeat this for the 18 + 9 pattern, again, using the more able children to help to take the answers beyond 18 + 79 = 97.

Lesson 5

Repeat the Starter from Lesson 4, but using different starting number sentences, such as 47 + 28 = 75 and 84 – 52. Keep the pace sharp. Review the mental calculation strategies that the children have used during the previous two lessons, giving further examples for each strategy, including adding and subtracting 10, 11 and 9, near multiples of decade numbers, and adding several small numbers. Discuss how using patterns of similar calculations, as covered in Lesson 4, can help to find answers. Provide each child with a copy of activity sheet 'Now I know!' to complete individually. This covers the strategies that the children have learned this week. (There are differentiated versions available for the less and more able children.) During the Plenary & assessment, review the answers to the core version of the sheet, using an A3 enlargement of it. Invite individual children to explain how they calculated their answers.

Name   Date

Missing numbers

Find the missing numbers in these number sentences.
Show your working.

1. 19 + [ ] = 25

2. 52 + [ ] = 64

3. [ ] + 45 = 63

4. 36 + [ ] = 93

5. 42 + 38 = [ ]

6. 64 + [ ] = 100

Now find four different solutions to this number sentence.

[ ] + [ ] = 40

[ ] + [ ] = 40

[ ] + [ ] = 40

[ ] + [ ] = 40

■ SCHOLASTIC

photocopiable

Name	Date

Now I know!

Write your answers to these questions.	Write your working out in here.
15 + 8 + 9 + 4 =	
17 + 5 + 3 + 6 =	
15 + 29 =	
18 + 31 =	

Write the answers to these number sentences.

Continue the patterns.

18 + 9 = ☐   97 − 5 = ☐

18 + 19 = ☐   97 − 15 = ☐

18 + 29 = ☐   97 − 25 = ☐

18 + 39 = ☐   97 − 35 = ☐

18 + 49 = ☐   97 − 45 = ☐

18 + 59 = ☐   97 − 55 = ☐

18 + 69 = ☐   97 − 65 = ☐

18 + 79 = ☐   97 − 75 = ☐

                      97 − 85 = ☐

                      97 − 95 = ☐

Pencil and paper methods of recording and solving word problems

Children are introduced to TU + TU and HTU + HTU using an empty number line. They use the empty number line for subtraction by counting up and by compensation. They also begin to record subtractions vertically. They use these methods to solve word problems and invent their own one-step and two-step word problems.

LEARNING OBJECTIVES

	Topics	Starter	Main teaching activities
Lesson 1	Pencil and paper procedures (+ and –)	● Derive quickly: doubles of multiples 5 to 100 (eg 75 × 2, 90 × 2) and all the corresponding halves.	● Use informal pencil and paper methods to support, record or explain HTU + TU, HTU + HTU.
Lesson 2	Pencil and paper procedures (+ and –)	As for Lesson 1.	As for Lesson 1.
Lesson 3	Pencil and paper procedures (+ and –)	As for Lesson 1.	As for Lesson 1.
Lesson 4	Pencil and paper procedures (+ and –) Problems involving 'real life', money and measures Reasoning about numbers or shapes Checking results	● **Add and subtract mentally a 'near multiple of 10' to or from a two-digit number…** by adding or subtracting 10, 20, 30… and adjusting.	● Use informal pencil and paper methods to support, record or explain HTU ± TU, HTU ± HTU. ● Solve word problems involving numbers in 'real life', money and measures, using one or more steps, including finding totals and giving change, and working out which coins to pay. ● **Explain methods and reasoning** orally and, where appropriate, in writing. ● Check with an equivalent calculation.
Lesson 5	As for Lesson 4.	As for Lesson 4.	As for Lesson 4.

Lesson overview

Preparation
Enlarge CD page 'Multiples of 5 cards' onto A3 card twice and cut out to make two sets of cards.

Learning objectives
Starter
● Derive quickly: doubles of multiples of 5 to 100 (eg 75 × 2, 90 × 2) and all the corresponding halves.
Main teaching activity
● Use informal pencil and paper methods to support, record or explain HTU ± TU, HTU ± HTU.

Vocabulary
tens boundary, hundreds boundary, add, subtract, how many more to make…?

You will need:
Photocopiable pages
'Addition empty number line' (page 178) for each child.

CD pages
'Multiples of 5 cards' for the teacher's/LSA's reference; 'Addition empty number line' less able and more able versions (Summer term, Unit 3) (see General resources).

Equipment
Blu-Tack; large 200–300 number line; squared paper.

Lesson ①

Starter

Play a class game of Pelmanism. Stick up the 'Multiples of 5 cards', face to the board. Divide the class into two teams, nominating a spokesperson for each team. Each team is allowed to come and reveal two cards. If the cards have the relationship of a double, then the team keeps the cards. If they have no doubles relationship, the cards are stuck back, face to the board and the other team has a go. The team with the most pairs wins.

Main teaching activities

Whole class: Explain to the children that they will be using an empty number line in order to help them to count on in multiples of 1, 10 or 100 as a strategy for addition. On the board write 65 + 34 and draw an empty number line.

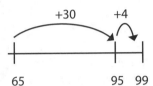

Discuss how 65 + 34 can be broken down in 65 + 30 + 4, counting on in tens for the 30 and in ones for the 4. Repeat for 54 + 37.

Now repeat this for examples which cross the hundreds boundary. Write on the board 75 + 38 and draw an empty number line. Explain that this example can be broken down like this: 75 + 38 = 75 + 30 + 5 + 3. Encourage the children to count in tens from 75 to 105, then add 5, then add 3. Now try 84 + 37 and some HTU + TU sums, such as 257 + 68 which breaks down into 257 + 60 + 3 + 5, and then for HTU + HTU, such as 348 + 279 (348 + 279 = 348 + 200 + 70 + 2 + 7).

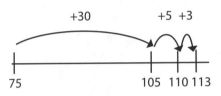

Individual work: Provide activity sheet 'Addition empty number line' for the children to complete.

Differentiation

Less able: Decide whether to use the differentiated sheet which includes just examples of TU + TU.
More able: There is a version of the sheet which includes more HTU + HTU examples.

Plenary & assessment

Review some examples from the core activity sheet. Invite individual children to draw an empty number line to demonstrate their addition strategy. Discuss whether different strategies were used by other children, and which they think was more efficient.

Lesson ②

Starter

Repeat the Starter for Lesson 1, but this time use only the decade cards from CD page 'Multiples of 5 cards'. Explain that one card has to be half the amount of the other. The children will quickly realise this is the same as yesterday's game but with halves, not doubles. For this version, introduce the rule that the second card they turn must be half the first card, so that having the correct order is crucial!

Main teaching activities

Whole class: Explain that today the children will use the empty number line in order to subtract by counting up from the smaller to the larger number. Write on the board 76 – 48 and draw an empty number line. Write an addition to show what is added to 48:

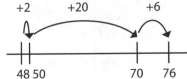

$$48 + 2 \rightarrow 50$$
$$+ 20 \rightarrow 70$$
$$+ 6 \rightarrow 76$$

So 20 + 2 + 6 = 22 + 6 = 28. Explain that 76 – 48 = 28. Repeat with another example, such as 94 – 57.

Paired work: Ask the children to work quickly in pairs to try 64 – 36 and 81 – 54.

Whole class: Review the two examples that the children have tried for themselves. Check that the majority understand the method and, if necessary, do some more examples with the whole class.

Now demonstrate the same method for HTU – HTU. Write on the board 654 – 367 and draw an empty number line to demonstrate: 3 + 30 + 200 + 54 = 287. Repeat for another example.
Paired work: Ask the children to work in pairs to complete examples of subtraction by complementary addition. Write on the board: 95 – 47, 61 – 38, 56 – 29, 123 – 45, 246 – 178 and 401 – 238.

Differentiation
Less able: Decide whether to limit the examples to just TU – TU and to work these as a group.
More able: Decide whether to include more HTU – HTU examples for this group.

Plenary & assessment
Review some of the examples from the board. Invite individual children to draw an empty number line and to demonstrate how they worked out the answer.

Lesson

Repeat the Starter from Lesson 1, then the Starter for Lesson 2 so that children practise deriving doubles and halves of multiples of 5. On the board write 83 – 57 and draw an empty number line:, as shown below.

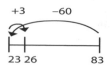

Write: 83 – 57 = 83 – 60 + 3 = 23 + 3 = 26. Repeat for 72 – 36 before deciding whether to demonstrate with an HTU – HTU example such as 782 – 357.

Show the children that this can also be written as:

782 – 357 = 782 – 400 + 43
= 382 + 43
= 425

```
    782
  – 357
    382   take 400
  +  43   add 43
    300
    120
      5
    425
```

Provide some examples of TU – TU by compensation for the children to try in pairs, such as 76 – 37, 81 – 35 and 62 – 34. (More able children may like to try some HTU – HTU examples, lining up the hundreds, tens and units on squared paper.) For the Plenary & & and assessment, review the examples on the board, drawing the empty number line each time and to ask a child to write in the appropriate numbers and a horizontal number sentence. Then ask: *How shall we round up? So how much shall we add back on?*

Lessons   overview

Preparation
Photocopy CD page 'Number problems' onto acetate to make an OHT.

Learning objectives
Starter
● **Add and subtract mentally a 'near multiple of 10' to or from a two-digit number…** **by adding or subtracting** 10, 20, 30… and adjusting.
Main teaching activity
● Use informal pencil and paper methods to support, record or explain HTU ± TU, HTU ± HTU.
● Solve word problems involving numbers in 'real life', money and measures, using one or more steps, including finding totals and giving change, and working out which coins to pay.
● **Explain methods and reasoning** orally and, where appropriate, in writing.
● Check with an equivalent calculation.

Vocabulary
tens boundary, hundreds boundary, add, subtract, how many more to make…? calculate, method, jotting

You will need:
Photocopiable pages
'Fruity problems' (page 179) for each child.

CD pages
'Number problems' for the teacher/s'/LSA's reference; 'Fruity problems' less able and more able versions (Summer term, Unit 3) (see General resources).

Equipment
Individual whiteboards and pens; OHP.

Lesson ④

Starter

Ask the children to write the answers to these addition questions on their whiteboards. Say: *What is 43 + 30? And 43 + 29? How did you work them out? What about 43 + 31?* Repeat for other examples, for example 56 + 40 and 37 + 50, so that the children have the opportunity to calculate by adding the multiple of ten before adjusting by one for the subsequent questions.

Main teaching activities

Whole class: Explain that you would like the children to use the empty number line methods that they have learned so far this week as an aid to solving problems. Uncover the first example on the OHT of CD page 'Number problems'. Ask: *How shall we solve this?* Invite a child to draw an empty number line on the board and to write in the additions. Write the number sentence: 45 + 36 = 45 + 30 + 6 = 75 + 5 + 1 = 80 + 1 = 81.

Repeat this for the second question on the OHT. First ask the children to explain what sort of problem it is (subtraction) and then invite a child to draw an empty number line to show how the problem could be solved. You may wish to do this both by counting up and by compensation. For counting up, write up: 25 + 5 + 60 + 1 = 91 so 91 – 25 = 5 + 60 + 1 = 66. Write also:

25 + 5 = 30
  + 60 = 90
  + 1 = 91
So 5 + 60 + 1 = 66.

For compensation, write: 91 – 25 = 91 – 30 + 5 = 61 + 5 = 66.

Individual work: Provide activity sheet 'Fruity problems' for the children to complete individually.

Less able: Decide whether to use the sheet which contains TU + TU and TU – TU only.

More able: There is a version of the sheet which contains HTU + HTU and HTU – HTU only.

Plenary

Choose another question from the OHT 'Number problems'. Invite a child to draw the empty number line and to explain what sort of problem it is. Work through the problem as a class and write up the equation. Then invite the children to suggest how they could check their answer. Explain that in the next lesson they will check their answers with an equivalent calculation.

Lesson ⑤

Repeat the Starter from Lesson 4, this time moving immediately to addition or subtraction of a near multiples of 10 such as 48 + 31; 56 + 29; 92 – 39. Discuss each question and answer method. Then, using the OHT 'Number problems' reveal problem 6. *What sort of problem is this?* (Addition then subtraction) Invite children to solve it, and work through this together on the board using empty number lines. Now write up 46 + 37 = and ask the children to solve it. Discuss their methods and the answer before they try 83 – 52 =. Ask the children to suggest how these number sentences could be checked (by using an addition calculation for subtraction and vice versa). Now, in pairs, ask the children to make up their own TU + TU number sentence and calculate the answer. Ask them to write a word number problem for these numbers. Then ask them to invent a TU – TU number sentence, calculate the answer and write a word number problem for these numbers. For the Plenary & assessment, invite pairs of children to set their word problems for others to try.

Name

Date

Addition empty number line

Write the answers to these addition sentences.

Show your working out on the empty number lines.

54 + 73 =

339 + 57 =

76 + 45 =

463 + 78 =

87 + 68 =

246 + 321 =

134 + 54 =

354 + 265 =

257 + 62 =

338 + 276 =

Name	Date

Fruity problems

Write the answers to these problems.

Use the empty number lines to help you.

Write a number sentence to show how you worked out the answer.

Question	Answer
1. Claire buys 56 bananas. James buys 137 oranges. How much fruit do they have altogether to give to Sam the giant? **Number line**	
2. Sam the giant eats 136 mangoes and 65 peaches. How much fruit has he eaten in total? **Number line**	
3. The supermarket has 76 pumpkins. Sam the giant buys 48 of the pumpkins. How many pumpkins are left in the supermarket? **Number line**	
4. Sam the giant collects some of the pumpkin seeds to make a necklace. He collects 93 seeds and uses 64 to make a necklace. How many seeds has he left? **Number line**	

Summer term
Unit 4 Capacity

Children use litres and millilitres to estimate, measure and compare capacities. They learn the relationship between litres and millilitres, read scales and write measurements in equivalent forms, such as 0.5l, 500ml, 1/2 litre.

LEARNING OBJECTIVES

	Topics	Starter	Main teaching activities
Lesson 1	Measures	● Derive quickly: doubles of multiples of 50 to 500 (eg 45 × 2).	● Read and begin to write the vocabulary related to capacity. ● Measure and compare using standard units (l, ml). ● Know the relationship between litres and millilitres. ● Read scales to nearest division (labelled or unlabelled).
Lesson 2	Measures	As for Lesson 1.	● Read and begin to write the vocabulary related to capacity. ● Measure and compare using standard units (l, ml). ● Know the relationship between litres and millilitres. ● Suggest suitable units and measuring equipment to estimate or measure capacity. ● Read scales to nearest division (labelled or unlabelled). ● Record estimates and measurements to the nearest whole or half unit, or in mixed units.
Lesson 3	Measures	● **Know by heart: multiplication facts for the 2, 5 and 10 times-tables.** ● Derive quickly: division facts corresponding to the 2, 5 and 10 times-tables.	● Read and begin to write the vocabulary related to capacity. ● Measure and compare using standard units (l, ml). ● Know the relationship between litres and millilitres. ● Read scales to nearest division (labelled or unlabelled). ● Record estimates and measurements to the nearest whole or half unit, or in mixed units.
Lesson 4	Measures	As for Lesson 3	As for Lesson 3.
Lesson 5	Measures	● Order a set of three-digit numbers.	As for Lesson 2.

Lesson overview

Preparation
Make an OHT of CD page 'Capacity'. Photocopy the 'Round the world cards' onto thin card and make multiple sets of the cards so there is a set per group of three children. Photocopy one set of 'Round the world cards' to A3.

Learning objectives
Starter
● Derive quickly: doubles of multiples of 50 to 500 (eg 45 × 2).
● **Know by heart: multiplication facts for the 2, 5 and 10 times-tables.**
● Derive quickly: division facts corresponding to the 2, 5 and 10 times-tables.
● Order a set of three-digit numbers.

Main teaching activity
● Read and begin to write the vocabulary related to capacity.
● Measure and compare using standard units (l, ml).
● Know the relationship between litres and millilitres.
● Suggest suitable units and measuring equipment to estimate or measure capacity.
● Read scales to nearest division (labelled or unlabelled).
● Record estimates and measurements to the nearest whole or half unit, or in mixed units.

Vocabulary
capacity, full, half full, empty, holds, contains, litre, half-litre, millilitre, container, equivalent

You will need:
CD pages
'Round the world cards' and 'Making a measuring jug' for each child; 'Round the world blanks' for each more able child; 'Capacity' and 'Measurements' for the teacher's/LSA's reference (see General resources).

Equipment
Whiteboards and pens; OHP; containers from 50ml to 4 litres; water; medicine spoons; five plastic bottles with three-digit capacity; five commercial containers with labels covered; small individual carton of fruit juice and can of cola; containers with smaller amounts measured in ml; teapot, cup, plastic bucket; 1-litre measuring jugs; labels.

Lesson ①

Starter

Ask the children to count with you in fifties to 500 and back. Repeat, extending the count to 1000. Now explain that you will say the number in the count and you would like the children to say its double. Begin with 50, so that the children say 100, then 100 (and 200), 150 (and 300) and so on. If necessary, remind the children that they can use the doubles of 5, 10, 15, and so on, to help them derive these facts.

Main teaching activities

Whole class: Begin by asking the children to give examples of capacity vocabulary, such as 'fill', 'empty' and 'litre'. Write the suggestions on the board. Now ask the children to write down as many facts as they can recall about capacity in about three minutes.

Now explain that this week the focus will be on capacity. Ask questions such as:
- *How many millilitres are there in a litre?* (1000)
- *How many are there in half a litre? A quarter of a litre?*
- *How many ways can you find of writing half a litre?* (1/2l, 500ml, 0.5l, half a litre)
- *How could you write 1 litre 250ml?* (1.25l, 1250ml, 1 1/4l, one and a quarter litres)
- *What size of jug would you need to measure a baby's bottle? Oil for a car? Bottled water?*
  Now ask:
- *Which is larger: 1500ml or one and a half litres? How do you know?*
- *What might you buy in litre containers?*

Show the OHT of CD page 'Capacity'. Ask individual children to mark the following measurements on different jugs: 100ml, 50ml, 1100ml and 240ml. (It will not be possible to do this on all jugs.) Ask the children which jugs it is easy to do this on, which more difficult, and why.

Group work: Ask the children to work in threes. They cut out the 'Round the world cards' and shuffle them. Then the child with the 'Start' card reads what is on their card. The player with the answer reads their card, and so on.

Differentiation

Less able: Begin with all the cards being dealt out and on show to start. Repeat this until the children are confident and can play the game in groups of three without adult intervention.

More able: When the children have mastered the original game, they can use the CD page 'Round the world blanks' to make their own game for another group to use.

Plenary & assessment

Using the enlarged set of 'Round the world cards', ask a child to come to the front of the class and hold any of the cards. Now ask another child to hold the next card. For each card, ask the child holding it to read out its measure. Determine where the smallest card will be placed, and ask how the two cards should be ordered. Continue until all 15 cards are held in an ordered line. Invite the children who are still sitting to suggest equivalent measurements for any of the cards, and write this on the board. For example, a quarter of a litre is 250ml, and 0.25l.

Lesson ②

Starter

Repeat the Starter for Lesson 1, but increase the pace of the question and answer so that the children are kept on their toes!

Main teaching activities

Whole class: Use the 'Round the world cards' with the whole class as a warm up activity. The children should have one card between two or three. They jump up when they have the answer and sit down straight afterwards. Encourage the children to build up their speed in completing the task.

Explain that the focus today is on being able to measure liquids accurately using a variety of measuring equipment. Display the OHT of CD page 'Capacity' and ask children to point to where a particular measurement would be for each jug, such as 50ml, 100ml, 250ml, 0.5l and so on.

Teach the children to look for clues to help them work out the scale of the jugs they are using, such as:

● *Look for any markings, especially numbers.*
● *Where is zero? Where is the 'full' mark?*
● *Estimate how much you think the container would hold. Do you think this is more than a litre of cola or less?*

Group work: Set up a carousel of activities, which the children can all attempt during today and the next two lessons. The activities are suitable for mixed-ability groups.

A. Make a measuring jug: Provide the children with CD page 'Making a measuring jug', gummed labels for writing the calibrations onto the containers, a variety of uncalibrated containers, each of which will hold at least 2 litres and two 1-litre measuring jugs. Ask the children to calibrate some containers to show the following measurements: 1/2l, 1l, 1 1/2l and 2l.

B. Round the world containers: Work with this group. Using the 'Round the world cards' the children find containers which they think will hold the amount on each card. They use a measuring jug to fill the container with the required amount of water, then place the appropriate 'Round the world card' beside the container. They then order all 15 measurements. You may wish to subdivide the children working at this activity into three groups, so that each group has five cards. Then the groups come together to order all their containers from holding the least to the most.

C. How much does it hold? Provide this group with a selection of containers with the capacity covered over. They estimate and then measure how much they think the label describes the container as holding. Discuss the space left at the top of containers that is there to avoid spillage.

Differentiation

Less able: Ensure that it is easy to read the measuring jugs given to these children for each activity.
More able: Challenge these children to record their answers in a variety of equivalent ways, building on the work of Lesson 1. This group can work with 4l containers (such as plastic milk cartons) for activity A. However, use smaller measuring containers for activity C such as 25ml.

Plenary & assessment

Review one of the activities during this and the subsequent two lessons.

● **Make a measuring jug:** Ask the children to explain what they had to do, what they found easy, and anything that was difficult. Discuss how they calibrated their containers. Discuss how accurate they think these calibrated containers will be and why. How could they calibrate a container in 100ml increments and 50ml increments?

● **Round the world containers:** Invite the children to explain what they had to do, what they found easy and anything they found difficult, and why it was difficult. Ask: *How did you order the containers?* Show the children the containers and discuss how a variety of shapes affects the level of water.

● **How much does it hold?** Invite the children to explain what they did, what they found easy, and anything they found difficult, and why. Uncover the commercial labels so that the contents is visible and invite a child to read how much the container would hold. Discuss how close this amount is to the children's estimates and measures. Discuss why there may well be differences, such as did the children fill the container to the same point as the manufacturer would? Ask for suggestions as to why the manufacturer would not fill the containers right to the top. (To save spillages when opening the container and to allow space for the contents to expand.)

Lesson 3

For the Starter write 'How many □ in □' on the board so that the children can generate some questions. Ask them to write a number sentence on their whiteboards, using their knowledge of the 2, 5 and 10 times-tables. Once every child has written a question, invite one to stand up to ask the class their question. The first person to offer the correct answer wins one point. (You might like to split the class into two halves and accumulate points.) For the Main teaching activity, use the OHT of CD page 'Capacity' and invite the children to estimate measurements. Draw in lines to represent the water level, ensuring they fall between the calibration marks, such as about 220ml. Invite the children to estimate the amount and to explain their estimate. Continue with the carousel of activities from Lesson 2 and review another carousel activity for the Plenary & assessment, using the suggestions in Lesson 2.

Lesson 4

Repeat the Starter for Lesson 3, but make this more of a game. Ask the teams to answer by having the correct number of children standing; for example, a child asks how many fives in 45 so the first team to have nine children standing wins a point. (This takes a bit of non-competitive practising first.) Then review equivalents with the children such as: *Which is greater 600ml or 0.5l? How do you know? How else might you record 0.5 litre?* Continue with the Carousel activities from Lesson 2 and use one of the Plenary & assessment Carousel activity suggestions from Lesson 2.

Lesson 5

For the Starter have a selection of plastic bottles/cartons of liquid with the three-digit capacity enlarged and stuck on the side. Turn the bottles so the children don't see the capacity at first. Ask a child to choose three of the bottles and invite the others to suggest how the bottles should be ordered for capacity. Now turn the bottles so that the children can read the capacity. *Are the bottles correctly ordered?* Repeat this for other choices of three bottles. For the Main activity, show the children a medicine spoon or teaspoon, a small carton of fruit juice and a can of cola. For each item, cover the ml measure and have two measurement cards taken from CD page 'Measurements'. To play in two teams one team starts and, if they make a mistake, the other team can take over. Add more items to the game as you feel necessary. The team who gets to the last item and guesses correctly is the 'winner'. You can extend this game to include three labels for each item. Now invite the children to suggest what would be suitable units and measuring equipment for measuring the capacity of each of the containers when empty. Discuss the suitability of each suggestion. In mixed-ability groups of four, give each child activity sheet 'How much?'. Ask them to discuss each item on the sheet and decide what the quantity would be, write their estimate and units. For the Plenary & assessment, discuss how easy or difficult the children found it to make these estimates. Now play 'Guess my capacity'. You will need a teapot, a cup and a plastic bucket. Each child writes their estimate for the capacity on their whiteboard. You choose the three nearest results of the teapot to come out. If no one is spot on with their estimate, they are each allowed to ask you one question before estimating again. Whoever is nearest this time wins a point. Continue with the other items. For each item ask: *What measuring container would you use to measure that? Why is that a good choice?*

Solving problems and symmetry

Children solve measures word problems which involve more than one step. They make symmetrical shapes with their bodies, both working alone and with a partner. They use mirrors to help them to find more than one line of symmetry and to draw the reflection of half a shape in order to complete the shape. They recognise that some shapes do not have lines of symmetry.

LEARNING OBJECTIVES

	Topics	Starter	Main teaching activities
Lesson 1	Making decisions	● Derive quickly all pairs of multiples of 5 with a total of 100 (eg 35 + 64).	● **Choose and use appropriate operations (including multiplication and division) to solve word problems**, and appropriate ways of calculating: mental, mental with jottings, pencil and paper.
Lesson 2	Making decisions	As for Lesson 1.	As for Lesson 1.
Lesson 3	Solving problems	● Say or write a subtraction statement corresponding to a given addition statement, and vice versa.	As for Lesson 1.
Lesson 4	Shape and space	● **Know by heart**: all pairs of multiples of 100 with a total of 1000 (eg 300 + 700).	● **Identify** and sketch **lines of symmetry in simple shapes, and recognise shapes with no lines of symmetry**. Sketch the reflection of a simple shape in a mirror line along one edge.
Lesson 5	Shape and space	As for Lesson 4.	As for Lesson 4.

Lesson overview

Preparation
Make an A3 enlargement of CD page 'How far?'.

Learning objectives
Starter
● Derive quickly all pairs of multiples of multiples of 5 with a total of 100 (eg 35 + 64).
● Say or write a subtraction statement corresponding to a given addition statement, and vice versa.
Main teaching activity
● **Choose and use appropriate operations (including multiplication and division) to solve word problems**, and appropriate ways of calculating: mental, mental with jottings, pencil and paper.

Vocabulary
calculate, calculation, mental calculation, method, jotting, answer, right, correct, wrong, what could we try next? how did you work it out? number sentence, sign, operation, symbol, equation

You will need:
Photocopiable pages
'Measures word problems' (page 188) and 'How far?' (page 189) for each child.

CD pages
'Hundred square' for the teacher's/LSA's reference (Autumn term); 'Measures word problems' and 'How far?' less able and more able versions (Summer term, Unit 5) (see General resources).

Equipment
Individual whiteboards and pens.

Lesson ①

Starter
Explain to the class that you would like them to play a bingo-type game. Ask the children to choose three numbers which are multiples of 5 and less than 100, and to write these on their whiteboards. Explain that you will then say a number that is a multiple of 5, and if the children have written the number that adds to this to make 100 they can cross it out. For example, if you say 55 and they have 45, they can cross 45 out. The first child to cross out all their numbers wins.

Main teaching activities
Whole class: The purpose of the activities over the next three days is to develop word-problem solving strategies within the context of measures. The children should attempt each problem using resources provided. The emphasis is on them talking through and demonstrating the problem, rather than being a pencil and paper exercise. To this end it is suggested that you have all measuring equipment available and assess how well the children select suitable equipment.

Begin with the following problem. Write it on the board and read it together: *A small apple weighs approximately 50g. How many apples approximately would you expect to have in a 1kg bag?*

Ask questions such as:
- *How many apples approximately would weigh 100g? How did you work that out?*
- *So how many would weigh 200g? 400g? 80g?*
- *How many grams are there in a kilogram?*
- *How many apples would weigh about 1kg? Why is it hard to say exactly the number of apples?* (They are a non-uniform size.)

Repeat for another problem such as: *The ball of string contains 35 metres of string. How many people can each have a length of string of 5 metres?*

Individual work: Provide each child with a copy of activity sheet 'Measures word problems'. Ask them to write the solutions to the problems and to show their working.

Differentiation
Less able: Decide whether to use the version of the activity sheet with smaller numbers.
More able: There is a version of the sheet available which involves larger numbers.

Plenary & assessment
Use the following problem with these measures written on the board: 1500m   1600m   1300m
Three children entered a race. After 30 minutes, runner One had run 500m, runner Two had run 1600m and runner Three had run 1300m.

Ask questions such as:
- *Who ran the fastest?* (Two) *How do you know?*
- *Who travelled the least distance?* (Three)
- *What is the total distance covered?* (1400m) *What calculation do you need to do?* (Find the total)
- *How many ways could you have found out the answer?*
- *What is 1400 metres in kilometres?* (1.4km) *How could you check it is the correct answer?*

Lesson ②

Starter
Repeat the bingo game from Lesson 1, but ask the children to write a different set of multiples of 5 onto their whiteboards.

Main teaching activities

Whole class: Explain that you will ask the children to solve a word problem. Write this on the board and read it together:

A farmer ploughs up 20kg of potatoes. He fills 10 sacks equally. How much does each sack hold? Then half of the sacks go to market. How many kg of potatoes are left?

Ask: *How shall we begin to solve this problem?* Elicit from the children that the problem is in a number of parts: how much each sack holds; how many sacks go to market; how many sacks of potatoes the farmer keeps; what the total weight of those sacks is. Then ask:

- *What are the important mathematical words in this problem?* (equally, how much, half)
- *What is the first calculation needed?* ($20 \div 10 = 2$)
- *What type of measurement is the first calculation? Is it a kg answer? A number of sacks?*
- *What is the second calculation?* ($10 \div 2 = 5$, so five sacks go to market. But the question asks how many kg of potatoes are **left**, so we need to calculate $5 \times 2kg = 10kg$.)

Paired work: Explain that you will write some word problems on the board. Ask the children to copy the problem into their jotters and, first of all, to underline the important mathematical words. Then ask them to break the problem down into what they need to find out, and to solve it. Write on the board:

1. *Seema buys 4 boxes of satsumas. Each box has 50 satsumas in it. She sells 100 of her satsumas at 6p each. How much money does she make?* (£6) *Each satsuma weighs about 50 grams. How much do the satsumas left weigh altogether?* (5kg)

2. *The swimming pool is 25 metres in length. Jodie swims on Monday and Friday. On Monday she swims 8 lengths. On Friday she swims twice as far as on Monday. How far does she swim altogether?* (600m)

Differentiation

Less able: Decide whether to work as a group to solve these (perhaps simplified) problems. Work together, identifying the mathematical vocabulary, and what has to be calculated.

More able: When everyone has finished the problems, challenge them to invent their own problem. Explain that they will be asked to set this for others to solve during the plenary and that it must have at least two parts to it.

Plenary & assessment

Review the two problems from the board. Ask: *What are the important mathematical words here? What do we need to find out? What order should we do this in? What type of number operations do we need to use?* Then ask the more able children to set their problems to the other children. (Do check these first and choose the ones that are suitable!) Ask similar questions as before to help the children to focus upon what is important in the problem and what they need to find out.

Lesson ③

For the Starter, write an addition sentence onto the board and ask the children to calculate the answer, and to write another addition and two subtraction sentences which use the same numbers. For example: $45 + 37 = 82$ and $37 + 45 = 82$; $82 - 45 = 37$; $82 - 37 = 45$. Keep the pace of this sharp. For group work, write on the board: *There are some apples in the box. 30kg is the weight of apples doubled with 2kg added. How much do the apples weigh?* Invite the children to pick out the key words, then to say what they must find out. After a minute or two, ask: *What did you do first? Yes, subtract 2 from 30. Why did you do that? What did you do next? Divide 28 by 2? Why did you do that? So how much do the apples weigh? Yes, 14kg.* Repeat this with another problem such as: *The petrol tank of Mr Smith's car holds 60 litres and it is full. He uses 25 litres on Monday and 17 litres on Tuesday. How many litres of petrol must he put in the tank to fill it up again?* (18 litres) For paired work, provide children with a copy each of differentiated activity sheet 'How far?' and ask them to solve the problems. Encourage them to begin by reading the problem through together, then underlining any useful mathematical vocabulary. Ask them to show their working out. For the Plenary & assessment, work through the core sheet of problems using the A3 version.

Lessons   overview

Preparation
Make an OHT from CD page 'Symmetry'.

Learning objectives

Starter
- **Know by heart:** all pairs of multiples of 100 with a total of 1000 (eg 300 + 700).

Main teaching activity
- **Identify** and sketch **lines of symmetry in simple shapes, and recognise shapes with no lines of symmetry**.
- Sketch the reflection of a simple shape in a mirror line along one edge.
- Read and begin to write the vocabulary related to position, direction and movement: for example, describe and find the position of a square on a grid of squares with the rows and columns labelled.

Vocabulary
size, bigger, larger, smaller, symmetrical, line of symmetry, fold, match, mirror line, reflection

You will need:

CD pages
'Lines of symmetry' for each child; 'Symmetry' for the teacher's/LSA's reference (see General resources).

Equipment
Gym mats; small safety mirrors; OHT; whiteboards and pens; pegs and pegboards.

Lesson

For the Starter, explain to the children that you will say a hundreds number and that they are to say the number that when added to your number makes a total of 1000. Begin by saying the hundreds numbers in order: 100, 200… with the children saying the complement to make 1000, so that they hear the ascending and descending pattern of numbers, then repeat with the numbers out of order. The Main activity needs to start in the hall. Ask the children to stand in a shape with a line of symmetry down the centre of their body. *What other shapes can you make with the imaginary vertical centre line?* The children now pair up with another child and each pair has a floor mat. Can they create a mirror image of their body shape with one hand touching? Can they create mirror images that have the following criteria: One foot and one hand on the floor? Makes a long thin shape? Has a right angle? Back in class, reveal the first shape on CD page 'Symmetry'. Ask: *Where is the line of symmetry?* Write 'symmetry' onto the board and point clearly along the line. Repeat this for the next shape, checking the lines with a safety mirror. For paired work, ask the children to work in twos. Provide them each with activity sheet 'Lines of symmetry' and ask them to check carefully each picture, decide whether the shape is symmetrical, then sketch in the lines of symmetry. For the Plenary & assessment, ask the children to decide which capital letters have line/s of symmetry. Use this opportunity to check that the children can use the vocabulary of symmetry and understand that shapes can have none, one or more than one line of symmetry.

Lesson

Repeat the Starter for Lesson 4, keeping the pace really sharp. Invite the children to make patterns with pegs and pegboards where the pattern has two lines of symmetry. Discuss how to use a mirror to check this by placing it along the horizontal and vertical lines and observe the reflection of half of the shape. More able children may recognise that shapes can have diagonal lines of symmetry too. For group work ask the children to work in twos. They both sketch half a shape, such as half a robot, half a butterfly, and check with a mirror whether or not their shape has a line of symmetry. If it has then they sketch the reflection. Encourage the children to draw shapes that do have lines of symmetry. For the Plenary & assessment, invite children to draw their half of a shape on the board for others to copy and then draw the reflection.

Name   Date

Measures word problems

Write the answers to these word problems.

Show your working out.

1. A large banana weighs about 200 grams. About how many large bananas weigh
1 kilogram? [   ]

> **Working out**

2. A bottle of cough medicine holds about 100ml of medicine. How many 5 millilitre
spoonfuls can be poured from the bottle of medicine? [   ]

> **Working out**

3. Two rolls of carpet tape measure 37 metres and 56 metres long. What is their
total length? [   ]
What is the difference between their lengths? [   ]

> **Working out**

4. Dilshad went on a sponsored walk for charity. For every kilometre he walked he
earned £4. He earned £36. How many kilometres did he walk? [   ]

> **Working out**

Name	Date

How far?

Write the answers to these problems.

Show your working out.

The problem

I walk 3500m in one morning. The next day I walk twice as far.
How far have I walked altogether?

_____

A mountain is 900m high. I walk halfway and twist my ankle.

How far did I get? _____

The total distance I walk is 36km over three days. On day one I
walked 15km, and day two I walked 12km.
How far did I walk on day three?

_____

Position, angles and investigating general statements about shapes

Children explore position in square grids. They compare angles with a right angle, and learn that a straight line is equivalent to two right angles through practical activities. They investigate a general statement about shapes.

LEARNING OBJECTIVES

		Topics	Starter	Main teaching activities
Lesson	**1**	Shape and space	● Count on in steps of 3 from any small number to at least 50, then back again.	● Read and begin to write the vocabulary related to position, direction and movement: for example, describe and find the position of a square on a grid of squares with the rows and columns labelled.
Lesson	**2**	Shape and space	● Begin to know the 3 times-table.	● Recognise that a straight line is equivalent to two right angles. ● Compare angles with a right angle.
Lesson	**3**	Reasoning about numbers or shapes	● Begin to know the 3 times-table.	● Investigate a general statement about shapes by finding examples that satisfy it. ● **Explain methods and reasoning** orally and, where appropriate, in writing.

Lesson   overview

Preparation
Make an OHT of CD page 'Untidy bedroom', and an A3 poster of 'Positional vocabulary'.

Learning objectives
Starter
● Count on in steps of 3 from any small number to at least 50, then back again.
● Begin to know the 3 times-table.
Main teaching activities
● Read and begin to write the vocabulary related to position, direction and movement: for example, describe and find the position of a square on a grid of squares with the rows and columns labelled.
● Recognise that a straight line is equivalent to two right angles.
● Compare angles with a right angle.
● Investigate a general statement about shapes by finding examples that satisfy it.
● **Explain methods and reasoning** orally and, where appropriate, in writing.

Vocabulary
left, right, up, down, forwards, backwards, sideways, across, row, column, grid, right angle, straight line, angle, is a greater/smaller angle than

You will need:
CD pages
'Angles' for each child; 'Untidy bedroom' and 'Positional vocabulary' for the teacher's/LSA' reference; '2cm² squared paper' for each child (see General resources).

Equipment
Counting stick, sticky labels; tiling computer program, or shape tiles and a magnetic or felt board; a box of 2D shape tiles, including squares, rectangles and triangles for each group.

Lesson ①

Starter

Hold the counting stick horizontally and label one end 0 and the other 30. Count along it on and back in threes, asking the children to join in with you. Now point to any position on the counting stick and ask the children to say the number that goes there. Keep the pace of this sharp. Then 'wipe' your hand along the stick to 'remove' the invisible numbers, and relabel the stick 1 to 31, before repeating the activity. Then label the stick ends 2 and 32 and repeat before, finally, doing it again for 0 and 30.

Main teaching activities

Whole class: Keep the class working together today. Put up CD page 'Positional vocabulary' and ask the children to think of sentences where each word could be used.

Now show the OHT of CD page 'Untidy bedroom'. Ask the children to use first the letter and then the number to answer the questions on the OHT using the words from the 'Positional vocabulary' poster. Ask: *Where is the football? What is to the left of the stripy sock? What item is in D4? In which corner is the television? Name an item between the bed and the bin. What is next to the dirty mug?*

Paired work: Provide each child with CD page '2cm² squared paper'. Ask them to label the columns (*x*-axis) with letters and the rows (*y*-axis) with numbers. Then invite them to draw a scene on their grid. Explain that they have just five minutes to do this part of the lesson, and so they must work quickly. Now, working with a partner, one child uses their grid and asks the partner to find the position on the grid of items such as: *What is the position of the hat? What is next to the dog?*

Differentiation

Less able: If the children are unsure about the activity, prepare your own grid in front of them, draw in some items and carry out the activity as a group task.

More able: Challenge the children to work with grids of ten along and up.

Plenary & assessment

On the board draw a 3 × 3 grid and label the *x*-axis with letters and the *y*-axis with numbers. Explain to the children that you would like them to play a game of noughts and crosses, in two teams.

Appoint two team captains and ask the captains to take turns to choose someone from their team to label a square, where the captain will draw a nought or a cross. The team that wins gains a point. Repeat this several times, but remind the captain that they must ask someone different each time so that everybody has a go. This game will give you the opportunity to check that the children understand how to find the position of a square and to label it using letters and numbers.

Lesson ②

Starter

Use the counting stick again, and label one end 0 and the other 3. Now count along it with the children and, for each position, say the relevant 3 times-table fact. Do this several times, keeping a good pace to the chanting. Now point to a place on the stick and ask for the fact for where your finger is pointing and repeat the activity.

Main teaching activities

Whole class: Explain to the children that in this lesson they will be comparing right angles with other angles to see which is greater. Ask them to take a sheet of paper, fold it in half and then across into quarters, making sure that the creases are firm. Then ask the children to identify the right angle, where the paper has all the folds. Now ask them to compare their right angle with angles that they can see around them, such as the edge of their desk. *Is this a right angle?* Now ask the children to

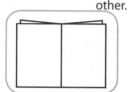

put two pieces of folded paper together so that the right angles touch, as if one is a reflection of the other. Suggest the children look at the straight edge that runs from one side of the two right angles to the other, explaining that a straight line can be seen as being the same as two right angles.

Individual work: Provide each child with a copy of the CD page 'Angles'. Ask them to use the right angle measurer that they have made from folded paper to check which angles are right angles, and which are larger/smaller than a right angle.

Differentiation

Less able: Decide whether to complete this activity as a group. Encourage the children to use the vocabulary of angles as they answer.

More able: Challenge the children to sketch some straight-line shapes and to label the angles 'L' for larger than a right angle and 'S' for smaller. They can mark the right angles with a 'R'.

Plenary & assessment

Use either a tiling computer program or some shape tiles on a magnetic or felt board. Ask the children to decide how to make a pattern with the tiles. Now reflect one of the tiles along one axis. Ask the children to describe how this changes the pattern. If there is time, the children may like to try this for themselves with shape tiles.

Lesson ③

Starter

Repeat the Starter for Lesson 2, this time including some division questions, such as: *What is 27 divided by 3?* Again, keep the pace sharp.

Main teaching activities

Whole class: Explain that today the children will be considering general statements about shapes and finding examples that fit. Ask the children to work in groups of between four and six, with a box of shape tiles in front of them. Explain that you are going to make a statement and that you would like each group to sort out their box of shapes, discarding those that do not fit the statements. Begin by saying: *The shape I am thinking of has four straight sides. All the sides are the same length. What shape is this?* (square).

Now ask: *Which shapes did you discard? Which did you keep when I said my shape has four straight sides?* (rectangles and squares) *How would you describe a rectangle?* Make a list of suggestions on the board, such as 'has four sides', 'all sides are straight', 'opposite sides are the same length' or 'all four angles are right angles'. Now say: *A square is a rectangle.* Invite the children to explain whether this is true (yes) and how they know. Ask: *Are all squares rectangles?*

Paired work: Ask the children to write some sentences that can be used to describe any triangle. Challenge them to sketch different triangles to show that their sentences are always true.

Differentiation

Less able: Work with this group, and encourage the children to use the vocabulary of shapes as they say sentences for you to scribe on the board.

More able: Ask the children to write some sentences to describe a pentagon.

Plenary & assessment

Invite children from each ability group to give examples of some of their sentences to describe triangles. Write some of these on the board and ask: *Is this always true? How can you tell?* Discuss how triangles always have three straight sides and three angles, that one of the angles could be a right angle but never two (because that would make a straight line).

Summer term
Unit 8
Multiples of 2, 5, 10, 50 and 100, and solving puzzles

Children learn to recognise two-and three-digit multiples of 2, 5 and 10, extending their understanding to include three-digit multiples of 50 and 100 by identifying the tens and units digits. They solve puzzles which involve finding sums and products, and are encouraged to record their results systematically.

LEARNING OBJECTIVES

		Topics	Starter	Main teaching activity
Lesson	1	Counting, properties of numbers and number sequences	● **Know by heart: multiplication facts for the 2, 5 and 10 times-tables.** ● Derive quickly: division facts corresponding to the 2, 5 and 10 times-tables.	● Recognise two-digit and three-digit multiples of 2, 5 and 10 and three-digit multiples of 50 and 100.
Lesson	2	As for Lesson 1.	As for Lesson 1.	As for Lesson 1.
Lesson	3	Reasoning about numbers or shapes	● Begin to know the 3 and 4 times-tables.	● Solve mathematical problems or puzzles, recognise simple patterns and relationships, generalise and predict. Suggest extensions by asking 'What if..?' ● **Explain methods and reasoning** orally and, where appropriate, in writing.
Lesson	4	As for Lesson 3.	As for Lesson 3.	As for Lesson 3.
Lesson	5	As for Lesson 3.	As for Lesson 3.	As for Lesson 3.

Lessons   overview

Preparation
Have ready the 0 to 9 cards from CD page 'Numeral cards for 0 to 20' and make enough sets for three sets per group of four children.

Learning objectives
Starter
● **Know by heart: multiplication facts for the 2, 5 and 10 times-tables.**
● Derive quickly: division facts corresponding to the 2, 5 and 10 times-tables.
Main teaching activity
● Recognise two-digit and three-digit multiples of 2, 5 and 10 and three-digit multiples of 50 and 100.

Vocabulary
how many times? count up to, two-digit, three-digit, multiples, pattern

You will need:
Photocopiable pages
'Multiples' (page 197) for each child.

CD pages
'Multiplication facts for 2, 5 and 10 times-tables' and 'Numeral cards for 0 to 20' (Autumn term) for the teacher's/LSA's reference; 'Multiples' less able and more able versions (Summer term, Unit 8) (see General resources).

Equipment
Individual whiteboards and pens.

Lesson

Starter
Using the cards from CD page 'Multiplication facts for 2, 5 and 10 times-tables', explain that you will call out a multiplication question and ask the children to say the answer quietly when you hold up your hand. Allow about five seconds of thinking time, then hold up your hand. This will keep the pace sharp.

Main teaching activities

Whole class: Explain to the children that today they will be learning about how to recognise two-digit multiples of 2, 5 and 10. Ask: *What is the last digit of a multiple of 10? Is it always a zero? Give me some examples of a multiple of 10.* Confirm that a multiple of 10 always has a zero as its unit digit. Write this on the board: 'Multiples of 10 end in 0'.

Now ask: *What could the last digit in a multiple of 5 be?* Agree that it will either be 0 or 5. Challenge the children to explain when it will be a 5 (when the multiple is odd, such as $7 \times 5 = 35$) and when it will be a 0 (when the multiple is even, such as $8 \times 5 = 40$). Write on the board: 'Multiples of 5 end in 0 or 5'. Now ask: *What could the last digit in a multiple of 2 be?* Confirm that these are 0, 2, 4, 6 or 8 and write on the board: 'Multiples of 2 end in 0, 2, 4, 6 or 8'.

Ask the children to begin to count from 0 to 100. Explain that if the number that they should say is a multiple of 2, they nod their head; if it is a multiple of 5, they stamp their feet; and if it is a multiple of 10, they stand up then sit down. This needs concentration!

Now invite the children to give three-digit examples of multiples of 2, 5 and 10, such as 104, and 260. **Group work:** Ask the children to work in groups of four with three sets of 0 to 9 cards. Ask them to shuffle the cards, then place them into a stack, face down. Each child takes three cards and makes as many three-digit numbers as they can that are a multiple of 2, 5 or 10. For each multiple made they gain a point. If a child has not made a multiple, but another child can see that by rearranging the digits they could make a multiple, then that child gains that point. For some selections it will be impossible to make a multiple of 2, 5 or 10, such as the cards 1, 3 and 7. Ask each child to record the three-digit numbers that they made and to give it a point if it is a multiple of 2, 5 or 10. At the end of ten turns, they count up the points to see who has won.

Differentiation

Less able: Decide whether to ask the children to play the same game, but make two-digit numbers.
More able: Challenge the children to play the game again, this time choosing four cards each time. The object is to make as many three-digit numbers which are multiples of 2, 5 or 10 as they can from each choice of four digits. The winner of each round this time is the child who makes the most multiples.

Plenary & assessment

Write on the board 1, 6 and 9 and ask: *Which three-digit numbers can I make with these digits? Which are multiples of 2? Will there be any multiples of 5? 10? Can you answer this just by looking at the digits? So what digits would we need to make multiples of 5 and 10?* (5 and/or 0) Repeat this for another three digits, before asking the children to write down any three digits that will give them a multiple of 5. Ask them to repeat this for multiples of 10, then of 2.

Lesson ②

Starter

Repeat the Starter from Lesson 1, but this time say a division fact. For example, for 6×5 ask: *What is 30 divided by 5?* Allow slightly more thinking time for this so that the children have time to derive the division fact from a multiplication one that they know.

Main teaching activities

Whole class: Explain that today the children will recognise three-digit multiples of 50 and 100. Ask: *What if the number has three digits? What would the last two digits be in a multiple of 100?* Write on the board: 'Multiples of 100 end in 00'. Repeat this for multiples of 50 and write on the board: 'Multiples of 50 end in 50 or 00'. Ask the children to give examples of multiples of 100 and of 50 to demonstrate that these statements are true. Ask the children to count on and back in fifties from 0 to 1000. Keep the pace of this count sharp. Now ask the children to write three multiples of 50 on their whiteboards, and to hold up their boards when you say *Show me!*

Individual work: Provide each child with a copy of activity sheet 'Multiples' and ask them to complete the activities. This covers work in Lessons 1 and 2 of this unit, and uses both two- and three-digit numbers.

Differentiation
Less able: Decide whether to use the version of the sheet which covers multiples of 2, 5 and 10 of TU numbers only.
More able: There is a version of the sheet available which includes three-digit numbers only and more challenging questions.

Plenary & assessment
Invite the children to say the rules for spotting multiples of 2, 5, 10, 50 and 100. Then say: *Write down three different three-digit multiples of 2, 5 and 10. Write down a three-digit number that is both a multiple of 5 and of 10. What else can you tell me about your number?* (It is also a multiple of 2 because the number will have 0 as its unit digit.) *Write down three different three-digit multiples of 50. Now what can you tell me about the multiples of 1000?* (It is a multiple of 50, 100 and 2. Some may know that it is a multiple of 4 also.)

Lessons overview

Preparation
Make an OHT of CD page 'Hairyonymus'.

Learning objectives
Starter
- Begin to know the 3 and 4 times-tables.

Main teaching activity
- Solve mathematical problems or puzzles, recognise simple patterns and relationships, generalise and predict. Suggest extensions by asking 'What if…?'
- **Explain methods and reasoning** orally and, where appropriate, in writing.

You will need:
CD pages
'Hairyonymus' for the teacher's/LSA's reference (see General resources).

Equipment
Counting stick; OHP; drinking straws.

Vocabulary
sum, product, total, difference, multiple, consecutive

Lesson

Starter
Say together the facts for the 3 times-table: 0 multiplied by/times 3 is 0; 1 multiplied by/times 3 is 3 and so on. Then ask the children questions about the 3 times-table, such as: *What is 8 multiplied by 3? What is 9 multiplied by 3?* Keep the pace sharp and encourage the children to begin to 'know' these facts by praising those with good recall.

Main teaching activities
Whole class: Explain that today, and during the following two lessons, the children will be solving number-based puzzles. Check that they understand the terminology of 'sum' and 'product' by asking them to think of a pair of numbers that have a sum of 19 and a product of 90. (10 and 9) Discuss the strategies that the children used to find the solution. Explain that it is useful to make jottings when finding solutions to puzzles and problems, because it helps you to remember what you have tried, what worked, and what did not.

Work through the following examples with the children.
Find a pair of numbers with: a sum of 10 and a product of 25 (5, 5); *a sum of 16 and a product of 60* (10, 6); *a sum of 12 and a product of 32* (8, 4).

Using the same products change the examples so they now read: *Find a pair of numbers with: a difference of 0 and a product of 25* (5 and 5); *a difference of 4 and a product of 60* (10 and 6); *a difference of 4 and a product of 32* (8 and 4).

Ask the children to consider whether these are possible. *A pair of numbers with: a sum of 1 and a product of 5* (No); *a sum of 0 and a product of 9* (No); *a difference of 0 and a product of 9.* (Yes: 3, 3) In each instance, ask the children for a clear example to show whether it is possible or not.
Paired work: Ask pairs of children to try an example you write on the board: *If the sum of a pair of numbers is 7, how many different products can you find?* (1 × 6, 2 × 5 and 3 × 4) Now ask them to think of another example and find how many products they can find for that.

Differentiation

Less able: Decide whether to work as a group. Encourage the children to discuss how they can work out some solutions and how they would record these. Then continue with the first investigation by extending it to: *If a sum of a pair of numbers is 10, how many different products can you find?* (1 × 9, 2 × 8, 3 × 7, 4 × 6, 5 × 5). Discuss any patterns that the children can see.
More able: Challenge the children to try several different sums, using small numbers.

Plenary & assessment

Review the children's findings for the sum of 7 example. Ask: *What pattern did you spot?* Check that the children understood that they could use the multiples of 1 and 6, 2 and 5, and so on, and that if ordered it is easier to spot if any products are missing.

Lesson

For the Starter. label the ends of a counting stick 0 and 40 and count along it in fours several times, then point to different positions on the stick and ask the children to name the number. Now repeat the counting along the stick, this time saying the 4 times-table facts aloud. Then point to different positions on the stick and ask the children to say the 4 times-table multiplication fact that belongs at that point. For the Main activity, write a puzzle on the board: *Using 2, 4 and 5, and the signs +, × and =, how many different answers can you make?* Invite the children to suggest how to begin the puzzle. Remind them that they may use the 2, 4 and 5 as many times as they need. Give the children about five minutes to try this, working in pairs. Then invite the children to feed back their results to the whole class. Discuss the importance of being systematic when approaching a problem. Remind the class that by recording everything that they try, even if it does not give the answer that they need, they will have a record of what has been tried, what worked, and what did not, so that they can spot patterns in their record. Show the OHT CD page 'Hairyonymus'. Ask the children to try this puzzle, working systematically in pairs. For the Plenary & assessment, review the day's learning. Write up the activity sheet findings in order as number sentences. For example: 2 + 2 + 2 + 2 + 2 + 5 = 15; 5 + 5 + 5 = 15; 5 + 10 = 15. Ask: *Is there any other combination that we could try? What other combinations could we have for the Hairyonymus babies? Why is this the only combination?* (We need to make a 5 or 10 in order to add to the teenager's or adult's hair.) Discuss how the children went about finding solutions and how they recorded these. Praise those who worked in a systematic way.

Lesson ⑤

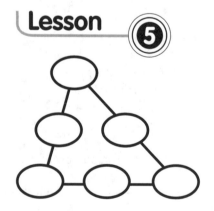

Repeat the Starter for Lesson 4, this time concentrating on using the counting stick to generate the 4 times-table facts. Draw a triangle with six circles. Ask the children to decide how to put the numbers 1 to 6 into the circles so that each side of the triangle totals 9. For their paired work, ask them to try the triangle totals again, this time making totals of 10, then 11, then 12. During the Plenary & assessment, review what the children did, and discuss how they recorded their work.

Name   Date

Multiples

1. Join the multiples of 2 to their label.

2. Join the multiples of 5 to their label.

3. Join the multiples of 10 to their label.

4. Now ring the numbers that are both a multiple of 5 and a multiple of 10.

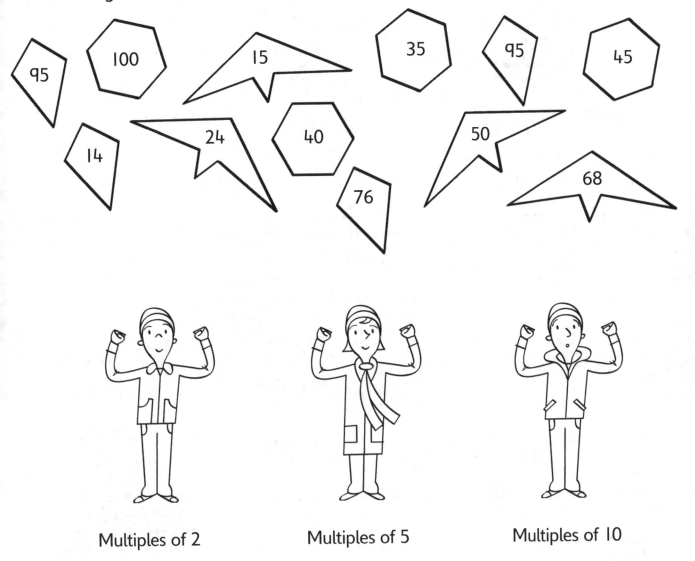

Multiples of 2   Multiples of 5   Multiples of 10

Now write the answers to these.

1. Write the multiple of 10 that comes before 130.

2. Write the next multiple of 5 that comes after 295.

3. Write three different multiples of 50.

4. Write three different multiples of 100.

Finding remainders and solving word problems

Children find remainders after division, firstly through practical activities which model the division, then through mental calculations. They learn to round up or down when appropriate, and use these skills when solving word problems.

LEARNING OBJECTIVES

	Topics	Starter	Main teaching activity
Lesson 1	Understanding multiplication and division	Derive quickly: doubles of multiples of 5 to 100 (eg 75 × 2, 90 × 2); and all the corresponding halves (eg half of 130).	Begin to find remainders after simple division.
Lesson 2	Understanding multiplication and division	As for Lesson 1.	As for Lesson 1.
Lesson 3	Understanding multiplication and division Problems involving 'real life, money and measures	As for Lesson 1.	Begin to find remainders after simple division. Round up or down after division, depending on the context. Solve word problems involving numbers in 'real life', using one or more steps. Explain how the problem was solved.
Lesson 4	Understanding multiplication and division Problems involving 'real life, money and measures	Derive quickly: doubles of multiples of 50 to 500 (eg 450 × 2); and all the corresponding halves (eg 900 ÷ 2).	As for Lesson 3.
Lesson 5	As for Lesson 4.	As for Lesson 4.	As for Lesson 4.

Lessons overview

Preparation
Make and A3 enlargement of the core activity sheet 'Rounding up and down'. Make an OHT of CD page 'Two-step problems'.

Learning objectives
Starter
● Derive quickly: doubles of multiples of 5 to 100 (eg 75 × 2, 90 × 2); and all the corresponding halves (eg half of 130).
● Derive quickly: doubles of multiples of 50 to 500 (eg 450 × 2); and all the corresponding halves (eg 900 ÷ 2).
Main teaching activity
● Begin to find remainders after simple division.
● Round up or down after division, depending on the context.
● Solve word problems involving numbers in 'real life', using one or more steps.
● Explain how the problem was solved.

Vocabulary
remainder, divide, divided by, divided into, left, left over, equal groups of

You will need:
Photocopiable pages
'Remainders' (page 202) and 'Rounding up and down' (page 203) for each child.

CD pages
'Remainders' and 'Rounding up and down' less able and more able versions (Summer term, Unit 9); 'Two-step problems' for the teacher'/LSA's reference (see General resources).

Equipment
Interlocking cubes or counters; OHP.

Lesson

Starter

Explain that you will say a multiple of 5 and that you would like the children to calculate its double. Say smaller multiples of 5, such as 5, 10, 15… up to about 50. Ask: *How did you work that out? If it is a double of a multiple of 5, what will its unit digit be?* (0) *How did you work that out?*

Main teaching activities

Whole class: Prompt the children to work in pairs with some counting apparatus, such as cubes or counters. Ask the children to count out 15 cubes. Now ask them to share them equally between them. Ask: *Do you both have the same amount of cubes? How many do you each have? Have all the cubes been used?* No. *You have one left over, or remainder 1.* Write '15 ÷ 2 = 7 remainder 1' on the board. Now ask the children to use their cube again, this time dividing the 15 cubes by 3, 4 and 5. Write the results on the board in the same way. Discuss how 15 comes in both the 3 and 5 times-tables: 3 × 5 = 15 and 5 × 3 = 15. Explain that when dividing, children will find that where there *is* a multiplication fact for the numbers, there will be no remainder. When there is *no* multiplication fact, they should look for the nearest fact which is less, and then count up to find the remainder. For example, for 18 ÷ 4, the nearest lower fact is 4 × 4 = 16, so 18 ÷ 4 = 4 remainder 2.

Ask the children now to work mentally to complete some divisions, some of which have remainders, and some of which do not, such as: 12 ÷ 3, 12 ÷ 5, 17 ÷ 5 and 17 ÷ 3.

Paired work: Ask the children to work in pairs, using the multiplication tables for 2, 3, 4, 5 and 10, to divide into the numbers 16, 19, 25 and 34, which can be written on the board. Ask them to write their answers as a division sentence and, where there is a remainder, to write this, too.

Differentiation

Less able: Decide whether to work with these children as a group. Concentrate on multiplication table facts with which the children are confident, such as 2, 5 and 10. Encourage this group to say each division as a sentence, using the vocabulary of division.

More able: Challenge this group to try to divide the numbers on the board by 6 and 8. They will need to think about doubles.

Plenary and division

Choose one of the numbers on the board. Ask the children to take turns to write up one of their division facts, such as 16 ÷ 2 = 8 or 16 ÷ 3 = 5 remainder 1. Discuss how they worked out their answers. Repeat this for the other numbers on the board so that the children can mark their own work. Now ask: *What would 75 divided by 10 be? How did you work out that 75 divided by 10 is 7 remainder 5?* Repeat this for another division and check who has understood, and who will need more practice, from the answers that you receive.

Lesson

Starter

Repeat the Starter from Lesson 1, this time using the multiples of 5 from 50 to 100.

Main teaching activities

Whole class: Ask the children to think of numbers that can be divided by 2 with no remainder. Ask: *What have the numbers in common?* (They are multiples of 2 and are even.) Now ask the same for dividing by 3, 4, 5 and 10. Say: *Tell me some numbers that will always have a remainder when divided by any of 2, 3, 4, 5 and 10.* (For example, 11, 13, 17 and so on.)

Now write on the board: $43 = 10 \times 4 + \square$. Ask: *How can we work out the missing number?* Discuss how 10×4 is 40, so 3 more will be needed to make 43. Write up further examples, such as $54 = 10 \times 5 + \square$. Ask the children to suggest an answer, and to explain how they worked this out.
Individual work: Ask the children to complete the activity sheet 'Remainders', which summarises the work from Lessons 1 and 2.

Differentiation

Less able: Decide whether to use the version of the sheet 'Remainders' which concentrates on facts from the 2, 5 and 10 times-tables.
More able: There is a version of the activity sheet which includes some facts from the 6 and 8 times-tables.

Plenary & assessment

Put the children into two teams, each with a captain. The captain's job is to choose a team member to answer the question (each child can go only once, so all have a turn) and to keep the score on the board. Explain that you will say a division sentence, and that you want the children to give the answer and, where there is one, the remainder. Ask them to say a complete sentence such as '36 divided by 5 is 7 remainder 1'. Use table facts that they know, such as those from the 2, 3, 4, 5 and 10 times-tables. This will give you an opportunity to check who has understood the concept of division and remainders, and who needs further help.

Lesson

Starter

Ask the children to derive the half fact for doubles of multiples of 5 to 100. Ask: *What is half of 200? What is 150 divided by 2?* Allow some thinking time so that the majority of the children have calculated the answer.

Main teaching activities

Whole class: Explain that in today's lesson the children will solve division problems and decide whether to round up or down. Say: *I have 23 cakes. The cake boxes hold 4 cakes each. How many boxes do I need for my cakes?* Discuss how 23 divided by 4 is 5 remainder 3, but that all the cakes must go into boxes, so the three cakes left over also need a box. So, in this case, the answer rounds up to six boxes.

Repeat with: *I have 37 cakes. The cake boxes each hold 4 cakes. How many boxes can I fill?* Discuss how $37 \div 4 = 9$ r1. So nine boxes can be filled, and that this is an example of rounding down.
Individual work: Provide the activity sheet 'Rounding up and down'. Ask the children to read each problem, write a division sentence and then decide whether to round up or down. They write the new answer.

Differentiation

Less able: There is a version of 'Rounding up and down' which uses just the 2, 5 and 10 times-table facts.
More able: There is a more challenging version of 'Rounding up and down' which also includes the 6 and 8 times-tables.

Plenary & assessment

Using the enlarged core version of 'Rounding up and down', review the problems with the children. Invite them to explain how they solved each question, whether they needed to round up or down, and why they made that decision.

Lesson ④

Starter
Explain that you would like the children to find the doubles of multiples of 50 to 500. Remind them that they have just practised doubling and halving for multiples of 5. Ask questions such as: *What is double 50? What will its last two digits be? How do you know that?* Repeat for other doubles such as: double 100, 350 and 400.

Main teaching activities
Whole class: Explain that this and the next lesson will be about solving problems. Say to the children: *I think of a number, double it and add 6. The answer is 66. What was my number?* (30) Invite the children to explain how they worked this out. Discuss how this problem is a two-step problem. Write on the board: 66 – 6 = 60. Half of 60 is 30.

Now ask the children to solve this problem: *I think of a number, halve it and subtract 3. The answer is 17. What was my number?* (40) Encourage the children to work with a partner to solve this, and to make jottings of what they did. Invite a pair of children to write up their jottings and solution on the board. Suggest the rest of the class say whether they solved the problem in the same way.

Individual work: Ask the children to solve similar problems from CD page 'Two-step problems'. Show these using the OHT. Ask the children to decide to record their work with jottings, and to write the answer as a sentence. This will encourage the children to work independently of a pre-formatted activity sheet.

Differentiation
Less able: Decide whether to work as a group to solve these problems. Encourage the children to make jottings, and to read their jottings back to you for you to check whether they are suitable.
More able: Challenge this group to make up some similar problems for themselves and to swap these with a partner's problems. They solve each other's problems.

Plenary & assessment
Using the OHT 'Two-step problems', review each problem in turn, and how the children responded to it. Discuss the types of jottings that the children made, and how useful these have been. Encourage the children to read out their answer sentences. Discuss the vocabulary used in these, and check that the children are using the vocabulary of multiplication, division, remainders and rounding appropriately. If the more able children have invented some problems of their own, ask them to share these with the whole class.

Lesson ⑤

Repeat the Starter from Lesson 4, this time asking for halves of 500, 600, 700, 800, 900 and 1000. Remind the children of the importance of making jottings if they cannot immediately see the answer to a problem. Ask them to solve this problem: *There are 64 chocolates in a box. If I put 10 chocolates on a plate, how many plates do I need to put out all the chocolates?* Discuss how this is a problem which will need rounding up and work through to the solution as a class. Ask the children to solve the problems on activity sheet 'The greengrocers'. This is available in differentiated versions. During the Plenary & assessment, invite children from each ability group to read out one of their problems from the sheet, and to explain how they solved it. Discuss rounding up and down to solve the problem.

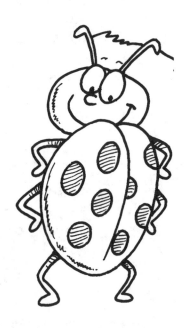

| Name | Date |

Remainders

Write the answers to these questions.

1. $16 \div 5 =$

2. $25 \div 4 =$

3. $36 \div 10 =$

4. $48 \div 5 =$

5. $31 \div 2 =$

6. $64 \div 10 =$

7. $28 \div 3 =$

8. $17 \div 3 =$

9. $84 \div 10 =$

10. $34 \div 4 =$

Now write in the missing numbers.

1. $45 = 10 \times 4 +$

2. $63 = 6 \times 10 +$

3. $18 = 4 \times 4 +$

4. $26 = 5 \times 5 +$

5. $31 = 10 \times 3 +$

| Name | Date |

Rounding up and down

Read these problems.

Write a division sentence to show your thinking.

Then decide whether you need to round the answer up or down.

Write the new answer.

Problem	Division sentence	Answer
35 children from class 3 are going to a party. They will travel there in cars. Each car will hold 4 passengers. How many cars will be needed?		
At the party, there are 42 children in all. The tables for party food each seat 5 children. How many tables are needed?		
There are 54 cakes in a box. If each plate will hold 10 cakes, how many plates can be filled with cakes?		
At home time, 42 children go home by minibus. 5 minibuses are ordered, and 4 of them are full. How many children go in each minibus?		

Using mental calculation strategies for multiplication and division

Children develop their understanding and ability to use calculation strategies, such as multiplying and dividing by 10 and 100. They solve money word problems and explain their methods and reasoning. They solve money problems and explain their methods and reasoning.

LEARNING OBJECTIVES

	Topics	Starter	Main teaching activity
Lesson 1	Mental calculation strategies (× and ÷)	● Begin to know the 3 and 4 times-tables.	● Use known number facts and place value to carry out mentally simple multiplications and divisions.
Lesson 2	As for Lesson 1.	As for Lesson 1.	As for Lesson 1.
Lesson 3	As for Lesson 1.	As for Lesson 1.	As for Lesson 1.
Lesson 4	Problems involving 'real life', money and measures Reasoning about numbers or shapes	● Say or write a division statement corresponding to a given multiplication fact.	● Solve word problems involving numbers in 'real life', money and measures, using one or more steps, including finding totals and giving change, and working out which coins to pay. ● Explain how the problem was solved. ● **Explain methods and reasoning** orally, and where appropriate, in writing.
Lesson 5	As for Lesson 4.	As for Lesson 4.	As for Lesson 4.

Lessons overview

Preparation
Make an OHT of 'Multiply and divide by 10 and 100'.

Learning objectives
Starter
● Begin to know the 3 and 4 times-tables.
Main teaching activities
● Use known number facts and place value to carry out mentally simple multiplications and divisions.

Vocabulary
product, multiply, multiplied by, multiple of, share, divide, divided by, divided into, left, left over, remainder

You will need:
Photocopiable pages
'Multiply and divide by 10 and 100' (page 207) and 'Multiplying and dividing' (page 208) for each child.

CD pages
'Multiply and divide by 10' less able version and 'Multiply and divide by 10 and 100' more able version; and 'Multiplying and dividing' less able and more able versions (Summer term, Unit 10) (see General resources).

Equipment
Counting stick; OHP.

Lesson ①

Starter
Label one end of the counting stick 0 and the other end 30, and count along it, forwards and back. Now ask the children to say a 'divided by 3' statement for each position on the stick, beginning at '0': 0 divided by 3 is 0, 3 divided by 3 is 1; 6 divided by 3 is 2 and so on. Do this several times.

Main teaching activities
Whole class: Explain that for this, and the following two lessons, the children will be using what they know to multiply and divide. Write on the board: $8 \times 10 = \square$ and ask for an answer. Repeat this for 9×100. Discuss how the digits move along one place to the left when multiplying by 10, and two places when multiplying by 100.

Now write up $500 \div 10$ and invite an answer. Discuss what happens to the digits, eliciting that this time they shift one place to the right. Repeat this for $700 \div 100$, and discuss how here the digits shift two places to the right.

Paired work: Ask the children to work in pairs with activity sheet 'Multiply and divide by 10 and 100', in which they play a simple game to practise multiplication.

Differentiation
Less able: Use the activity sheet which concentrates on multiplication and division by 10.
More able: This activity sheet requires the children to think about strategies as they play the game.

Plenary & assessment
Play the game again as a class using an OHT of the core version of 'Multiply and divide by 10 and 100'. The children can be divided into two teams with captains who decide who chooses a number and multiply/divide. A different child should be chosen each time so that everybody has a go.

Lesson ②

Repeat the Starter from Lesson 1, this time for division by 4, asking questions such as: *What is 36 divided by 4?* Write on the board 30×2 and ask for an answer before repeating for multiples of 5 up to 50. Now ask: *What is half of 80? 70? 90? How did you work this out?* For the Main activity, explain that you would like the children to use their knowledge of the 2, 3, 4 and 5 times-tables to multiply 10, 20, 30 40 or 50. Write up $2 \times 3 =$, ask for the answer and note it down. Repeat for $20 \times 3 =$. Repeat for other examples. Ask: *What is one-third of 30? One-fifth of 50? One-tenth of 100? How did you work that out?* Write on the board the multiples of 10 to 50. Underneath write ×2, ×3, ×4, ×5, ×10. Ask the children to write out the results of multiplying each of the multiples of 10 by 2, 3, 4, 5 and 10. For the Plenary & assessment, ask questions such as: *What is 700 divided by 100? What is one-hundredth of 300? What is one-tenth of 50? 800? What is double 25? 45? What is half of 80? 50? What is a quarter of 40?*

Lesson ③

Repeat the Starters from Lessons 1 and 2, so that the children derive both sets of division facts for 3 and 4 times-table facts. Write on the board 20×2 and ask for an answer. Now write 3×2 and repeat. Write up 23×2 and ask: *How can we work this out?* Children may suggest combining the two previous answers. Repeat for other examples, such as 31×3, 42×2, 22×4, 11×5. Provide copies of differentiated activity sheet 'Multiplying and dividing' and ask the children to work individually to write the answers. For the Plenary & assessment, invite the children to take turns to choose one of the questions from their sheet and explain to the others how they calculated their answer.

Lessons ④ ⑤ overview

Learning objectives

Starter
- Say or write division a statement corresponding to a given multiplication fact.
- **Know by heart:** all pairs of multiples of 100 with a total of 1000.

Main teaching activities
- Solve word problems involving numbers in 'real life', money and measures, using one or more steps, including finding totals and giving change, and working out which coins to pay.
- Explain how the problem was solved.
- **Explain methods and reasoning** orally, and where appropriate, in writing.

Vocabulary
money, total, amount, value, spend, pay, change, mental calculation, jotting, answer, number sentence

You will need:
Equipment
Whiteboards and pens; pots of mixed coins; pots of mixed coins and mixed notes.

Lesson ④

Starter
Say a multiplication fact, such as 4 × 5. Ask the children to work in pairs to write the two multiplication facts and two division facts, with answers, from your starting point. Use the 2, 3, 4, 5 and 10 times-tables.

Main teaching activities
Whole class: Explain that today and in the next lesson the children will be solving money problems. Begin with an investigation. Ask the children to use the pots of money on their tables and, working in groups, to decide what different amounts of money they can make if they choose two silver coins each time. Give the children about five minutes to do this. Invite a response from each group and write these on the board. Ask: *How did you find your solutions?*

Paired work: Ask the children to work in pairs. Set the challenge: *How many different amounts can you make with four silver coins?* Ask the children to record their work and remind them that it will be an advantage to them if they think about doing this systematically.

Differentiation
Less able: Decide whether to ask the children to use just three silver coins each time.
More able: Challenge the children to work with five silver coins each time.

Plenary & assessment
Invite the children from the core group to feed back their results. Write these on the board, ordering them so that only one coin changes each time. Discuss the patterns of results that are revealed.

Lesson ⑤

200

For the Starter, ask the children to say the complement of the hundreds number that you say which makes a total of 1000. For example, if you say 300 they say 700. Keep the pace of this sharp. Set another challenge during the Main teaching activity. Ask: *If I buy a toy which costs 36p and use two silver coins to pay for this, what change might I get?* Write similar problems on the board and ask the children to work through them in pairs. Provide pots of coins and notes where children would find these useful. During the Plenary & assessment review the responses to the problems, and discuss the jottings that the children made and how these were useful in solving the problem.

Name   Date

Multiply and divide by 10 and 100

Play this game with a friend.

You will need some counters in two colours.

Take turns to choose a number from the grid. Then decide whether to multiply or divide your number by 10 or 100.

Say your answer.

If your friend agrees, cover your answer on the grid with a counter.

The winner is the one with the most counters on the grid when all the numbers have been covered.

1	2	3	4	5	6	7
8	9	10	20	30	40	50
60	70	80	90	100	200	300
400	500	600	700	800	900	1000

Name	Date

Multiplying and dividing

Write the answers to these questions.

1. 6 × 10 = ☐

2. 5 × 100 = ☐

3. 6 × ☐ = 600

4. 7 × ☐ = 70

5. 700 ÷ 100 = ☐

6. 400 ÷ 10 = ☐

7. What is one tenth of 90? ☐

8. What is one hundredth of 300? ☐

9. What is double 45? ☐

10. ☐ × 2 = 70

11. 90 ÷ 2 = ☐

12. ☐ ÷ 2 = 40

13. 60 × 2 = ☐

14. 20 × ☐ = 100

15. 33 × 3 = ☐

16. 13 × ☐ = 26

17. What is 11 multiplied by 5? ☐

18. What is 24 multiplied by 2? ☐

19. What is 12 multiplied by to make 24? ☐

20. What is 100 divided by to make 10? ☐

Fractions

Children learn about placing fractions onto a number line, and how to make comparisons between them. They recognise the position of common fractions on the number line, and state which is greater or smaller than given fractions. They estimate simple fractions of quantities and measures.

LEARNING OBJECTIVES

	Topics	Starter	Main teaching activity
Lesson 1	Fractions	● **Read and write whole numbers to at least 1000** in figures and words.	● Compare familiar fractions: for example, know that on the number line one half lies between one quarter and three quarters.
Lesson 2	Fractions	As for Lesson 1.	As for Lesson 1.
Lesson 3	Fractions	● **Count on or back in tens or hundreds, starting from any two- or three-digit number.**	As for Lesson 1.
Lesson 4	Fractions	As for Lesson 1.	● Estimate a simple fraction.
Lesson 5	Fractions	● **Round any two-digit number to the nearest 10 and any three-digit number to the nearest 100.**	As for Lesson 4.

Lessons overview

Preparation
Make OHTs of CD pages 'Fraction number lines', 'Fraction cards', 'Estimates' and 'Fraction shapes.' Cut out the fraction cards.

Learning objectives
Starter
● **Read and write whole numbers to at least 1000** in figures and words.
● **Count on or back in tens or hundreds, starting from any two- or three-digit number.**
● Round any two-digit number to the nearest 10 and any three-digit number to the nearest 100.

Main teaching activity
● Compare familiar fractions: for example, know that on the number line one half lies between one quarter and three quarters.
● Estimate a simple fraction.

Vocabulary
part, equal parts, fractions, approximately, one whole, one-half, one-quarter, one-third, two-thirds, one-tenth

You will need:
Photocopiable pages
'Fraction estimate' (see page 213) for each child.

CD pages
'Fraction cards', 'Fraction shapes', 'Estimates' and 'Number lines' for the teacher's/LSA's reference, and 'Fraction number lines' for the teacher's/LSA's reference and for each child (Autumn term); 'Fraction estimate' less able and more able versions (Summer term, Unit 11) (see General resources).

Equipment
Individual whiteboards and pens; OHP; coloured OHP pens; large sheets of paper; coloured pencils; metre rules marked in centimetres; counting stick; counters.

Lesson ①

Starter

Explain that you will say a number. Ask the children to write it in numerals on their whiteboards. When you say *Show me*, the children hold up their boards. Say, for example: 132, 246, 987, 205, 440 and 900.

Main teaching activities

Whole class: Explain that the work for this unit is on fractions and that in this lesson the children will be placing fractions on a number line. Show the OHT 'Fraction number lines' and write on one number line 0 at the beginning and 1 at the end. Point to the mid-point of the line and ask: *What fraction is this?* Agree that it is 1/2 and place that fraction card in place. Place the other fraction cards from CD page 'Fraction cards' around the edge of the OHT so that the children can see what these are. Ask: *What other cards could go here?* Praise those who suggest 2/4 and 5/10 and ask for explanations of why these are correct. Place the fifth cards and tenth cards.

Mark a second number line from 3 to 4 and ask: *What number is halfway between 3 and 4?* Write in 3 1/2 . Point to other positions on the line and ask the children to say which fraction would go there. Draw a line on the board and ask the children to help you to put in all the fractions of halves and quarters from 0 to 10. Do this systematically: 0, 1/4, 1/2, 3/4, 1, 1 1/2… 10. When the line is complete, read it forwards and backwards several times until the children are confident. Cover the line over with some large sheets of paper and ask questions such as: *What number is halfway between 5 and 6? What is between 4 1/2 and 5? Tell me any number between 8 and 9.* Write down the children's responses, then uncover the line so that they can check that the answers are true.

Paired work: Provide each pair with a copy of CD page 'Fraction cards'. Ask the children to cut out the cards and to place them, shuffled, in a pile. They take turns to take a card and place the cards in front of them. The object is to work together to make a fraction line for halves, quarters, fifths and tenths, placing the fractions in order.

Differentiation

Less able: Decide whether to work as a group so that all the children work together to decide where the cards should go. Encourage them to read each card and say where it belongs in the line.
More able: Challenge the children to make their own fraction line, using a copy of CD page 'Fraction number lines'. They can decide which set of fractions they would like to use.

Plenary & assessment

Using the OHT 'Fraction number lines', invite a child to write in the fractions for halves on the first line. Agree that the start is 0, 1/2 is at the mid-point, and 1 is at the far end. Repeat this for tenths and fifths. Now discuss quarters. Explain that there are only four quarters in a whole, so that the children will need to look at the mid-point between 0 and 1/2 for 1/4 and the mid-point between 1/2 and 1 for 3/4.

Lesson ②

Repeat the Starter from Lesson 1, but ask the children to write the numbers in words. Include some more difficult numbers such as 408 or 560, as well as numbers such as 562 or 149. For the Main activity, show CD page 'Fraction shapes', with all but the top shape covered. Ask the children to count how many squares make up this shape (10). Now invite a child to colour in quickly 1/10 of the shape. Repeat this for 1/5 using a different colour. Now ask a child to colour in half of the shape, using a different colour again. Ask: *How many squares will you need to colour? So what fraction has been coloured? What fraction is not coloured?* (1/5) Repeat this for another shape. For individual work, ask the children to draw a row of 20 squares, and to colour it as follows: *Twice as much of one colour as another; A maximum of four colours; One-tenth one colour; One-fifth another colour.* For the Plenary & assessment, invite children to explain how they coloured each row of 20 squares. Ask: *Which fraction*

did you colour first? Was it helpful to follow the instructions in order, or not? In what order did you colour the squares? Was that a good choice? Why/why not?

Lesson 3

Starter
Ask the children to count together, in tens or hundreds from any two- or three-digit number that you say. Say, for example: *Count on in tens from 63. Stop. Now count back in tens.* Repeat this for other starting numbers, and then for counting in hundreds.

Main teaching activities
Whole class: Explain that today, you would like the children to compare two fractions and to say which is greater and which is less. Using the OHT 'Fraction number lines', invite a child to mark on the line 0 and 1 at the two ends, and then the position of 1/2. Invite another child to mark on 1/4. If necessary, remind the children that this will come mid-way between the points of 2/10 and 3/10. Now ask: *Which is greater: 1/2 or 1/4? How can you tell?* Repeat this for other fractions, such as 3/4, and ask the children to describe its position on the number line in terms of halves and wholes.
Paired work: Ask the children to work in pairs. They will need copies of CD page 'Fraction number lines' and ten counters. Ask the children to take turns to take some of the counters, and to write onto the number line what fraction they have. They also mark in the fraction that is left. They then say which fraction is the greater. Encourage the children to use equivalent fractions, such as 5/10 and 1/2, wherever possible.

Differentiation
Less able: Decide whether to ask the children to work in tenths.
More able: Challenge the children to draw their own fraction number lines, and to work with 12 counters. This will mean that they can work in twelfths, sixths, quarters and halves.

Plenary & assessment
Review together some of the fractions that the children made. Discuss how these can be put into simpler, equivalent forms, where appropriate. Draw an empty number line on the board and encourage the children to place their fractions appropriately.

Lesson 4

Starter
Repeat the Starter from Lesson 3, this time start by counting back from a three-digit number until you say Stop, then forward again. Repeat this, asking the children to count around the class, until you say Stop, then forward again.

Main teaching activities
Whole class: Show the OHT of CD page 'Estimates'. Ask the children to estimate what time the first clock shows. If children respond with an answer such as 2.28, ask them to estimate to the nearest quarter of an hour (about half past 2.) Repeat this for the next clock. Now look together at the first cake and ask for an estimate of what has been eaten. Say: *So how much is left?* Repeat this for the second cake.

Show the children the metre rule and ask an individual to point to a measurement that they choose, such as 86 cm. Now ask: *Where do you think half of this measurement will be?* Repeat this for other measurements.

Paired work: Ask the children to work in pairs and give them a number line each. If using CD page 'Number lines', which mark decades, the children should write in their chosen number, such as 64, and mark the point on the line. They take turns to mark a point on their number line and ask their partner to estimate what half of that number would be and to mark its position on the line.

Differentiation

Less able: The children may find this activity easier if they use a metre rule with all centimetres marked.

More able: When the children are confident with this activity, challenge them to work mentally, without the aid of the number line.

Plenary & assessment

Using the counting stick, label the ends 0 and 100, and count in tens along the stick. Now ask the children to look carefully at where you place your finger, such as at approximately, 86. Invite them to say the number and then to calculate where the halfway point would come (43). Repeat this for different numbers. When the children are confident, ask one child to point to a place on the stick and the others to say the approximate number. Now ask another child to point to the approximate halfway point, and to say what the number at that point would be.

 Lesson

Starter

Explain that you will say a two-digit number. Ask the children to round it up or down to the nearest 10. Invite the children to say the rule for rounding – that is, 1 to 4 rounds down; 5 to 9 rounds up. Choose numbers such as 28, 63 and 55. Repeat this for rounding to the nearest 100, using three-digit numbers this time.

Main teaching activities

Whole class: Put ten counters onto the OHP. Give the children time to count these, then turn off the OHP light and move some of the counters to one side. Explain that you will turn the light back on for just a moment. Ask the children to look at the counters still in the centre of the OHP and to estimate what fraction of the original quantity that is. Switch the light on for a couple of seconds (not long enough for counting!) and then turn it off again. Ask: *What fraction do you estimate is left?* Repeat this several times, before increasing the quantity of counters to 20 and repeating. Encourage the children to use fractions of halves and quarters.

Individual work: Provide the children with a copy of activity page 'Fractions estimate'. Ask them to estimate the fractions that they can see, and to complete the sheet.

Differentiation

Less able: There is a simpler version of the activity sheet which uses a more limited range of fractions.

More able: There is a version of the sheet which uses more complex fractions.

Plenary & assessment

Put about 40 counters onto the OHP. It may help to count these on for the children. Now, with the light on the OHP turned off, remove some of the counters to the edge of the screen, turn the light back on for a couple of seconds and ask for an estimate of the fraction left. Repeat this several times so that you have an assessment of their ability to estimate fractions of quantities.

| Name | Date |

Fraction estimate

Estimate and write the fractions that you can see.

Now answer these questions.

Approximately what fraction is:

110g of a kg

260ml of a litre

22 minutes of an hour

Addition and subtraction, solving problems and explaining

Children develop their mental, and mental with jottings, methods of adding small numbers. They begin to use the column method for addition, and the column decomposition method for subtraction. They solve problems, reading and using a calendar.

LEARNING OBJECTIVES

	Topics	Starter	Main teaching activity
Lesson 1	Understanding + and –	● **Add and subtract mentally a 'near multiple of 10' to or from a two-digit number**… by adding or subtracting 10, 20, 30… and adjusting.	● Extend understanding that more than two numbers can be added: add three or four two-digit numbers with the help of apparatus or pencil and paper.
Lesson 2	Pencil and paper procedures (+ and –)	● As for Lesson 1.	● Use informal pencil and paper methods to support, record or explain HTU ± TU, HTU ± HTU.
Lesson 3	Pencil and paper procedures (+ and –)	● Round any three-digit number to the nearest 100.	● As for Lesson 2.
Lesson 4	Pencil and paper procedures (+ and –)	● As for Lesson 3.	● Use informal pencil and paper methods to support, record or explain HTU ± TU, HTU ± HTU. ● Begin to use column addition and subtraction for HTU ± TU where the calculation cannot easily be done mentally.
Lesson 5	Problems involving 'real life', money and measures Pencil and paper procedures (+ and –) Reasoning about numbers or shapes Measures	● **Order whole numbers to at least 1000**, and position them on a number line.	● Solve word problems involving numbers in 'real life', money and measures. ● Begin to use column addition and subtraction for HTU ± TU where the calculation cannot easily be done mentally. ● **Explain methods and reasoning** orally, and where appropriate, in writing. ● Use a calendar.

Lessons overview

Preparation
Make an OHT of CD page 'Hundred square'.

Learning objectives
Starter
● **Add and subtract mentally a 'near multiple of 10' to or from a two-digit number…** by adding or subtracting 10, 20, 30… and adjusting.
Main teaching activity
● Extend understanding that more than two numbers can be added: add three or four two-digit numbers with the help of apparatus or pencil and paper.

Vocabulary
look at, point, show me, vertical, horizontal, diagonal, greatest value, least value, before, after, next, last

You will need:

CD pages
'Hundred square' (Autumn term) (see General resources).

Equipment
OHP and pens; pots of money including mixed coins and £5 notes.

Lesson

Starter
Using the hundred square, ask the children to answer the following: *Which number has the greatest/least value? If I start on the number 39 and add 9/19/29, where will I end? How did you work it out?* (Model jumping to nearest 10 and then moving back one with your OHT and marker pen.) *If I start on the number 79 and subtract 9/19/29, where will I end? With a partner, work out a calculation that subtracts 9 at least three times.*

Main teaching activities
Whole class: Explain that the purpose of the lesson is to teach the children how to add three or four two-digit numbers efficiently. First, spend some time discussing which of the following additions would be easy to do mentally, or mentally with jottings, or are too hard to do mentally:
20 + 20 + 30 = (70)   40 + 20 + 19 = (79)   29 + 29 + 29 = (87)   47 + 18 + 26 = (91)
Work through the answers, asking: *Which number did you start with? Why? Which numbers are easiest to add? What kind of jottings would you make?*

Show the OHT 'Hundred square' and explain that this can be used for addition. Write on the board: 19 + 63 + 54 + 97. Ask: *How shall we start to total these?* The suggestion of adding 97 and 63 would be useful. Explain that this is the same as 97 + 3 + 60 = 160. Now add 54 and 19. If children cannot do this mentally (add 20 and subtract 1 for the 19), demonstrate this on the hundred square. Now total 160 and 73. Suggest that the children break this down, too: 100 + 60 + 70 + 3 = 100 + 130 + 3 = 233. Repeat for another example, such as adding money: £2.54 + £0.63 + £5.50.
Paired work: Write on the board: £1.75, £1.30, £5.50, £3.24, £2.66 and £0.45. Ask the children to work in pairs to choose three amounts of money and, making jottings, find the total. Provide pots of money, but suggest that the children use these only if they are stuck. Repeat six times.

Differentiation
Less able: Decide whether to work as a group. Provide pots of money to help.
More able: Challenge the children to work these without the aid of the pots of money.

Plenary & assessment
Review what the children have done. Choose one or two examples to work through together. For example: £1.75 + £5.50 + £3.24 = £1 + £5 + £3 + 75p + 50p + 24p = £9 + 70p + 50p + 20p + 5p + 4p = £9 + £1.40 + 9p = £10.49.

Lessons overview

Preparation
Make an OHT of CD page 'Hundred square'.

Learning objectives
Starter
- **Add and subtract mentally a 'near multiple of 10' to or from a two-digit number...** by adding or subtracting 10, 20, 30... and adjusting.
- Round any three-digit number to the nearest 100.
- Begin to use column addition.

Main teaching activity
- Use informal pencil and paper methods to support, record or explain HTU ± TU, HTU ± HTU.

Vocabulary
add, subtract, column, place, place value

You will need:
Photocopiable pages
'Column addition for HTU' (page 219) for each child.

CD pages
'Hundred square' for the teacher's/LSA's reference (Autumn term); 'Adding in columns' for each child; 'Column addition for TU' less able version and 'Column addition for HTU' more able version (Summer term, Unit 12) (see General resources).

Equipment
Whiteboards and pens; flipchart; squared paper.

Lesson ②

Starter

Repeat the Starter for Lesson 1, but this time extend it by taking the children on 'number walks'. This involves the children listening to your calculation and then making jottings as the number walk progresses. Only accept an answer right at the end. For example: *I start on the number 15, double it* (pause for jotting), *then I move onto add the number 20* (pause). *I halve this number and add 3* (pause). *What is my final answer?* (28)

Main teaching activities

Whole class: Explain that today, and for the following two lessons, the children will be using column addition and subtraction. Explain that this can be done by adding the most significant digits first. Write on the board: 58 + 34 = (50 + 30) + (8 + 4) = 80 + 12 = 92.

Now write up:
```
  5 8
+ 3 4
  8 0
  1 2
  9 2
```

Alternatively, if your school policy is to begin with the least significant digits, write up: 58 + 34 = (8 + 4) + (50 + 30) = 12 + 80 = 92 and: Repeat for another example, such as 47 + 56 (103).

```
    5  8
+   3  4
    1  2
    8  0
    9  2
```

Paired work: Ask the children to work in pairs to find totals on CD page 'Adding in columns'. Remind them to set their work out in the way that has been practised during the whole-class activity.

Differentiation

Less able: Decide whether the children are ready to tackle this work. If they are not, then continue to work horizontally. If tackling the activity sheet, work as a group. Write each example onto the flipchart for the children to copy down, then work together to find the totals. Talk the process through. When the children are confident, encourage them to explain the process to the others in the group.
More able: If the children finish the activity sheet quickly, provide some examples of HTU + TU, such as 164 + 58 (222).

Plenary & assessment

Review some of the examples which the children tried. Ask them to write up, in columns, what they tried and ask questions such as: *How did you work this one out? Did anyone total in a different order? Which did you find easier?* This will give you an opportunity to check whether the children have understood the method.

Lesson ③

Starter

Ask: *What are the rules for rounding up or down to the nearest 100?* Check that the children are clear that if the tens digit is a 1, 2, 3 or 4, that the number rounds down to the nearest 100, and if the tens digit is a 5, 6, 7, 8 or 9, it rounds up. Ask the children to say the rounded number when you hold up your hand, allowing no more than five seconds of thinking time. Say: *Tell me the rounded number for: 523, 665, 809 and 651.*

Main teaching activities

Whole class: Explain that in this lesson the children will learn about column addition for adding two-digit numbers to three-digit numbers, and for three-digit numbers to three-digit numbers. Write on the board 256 + 67 = and ask the children to suggest how to solve this, working horizontally. For example: 256 + 67 = 200 + 50 + 60 + 6 + 7 = 200 + 110 + 13 = 323. Now write the same addition in columns (see page 217).

```
  2 5 6
+   6 7
  2 0 0
  1 1 0
    1 3
  3 2 3
```

```
  2 6 4
+ 3 7 7
  5 0 0
  1 3 0
    1 1
  6 4 1
```

This example has been worked adding the most significant digits first. If your school policy is to start with the least significant digits, then refer back to the example given for Lesson 2.

Repeat this for another example, such as 497 + 63. Then provide an example of adding HTU to HTU, such as 264 + 377: 264 + 377 = (200 + 300) + (60 + 70) + (4 + 7) = 500 + 130 + 11 = 641. Repeat this using column addition, reminding the children that the columns must line up for place value.

Individual work: Ask the children to complete the additions on activity sheet 'Column addition for HTU'. It would be helpful to leave an example on the board to act as a reminder to the children of how to set out the examples.

Differentiation

Less able: There is a less complex activity sheet called 'Column addition for TU'.
More able: There is a version of the sheet 'Column addition for HTU', which includes totals beyond 999.

Plenary & assessment

```
  1 2 7
+   7 8
  1 0 0
  □ □
    1 5
  2 0 5
```

Play 'Spot the missing number' with the class. The children will need to explain how they have decide upon the missing digit. Use 127 + 78. Ask: *As the unit answer is 5, what possibilities could there be for the empty units box? (Multiples of 5). What explanation is there for having 200 in the answer?* Children may now like to work in pairs to invent their own example to try with the whole class.

Lesson ④

Starter

Repeat the Starter from Lesson 3. This time increase the pace.

Main teaching activities

Whole class: Explain to the class that in today's lesson they will be learning again about how to do column subtraction (Spring term, Unit 3). Write on the board: 82 – 56 and ask the children to try this for themselves in horizontal form. Now write: 82 – 56 = (82 – 50) – 6 = 32 – 6 = 26.
Show the children the simplified column method of recording this:

```
  82    =    80 + 2    =    70 + 12
– 56    =    50 + 6    =    50 +  6
                             20 +  6 = 26
```

Discuss how 80 + 2 is the same as 70 + 12, and that this makes it much easier to subtract 50 + 6.
Repeat this for another example, such as 57 – 28, then ask the children to work in pairs to solve one for themselves, such as 64 – 37 (27).
Paired work: Write on the board the following subtractions: 94 – 37, 86 – 59, 67 – 28, 65 – 28 and 82 – 35. Ask the children to work in pairs to find the solutions using column subtraction. Remind them how important it is to line up the digits correctly for place value. Provide squared paper for the children to record their work.

Differentiation

Less able: Decide whether to ask the children to continue to work horizontally to find the solutions.
More able: If the children are confident with this method, suggest that they work individually so that you can check their level of confidence.

Plenary & assessment

Ask the children to complete the following subtraction by their preferred method: 85 – 38 = □. This will enable you to check which method for subtraction the children prefer. At this stage, some children may prefer to work horizontally.

Addition and subtraction, solving problems and explaining
Unit 12

Lesson overview

Preparation
Make an OHT of CD page 'Calendar'.

Learning objectives

Starter
● **Order whole numbers to at least 1000**, and position them on a number line.

Main teaching activity
● Solve word problems involving numbers in 'real life', money and measures.
● Begin to use column addition and subtraction for HTU $\pm$ TU where the calculation cannot easily be done mentally.
● **Explain methods and reasoning** orally, and where appropriate, in writing.
● Use a calendar.

Vocabulary
now, soon, early, late, earliest, latest. how often? always, never, often, sometimes, usually

You will need:

Photocopiable pages
'Calendar challenges' (page 220) for each child.

CD pages
'Calendar' for the teacher's/LSA' reference; 'Calendar challenges' less able and more able versions (Summer term, Unit 12) (see General resources).

Equipment
OHP.

Lesson

Starter
Write up sets of three, three-digit numbers on the board. Draw an empty number line, marked 0 and 1000 at the ends and invite the children to write the numbers on the number line, in order. Repeat this for other numbers.

Main teaching activities
Whole class: Explain that the problems focus around the use of a calendar. Show the children the OHT for 'Calendar'. Ask questions such as:
● *What day is 12 March?*
● *How many weekends are in each month? How many days/weeks/months are there in a year?*
● *What day is your birthday on this year?*
● *What special dates could we mark on our calendar?* (eg, Ramadan, Divali, Christmas, Easter)
● *How could we work out how much pocket money Tony gets per year if he receives 50p per week?*
Discuss the number of months and the number of days in each month. Ask: *How many days are there in February? Is this always true? When will the next leap year be? How many days will there be in February then?*
Individual work: Provide copies of activity sheet 'Calendar challenges', for the children to work individually to find solutions to the questions.

Differentiation
Less able: There is a simplified version of the activity sheet available.
More able: There is a version of the sheet available with more challenging questions.

Plenary & assessment
Use the questions from the more able group's activity sheet, which could involve the rest of the class having to read the answer from the OHT of 'Calendar'.

Ask the children to work in pairs at this problem: *Each month I receive a magazine through the post. The magazine costs £1.50 and the postage is £1. How much do I pay every year?* Model one child's thinking by writing what is said up on the board for the class to see. There may be variations in how the problem is tackled, so use these for discussion.

Name		Date

Column addition for HTU

Use these six numbers to make as many different adding calculations as you can.

Set the numbers out under each other in columns.

124	143	255	217	329	434

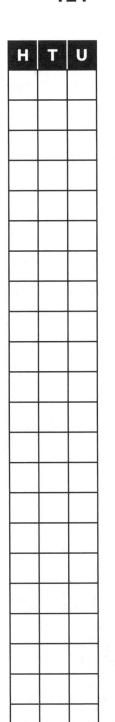
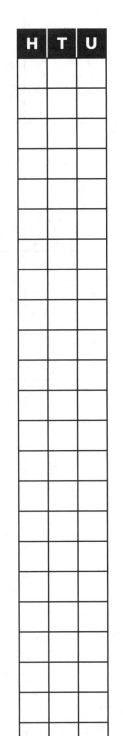
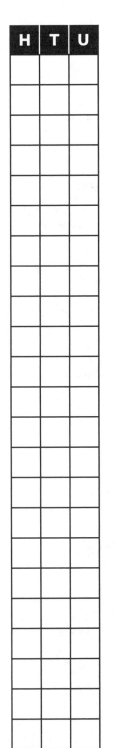
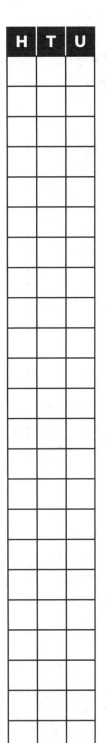

Name	Date

Calendar challenges

Solve the following challenges using the calendar.

Challenge	Workings	Answer
Daniel walked 2km each day. He started on 1st February and finished in the evening on 8th February. How far did he walk?		
Jeunell had 30p every Saturday during February. How much more money did she need to get £2.50?		
Ronell ran 5km every other day starting on the 19th February. How far did she run during February?		
Pablo spends 65p on crisps every Tuesday. How much did he spend in February?		
Sarah goes to Girl Guides every Friday. What date was her last meeting in February?		
I want to meet my friend on the second Saturday in February. What will the date be?		

SCHOLASTIC
photocopiable

Handling data

Children revise what they know about using Carroll, Venn and bar charts. They use a scale.

LEARNING OBJECTIVES

		Topics	Starter	Main teaching activity
Lesson	1	Organising and using data	● **Know by heart: all addition and subtraction facts for each number to 20.**	● **Solve a given problem by organising and interpreting numerical data in simple lists, tables, and graphs,** for example: simple frequency tables; pictograms – symbol representing two units; bar charts – intervals labelled in ones then twos; Venn and Carroll diagrams (one criterion).
Lesson	2	Organising and using data	As for Lesson 1.	As for Lesson 1.
Lesson	3	Organising and using data	● Derive quickly: all pairs of multiples of 5 with a total of 100 (eg 35 + 65).	As for Lesson 1.
Lesson	4	Organising and using data	As for Lesson 4.	As for Lesson 1.
Lesson	5	Organising and using data	As for Lesson 1.	As for Lesson 1.

Lessons overview ① ② ③ ④ ⑤

Preparation
Make OHTs for CD pages 'Data collection', 'Graphs', 'Venn diagrams', 'Sunflowers' and 'Carroll diagrams'.

Learning objectives
Starter
● **Know by heart: all addition and subtraction facts for each number to 20.**
● Derive quickly: all pairs of multiples of 5 with a total of 100 (eg 35 + 65).
Main teaching activity
● **Solve a given problem by organising and interpreting numerical data in simple lists, tables, and graphs,** for example: simple frequency tables; pictograms – symbol representing two units; bar charts – intervals labelled in ones then twos; Venn and Carroll diagrams (one criterion).

Vocabulary
table, chart, Venn diagram, axis, diagram, least popular, group, set, interpret, count, tally, Carroll diagram, pictogram, bar chart, frequency table

You will need:
CD pages
'Venn diagrams' (Spring term), 'Using scales', 'Graphs', 'Sunflowers' and 'Carroll diagrams' for the teacher's/LSA's reference, 'Data collection' for the teacher's/LSA's reference and for each child; 'Using scales' less able and more able versions (Summer term, Unit 13) (see General resources).

Equipment
OHP, OHP pens; squared paper; data handling package for the computer; boxes of assorted shapes for sorting; sugar paper.

Lesson ①

Starter

Explain to the children that you will say a number and that you want them to put up their hands when they have thought of an addition fact with that number as the answer. Say, for example, *18*, and allow the class up to five seconds of thinking time. Then ask for answers.

Main teaching activities

Whole class: This lesson and the next focuses on developing the skill of constructing appropriate lists, tables and graphs. Show the children the OHT of 'Data collection'. Ask:

- *What do you think this list is all about?*
- *How could we group the items?*
- *Can we work out how many children are in the class?*
- *Which category is the best to use to tell us how many children are in the class?* (Ways of getting to school)
- *Why wouldn't the pets category be helpful?* (We can't be sure whether it tells about pets we have, would like or whether some children have more than one pet.)
- *What can we do about the tally marks to make things easier?* (Write in numbers)

Now think of titles for each list, for example 'The numbers and type of pets in 3H', 'Our favourite colours' and 'How we travel to school'. Then work with the children to total the scores for each one. Ask the class to reason why the colours and the travelling lists will have the same total.
Rearrange the data with the class to make frequency tables:

Cats	9
Rabbits	6
Dogs	4
Hamsters	11

Red	5
Yellow	5
Green	10
Blue	10

Bus	12
Car	2
Bike	6
Walk	10

Ask questions such as: *How many children walk/cycle to school? Which pet appears to be the most popular? How would the data change if we said who would like a dog/cat? Would this data be different in another class? Why?*

Remind the children that data like this can be put into graphs. Show the OHT of 'Graphs' and discuss the scale, headings of the columns, the title, and what can be deduced from the graphs.
Paired work: Provide each child with a copy of CD page 'Data collection', and some squared paper. Ask them to work together to make sensible frequency tables for the data, then to make a bar chart and pictogram for each of their frequency tables.

Differentiation

Less able: Work with this group to produce a giant pictogram and bar chart for later use.
More able: Allow this group to work in pairs using a graph computer package to present their data.

Plenary & assessment

Invite the less able children to show their poster, and compare these. Ask: *Which do you prefer for this data: a pictogram or a bar chart? Why?* Now ask the more able children to show what they produced using the computer package. Encourage the children to explain how they inputted the data, and which was easier to make and why.

Lesson ②

Starter

Repeat the Starter from Lesson 1. This time, however, ask the children to give a subtraction fact for the number that you say. The number is the result of the subtraction. Keep the pace sharp.

Main teaching activities

Whole class: Explain that today is all about working to a scale. Count together in twos from 0 to 20, and explain that when working to a scale, each step along the scale stands for, in this case, two things. Uncover the bar chart from the OHT of 'Sunflowers' and ask the children to look at it carefully. Explain that this is a bar graph. Point to the scale and explain that the increases by two each time. Ask questions such as: *How many sunflowers are about 150cm tall? How many are taller than that? How did you work that out? How many sunflowers are taller than 160cm but shorter than 200cm?* Now reveal the second half of OHT 'Sunflowers', which has the same data as a pictogram. Ask the children to look carefully at this and explain the scale: that one sunflower icon represents two sunflowers.

Individual work: Ask the children to work individually to draw a bar chart and a pictogram for the information given on activity sheet 'Using scales'. They are asked to use one square, or icon, to represent two. Invite two children to use the computer package to carry out this work. Suggest another two children draw their graphs on large sheets of paper, for the Plenary & assessment.

Differentiation

Less able: There is a version of the activity sheet which uses scales of 1:1.
More able: There is a version of the activity sheet which uses scales of 5:1 and 10:1.

Plenary & assessment

Ask the two children who drew their graphs on large sheets of paper to show the rest of the class what they did. Ask questions about the information in the bar chart, such as: *Which fruit was the most popular? How can you tell this? How many children like pears?* And for the pictogram: *What does one picture represent? So how many children ate meat feast pizza?*

Lesson 3

Combine the Starters for Lessons 1 and 2, so that for a given number, children give both addition, then subtraction facts for it. During the Whole class work, ask the children to work in groups of about 8 and decide what information they will collect about their group. Ask them to devise a data collection chart, frequency table, and then to put their data onto both a pictogram and a bar chart, using a 2:1 scale. During the Plenary & assessment, invite each group to display their work for others to see, and ask questions about the data.

Lesson 4

Starter

Explain that you will say a multiple of 5 and would like the children to say the multiple of 5 which, added to yours, makes 100. Keep the pace of this sharp. Say your number, allow about five seconds thinking time, then hold up your hand for the children to say their number together.

Main teaching activities

Whole class: Explain that during this lesson, the children will be putting data into Venn diagrams. Show the OHT of CD page 'Venn diagrams' and explain that you would like the class to help to sort some numbers into it. Write 'Multiples of 2 from 0 to 40' into the title bar and label the circle 'Multiples of 4'. Say together slowly the numbers from 0 to 40 and, for each one said, the children decide where to place it. Discuss what the numbers inside the circle have in common (they are all multiples of 4) and those outside the circle (they are multiples of 2 but not of 4).

Introduce two criteria sorting, with four regions. Ask the children to sort the numbers 0 to 10 for the criteria 'Even' and 'Multiple of 5'. Discuss where the numbers go, and what sits within the intersection (where the two circles cross). Explain that this part of the diagram belongs to both 'Is even' and 'Is a multiple of 5'.

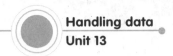

Paired work: Ask the children to sort the numbers from 0 to 60 on large sheets of sugar paper. They are sorting for 'Is a multiple of 3' and 'Is even'.

Differentiation

Less able: Decide whether to limit the number range to 0 to 30.

More able: Challenge the children by asking them to sort the even numbers from 0 to 100, with the criterion 'Is a multiple of 6' and 'Is a multiple of 5'.

Plenary & assessment

Draw a large Venn diagram on the board and invite the children to explain where each number, from 0 to 60 will go. Ask: *What will go into the intersection? (*Numbers which are both a multiple of 3 and are even, such as 6, 12, 18).Now invite the more able children to show their sorting. Invite the other children to explain what will go into the intersection.

Lesson ⑤

Starter

Repeat the Starter for Lesson 4, this time increasing the pace slightly.

Main teaching activities

Whole class: Explain that today the children will use Carroll diagrams for sorting. Show the OHT of CD page 'Carroll diagrams', and explain that you would like the children to sort eight of their classmates. Invite eight children to the front, then sort them by age. Write 'Is eight' into the left-hand box and 'Is not eight' into the right-hand box. Invite the children to write their own names into the correct box for their age. Ask: *What should the title be for this Carroll diagram?* Write in an appropriate suggestion, such as 'Ages of red group'.

Now, using a fresh Carroll diagram on the OHT, ask the children for their suggestion of something that they could sort for another group of eight children. Suggestions might include their gender or type of shoes. Ask: *What will the title be? How shall we label each box?* Then ask the eight children to again write their names into the appropriate box.

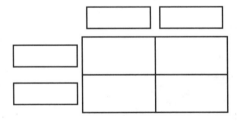

Draw a four-region Carroll diagram on the board and label it. Discuss how the numbers go into each box. Discuss, in particular, the bottom right-hand box, and ask the children to label these: 'Not greater than 10' and 'Not a multiple of 2'.

Group work: Provide each group of about four children with a box of assorted shapes. Ask them to choose their two criteria, draw a large four-region Carroll diagram and sort their shapes. They record by drawing in the shapes.

Differentiation

Less able: If possible, use a graphing program which will graph Carroll diagrams with this group.

More able: Challenge the children to sort the numbers 25 to 75 by the two criteria: 'Is a multiple of 5' and 'Is a multiple of 4'.

Plenary & assessment

Invite children from the core group to display their work. Invite the other children to check the title and box labels. Point to each of the four boxes in turn and ask: *What fits here?* If the less able children have used a graphing package, ask them to explain what they have done and to show their work. Now ask the more able children to display their four-region Carroll diagram and to explain what has gone into each of the regions. Ask questions about their data, such as: *What can you tell me about the numbers in this box?*